THE SPIRIT
OF THE
APPALACHIAN TRAIL

THE SPIRIT
OF THE
APPALACHIAN TRAIL

COMMUNITY, ENVIRONMENT, AND BELIEF
ON A LONG-DISTANCE HIKING PATH

Susan Power Bratton

THE UNIVERSITY OF TENNESSEE PRESS / KNOXVILLE

Library of Congress Cataloging-in-Publication Data

Bratton, Susan Power.
The spirit of the Appalachian Trail: community, environment, and belief on a long-distance
hiking path / Susan Power Bratton.
p. cm.
Includes bibliographical references and index.
ISBN-13: 978-1-62190-191-4
1. Hiking—Appalachian Trail.
2. Hiking—Appalachian Trail.—Religious aspects.
3. Spiritual life.
I. Title.

GV199.42.A68B74 2012
917.404—dc23
2011041687

CONTENTS

FIGURES

TABLES

PREFACE
HILL WALKING, HEART AND SOUL

I grew up between two cultural traditions, both of which considered walking as a healthful avocation. One influence was the Protestant middle class of the eastern U.S. seaboard—sponsors of children's YMCA and church camps. Scrambling through patches of oak forest, bordered by bramble-filled old fields, we took short hikes, studied nature (sort of), and really did sing "Kumbaya" around woodland campfires. During a summer adventure in western Maryland, the counselors announced to a cabin full of preteens that we were scheduled for an all-day excursion on the longest footpath in the country. Thus chaperoned by out-of-shape Presbyterian adults, and a college student or two, I undertook my first five-mile hike on the Appalachian Trail (AT). The leaders treated this challenge as a nonnegotiable component of the spiritual formation provided by pillow fights in rustic cabins, and jugs of Kool-Aid (aka bug juice) in a log-sided dining hall. Despite the slow pace of a disorganized party of kids, the distance proved too much for toes squeezed into new hiking shoes. Tears were running down my cheeks as I limped back to the bus. Many more relaxed days were spent, though, roaming the creeks and meadows of home. Parental values blessed my growing passion for withdrawing for an hour or two to woodlots populated with white oaks, tulip trees, and dogwoods. Ambling along fence rows and stalking bass at the neighbor's pond kept me and my siblings out of trouble (really), and was better than having us indoors lying on the floor in front of the television.

The second source of walking tradition was my mother's Irish upbringing and nursing experience in the United Kingdom. During a childhood visit to Eire, my Uncle Tommy drove us Yanks to the "V" in the Knockmealdown Mountains and introduced us to the panorama of the Tipperary plain, with its checkerboard of hedges and verdant fields. A mountain loomed behind Uncle Jimmy's cottage, and we splashed through the boggy sheep pastures and dodged boulders while enjoying our travels across the misty heath. These vistas were as much about family and heritage as they were about nature and beauty. We toured Blarney Castle, the high crosses at Cashel, and St. Declan's round tower. In this devout, rural realm, Uncle Tommy's bus company carried pilgrims to local holy wells in Counties Waterford and Cork, and transported them to faraway sacred sites on the mysterious west coast or in mountains far to the north. Glendalough, in the Wicklow Mountains, and Crough Patrick in wild Mayo were extraordinary places we could seek out later, when we were adult enough to manage the daunting topography.

Following my freshman year of college, a German program to encourage student exchange found me a summer job in the scenic Eifel region of Germany. My employers were Roman Catholic nuns who ran a hotel welcoming tourists drawn to nearby spas and mature coreligionists seeking spiritual and physical restoration. Having bought a walker's map, I began to explore the network of public footpaths adjoining the village. Roaming solo, I would greet hotel guests, some out for exercise, others strolling along with a rosary. The nuns, like my parents, thought I was better off surprising dairy farmers mending gates, rather than spending my spare time lounging in the employee common room. Sister Hildegard remarked on my speedy adaptation to the slopes above Moselle River tributaries, and affirmed the benefits of *Wanderen*—walking for walking's sake. She smiled when she noticed a paperback selection of Heinrich Heine's poems had joined W. B. Yeats in my old-fashioned canvas pack.

When I returned to Europe as a college junior, my mother, worried that I might waste my summer, found a natural history field school in Scotland and promised to pay the tuition. As a British naval nurse, stationed in Aberdeen and the Orkney Islands, she had fallen in love with the Highlands, the summer flowers, and the stormy coasts. So, as a budding biologist, I spent a month in the Cairngorm range, stomping through drizzle, learning to distinguish moss species, and ducking wind on heather-crowned peaks as August rain turned to sleet. At the time, field ecology seemed too physically difficult a profession to pursue. On returning to Columbia University, I reflected on the joys of cross-country exploration, and decided I would much rather be soaked on the shores of a lough than trapped in a complex of buildings with only narrow green strips between them. I volunteered for another field school in the Colorado Rockies the next summer.

Woven subtly through the supervised camping and independent rambles of my youth was a cultural consensus that walking though the wilds and the countryside is spiritually beneficial. Cultural traditions as diverse as early medieval monastic withdrawal to the wilds, romantic appreciation of the rural scene, and progressive Protestant physical self-discipline converged in a common channel. In Irish folk Catholicism, the respectful journey to St. Kevin's favored retreats, between an icy lake and two looming peaks, was overtly religious, as was the climb to the top of St. Patrick's holy mountain. The German perspective ranged from nature-centered monism to an ailing bishop seeking the quiet of rural paths to aid his concentration for prayers. The Presbyterians, while rejecting the belief that visiting a saint's hermitage might accelerate progress to heaven, believed walking could enhance reflection and an understanding of God as Creator. My first Appalachian Trail hike, with its painful finish, was religious training, even if it lacked ritual. Later, as a graduate student and professional, when I began to work in the Great Smoky Mountains as an ecologist, I returned to the Appalachian Trail, not merely as a route to scattered scientific sampling sites, or a wilderness corridor for a pleasurable Saturday jaunt, but as an environment in which to unwind, reflect, and hold a relaxed, yet intense, conversation with God.

WILDERNESS SPIRITUALITY, MINDFUL WALKING

The growing academic interest in nature religion, pilgrimage from secular to sacred, wilderness spirituality, and the meaning of walking has generated a literature reaching far beyond the heritage of European Christianity. One of my earlier books, *Christianity, Wilderness and Wildlife: The Original Desert Solitaire*, and Belden Lane's *The Solace of Fierce Landscapes: Exploring Desert and Mountain Spirituality*, examine the explicitly religious aspects of wildland experience, through a Christian lens.[1] Looking across the religious spectrum turns up similar publications for other spiritual traditions, ranging from the established and mainstream to the experimental and alternative. One increasingly prominent genre is the guides to personal renewal, enrichment, and healing in natural settings. Jamie Korngold, for example, has written *God in the Wilderness: Rediscovering the Spirituality of the Great Outdoors with the Adventure Rabbi* for Jewish backpackers and kayakers. Rabbi Korngold recommends recovering our awe of nature, and, invoking Psalm 23, taking advantage of the restoration and comfort the living environment offers.[2] Rabbi Mike Comins has similarly penned *A Wild Faith: Jewish Ways into Wilderness, Wilderness Ways into Judaism*.[3] Comins simultaneously grounds his perspective in Torah and considers the possibility for a Jewish medicine wheel—a geographic articulation of a nature-based cosmology imported from American Indian religion. In *Renewal in the Wilderness: A Spiritual Guide to Connecting with God in the Natural World,* John Lionberger argues that the benefits of wilderness experience are universal, and that most of the world's religions were born in the wilderness. Lionberger reviews the desert origins of Judaism and Islam and the ancient hermitages of Taoism and Hinduism. He provides instructions for testing one's own limits, finding fresh vision and seeking physical and emotional recovery in environments relatively free of human developments.[4]

A second wellspring is the growing inventory of accounts of trail establishment, and of the origins of walking for walking's sake. Included are region-specific histories, such as Laura Waterman and Guy Waterman, *Forest and Crag: A History of Hiking, Trail Blazing, and Adventure in the Northeast Mountains,*[5] and literary strolls, such as Rebecca Solnit's *Wanderlust: A History of Walking,* which strides along with the Sophists, William Wordsworth, Lenten pilgrims, and even the suburban treadmill.[6] Mindful or contemplative walking, a staple of Eastern and Western mysticism, is experiencing a revival, and has surfaced as "mindful hiking" in recreational frameworks.[7] A parallel trend is the expansion of research on pilgrimage from the explicitly to the implicitly religious, and from the established context of world religions to the informal, postmodern, and novel. Jill Dubisch and Michael Winkelman, in *Pilgrimage and Healing,* for example, include chapters on the Vietnam veteran's motorcycle pilgrimage[8] and the Burning Man Festival, held in the Nevada desert since 1991.[9] Such studies are increasingly respectful of the participant's self-reported motives, outlooks, and perceived benefits. Led by anthropologists, such as Victor and Edith Turner, scholars of comparative religion have become increasingly aware that the pilgrimage, or ritual landscape, is itself symbolic and a form of sacred text, read with boots, staffs, and bare feet.

In the period following the World Wars, the failure of religious principles to stop the death-dealing rampages armed by heavy industry, and Christian culpability in atrocities such as the Holocaust, led to sweeping critiques of Christian ethics—and its fundamental validity. Environmental and wilderness historians of the 1960s through 1980s argued that Christianity, and de facto Judaism, were disrespectful of undeveloped nature from their very origins. Roderick Nash's

evil in world
cause distruct
of ethics

well-circulated summary of Euro-American attitudes toward wilderness presented the Pilgrim "forefathers" of the republic as destroyers of primal forests because of their literal Biblical interpretation and fear of the demonic.[10] This put religious commentaries on backcountry hiking on the defensive—to say the least. Prior to a 1980s wilderness conference, a session chair attempted to limit my platform presentation on Biblical images of wilderness to four minutes, while other speakers had up to twenty. I called the former divinity student–turned recreational sociologist and he claimed the topic was unimportant, and that no one would be interested. Also because I was one of the few women presenting, I decided to stay on the phone until he gave in, and he ultimately compromised at twelve minutes, while still awarding more intellectually acceptable topics the full twenty. My paper packed the room, although some of the attendees may have been hoping there would be a further academic scuffle.

Considering how innately imbedded in spirituality the Western walking ethos appears to be, I have always found this period of denial puzzling. Many scholarly studies of outdoor recreation have been the product of federal and state agencies, which, indeed, have held religion to be beyond their mandate or too controversial to scrutinize—which partially explains the dearth of quantitative research. My own experience, ambling across hundreds of miles of the Appalachian Trail and many other footpaths, is that backpackers range from the oblivious and incompetent, who have no idea why they bought an expensive waterproof rain suit and attempted a multiday hike in the first place, to the seasoned and sensitive, who relish every turn in the treadway, and arrive where they intended with their socks still dry. Hikers offer similar variety in spiritual perspectives, from individuals who see wilderness as a relief from the pressures of the greater culture, including the pressures of organized religion, to those who find that their denominational background is compatible with natural aesthetics, to the disciplined practitioners of outdoor meditation, who expect to find God in nature, or seek an ambiance favorable for deep, undistracted reflection.

Rather than asking if wilderness and outdoor recreation have spiritual benefits, this volume is intended to investigate specifically how long-distance walking might enhance spiritual wellness. The research design assumes that hikers of different religious preferences, levels of religious commitment, and generations may experience a mega-hike or extended wilderness sojourn in different ways. I have, over the decades, enjoyed moments of contemplation with friends, as we viewed the sunset from an open summit, and equally savored conversations with strangers at backcountry shelters, as they mused over their life goals and the meaning of their long-planned Appalachian Trail hike. The first 2,000-milers I ever met on the Appalachian Trail were two gray-haired women, one in her fifties and the other in her sixties, who had vanquished a section of the AT together each summer. They were just about to finish, and in celebration of completing the last long stretch above five thousand feet, they sat down on the summit of Thunderhead in the Great Smokies and made a pot of tea. Their exhilaration as they eyed their final miles from the promontory, with its spectacular 360-degree view, conveyed a sense of fulfillment many people will never feel. This study is an expansion of these casual assemblies and the positive outlook on humanity and wild nature they produce. My purpose is not to advocate for the physical management of national trails and hiking venues as much as it is to reflect on their importance to us, and to consider why, in an era of tight budgets, we should continue to care for them. Our concepts of religion and nature are dynamic; to determine where we should head on our trek, it helps to know where we are right now.

READING THIS VOLUME

Readers will have varying motives for perusing this volume. Former Appalachian Trail end-to-enders may find that some sections, particularly chapter 2, with its geographical descriptions, offer little that is unfamiliar, thus they may wish to speed ahead. In contrast, someone planning a trip will find the first part of the volume a useful orientation to the Appalachian Trail landscape. To make the text more accessible, I have dropped digits from some of the statistics, and placed more tedious discussions of academic matters, such the models for the survey design, in the end notes. The photography, completed in the summer of 2009, does not parallel my own walking experience, because I do not always take a professional-quality camera along. I have spent much more time among the oaks of Pennsylvania and western Maryland than the illustrations suggest. The photography includes a high proportion of shots of the off-trail support network, and far fewer flowers, birds, and boulders than one would see on an end-to-end hike.[11] They are intended to reinforce the text and offer visualization of the cultural and natural context.

ACKNOWLEDGMENTS

This volume is dedicated to all the individuals who have worked to establish, maintain, and interpret Appalachian natural areas and hiking trails, including those who have passed on. I fondly remember Carlos Campbell, Anne Broome, Don Defoe, Al Radford, Robert Whittaker, and Stan Murray (among many others) and their sheer commitment to the Great Smoky Mountains National Park, upland conservation, or the AT. This book is also dedicated to the many friends, coworkers, and students, including the gang from Uplands Lab, who have provided good company, and perhaps a folk song or two, on the slopes, summits, and wooden porches of the Appalachians. We have all gone our different directions, yet I was thinking about you all (Peter, Rita, Mary, Ken, Charlie, Lee, Jill, Glen, Barb, Chris, Bart, Matt, Hal, Lars, Don, Austin, Haines, and others) as I wrote the manuscript. Finally, I would like to thank all the wonderful trail angels and hiking club members (particularly the volunteers from St. Thomas Episcopal Church in Vernon, New Jersey) who assisted with this study and have cared for my fellow hikers over the years. You are incredible; may your work live on.

CHAPTER 1

THE APPALACHIAN TRAIL AS SPIRITUAL EXPERIENCE

LONG WALKS AS PILGRIMAGE

national trail(s)

Although landscape architects, designers, and planners have appreciated the built or developed environment as an expression of human integration with the greater geologic and biotic milieu, some very important human constructions are, more often than not, left out of the dialogue about spirit and nature. One of the most obvious forms of human endeavor fostering spiritual interaction with both natural and cultural environments is the pilgrimage path, and its modern analogue, the national trail. Because a scenic footpath is not an explicitly religious structure, like a church or a temple, sociologists do not usually analyze the bands of walkers struggling along these narrow, rock-strewn routes in terms of their religious or spiritual experience. Conversely, students of pilgrimage focus on forays tied to religious traditions, such as Christianity and Hinduism.

Paths, trails, and other cross-country routes may originate in economic or military activity. Ancient roads typically follow the lines and curves of least resistance, connecting trading centers, fortifications, and watering places. Not every thoroughfare is practical or commercial. Some routes are processional or ritual. Entry arches welcoming victorious armies, religious paths to hillside shrines, and even gravel entries through wrought iron cemetery gates make declarations about the meaning and ends of human life. Human beings have invented routes to "nowhere" and have trudged hundreds of kilometers to uninhabited peaks to nurture their souls or receive a vision. Circuitous chalk steps lead to hillside springs, promising physical healing. Unmarked sacred tracks, beaten over centuries by hunters, monks, and shamans, celebrate rites of passage and contact with the ancestors. Buddhists, Bons, and Hindus walk resolutely to the high valleys of the Himalayas and circumambulate majestic Kailas, though deeming the peak

religious/nationalstic

too sacred to climb.[1] Since late antiquity, Christians have connected the country-side to cities via pilgrims' roads, and struggled up holy mountains, such as Mount Brandon in Ireland (Saint Brendan's Mountain) or Mount Sinai in Egypt.[2]

Prior to the nineteenth century, long-distance trails not committed to prac-tical uses, such as driving livestock to market, connecting villages, speeding cav-alry patrols, or transporting goods, were primarily pilgrims' ways or prescribed tracks for religious quests. In the days when horses were elite transportation, wealthy landowners built walking and riding paths in gardens and forests for aesthetics and enjoyment. Often, these too have imbedded religious meaning. The features of a Japanese stroll garden, for example, incorporate Buddhist and Shinto concepts of order in nature.[3] The decorative bridges and lanterns are simul-taneously religious objects, symbolizing cosmic harmony and the concepts of yin and yang.

The modern era has brought national and regional trail and scenic road sys-tems, intended for the recreationist and tourist. Some seek out pleasant scen-ery, while others memorialize historic events, extending from the tragic Trail of Tears to the nation-building explorations of Lewis and Clark. Such trails are so inherently environmental that they superficially appear to be above criticism. Whether of folk origin or the product of landscape architects, routes "not for bus-iness or conquest" immerse the wanderer in the open air and natural settings. Yet, the selection of these passageways and their placement in the landscape is saturated with cultural values and the dialogue between human beings and na-ture. The type of experience they promise has converged with that of the historic pilgrims' roads, such as the walking or horseback route to Santiago de Compos-tela, in Spain, which are increasingly absorbing recreational traffic.

This volume is dedicated entirely to the Appalachian Trail, the first and best-known long-distance interstate hiking trail established in the United States (fig. 1.1). The Appalachian Trail, also affectionately known as the AT or simply the trail, extends from Maine to Georgia, running up and down the backbone of the Appalachian Mountains. The AT, designated the first national scenic trail in 1968, was once the only interstate trail of its kind.[4] The Appalachian Trail is now one of the Triple Crown of U.S. hiking—the other two are the Continental Divide Trail, following the Pacific/Atlantic watershed divide of the Rocky Moun-tains, and the Pacific Crest Trail, beginning in the volcanic Cascade Mountains and winding south to Mexico through the California Sierras. National scenic and recreational trails now extend coast to coast, and follow single mountain ranges and topographic features, such as the Ozark Mountains or the moraines and eskers of the Great Lakes region.

Fig. 1.1. Appalachian Trail sign, Massachusetts, announcing Maine to Georgia.

Spirituality and Religion

Leaving a job or taking time off between college and employment and then heading out to the woods to walk a national trail is a major personal undertaking. The purpose of this project is to investigate one aspect of the trail: its impact on long-distance hikers in spiritual and religious terms and its potential for promoting spiritual well-being. Although academics continue to discuss the differences between spirituality and religion, a potential definition of spiritual well-being is a "high level of faith, hope, and commitment in relation to a well defined world-view or belief system that provides a sense of meaning and purpose to existence in general, and that offers an ethical path to personal fulfillment which include connectedness with self, others and a higher power or larger reality."[5] Though religion and spirituality overlap, an individual may have spiritual experience without belonging to a religion or a denomination. A religion is distinguished by community, coda, and cult and defined by rituals such as worship services, practices such as prayers, and rules or beliefs held in common by its members. A religion also has a community, consisting of its congregations, parishes, temples, clans, orders, or other social units. Spirituality is a personal state or amalgamation of interactions with the environment, other people, and the transcendent, which may be actualized through organized religion or may emerge independently. In Western religion, the word *spirit* "has come to denote those invisible but real qualities which shape the life of a person or community—such as love, courage, peace or truth—and a person's own 'spirit' is their inner identity, or soul, the sum of those invisible but real forces which make them who they are."[6]

The research for this book draws on five sources of information: a series of interviews with volunteers and the support network along the Appalachian Trail corridor, a paper survey of long-distance AT hikers collected in 2007–8, hikers' logs and postings, published trail diaries and memoirs, and personal observations and conversations with numerous members of the AT "community." The first question, of course, is do hikers perceive their undertaking as a spiritual quest or venture? What are their motives? Can the trail function as a source of spiritual and personal ethical formation for hikers? Because the trail isolates hikers from their families and home communities, it de facto has an impact on their religious or spiritual lives. Are these effects beneficial? Can a long sojourn on the AT initiate spiritual change?

The mountain setting of the Appalachian Trail is distinctive and offers repeated encounters with unsurpassed natural beauty. Do today's hikers perceive aesthetic engagement with nature as spiritual? Because they are in a unique environment, are they experiencing anything different than they experience at home in spiritual terms? How important are interactions with other hikers, or, conversely, do the hikers experience solitude or even isolation? Do they feel close to God, or isolated from their previous belief system and home communities?

Long-distance walking is an intentional spiritual practice for many of the world's religions. Throughout this book the analysis compares the spiritual experience of Appalachian Trail hikers to the spiritual benefits that religious walking pilgrimage is reputed to provide. Can a long-distance walk assist someone in making a life transition or gaining a greater understanding of the needs of other people? Can hiking provide relief from stress? Does the trail experience result in any major changes in personal relationships, coping, or religious preferences or practices?

THE ORIGINS OF THE APPALACHIAN TRAIL

Prior to the installation of the Appalachian Trail, hotels, tourist camps, national parks, and even hikers themselves cleared recreational paths to summits and along ridges. The Long Trail of Vermont, begun in 1910, crossed a state end to end and an entire mountain range, the Green Mountains. In 1921, Benton MacKaye, a northeasterner and Harvard-trained professional forester and regional planner, proposed a foot trail from Mount Washington, the highest mountain in New England, to Mount Mitchell, NC, the highest peak in the entire Appalachians and, indeed, the highest east of the Mississippi River. MacKaye, in fact, imagined a series of camping communities, which would provide opportunities "for recreation, recuperation, and employment" along the Appalachian skyline. He proposed the walking trail to connect these "recreational communities" and to provide "shelter camps," "after the function of the Swiss chalets." These camps would in turn blossom into entire villages, which might be organized "for recreation, for recuperation and for study."[7] Today, we have just the trail and the shelters or huts, with the corridor avoiding the ever-denser clusters of summer homes dotting the Appalachians from base to top.

Fig. 1.2. The Appalachian Trail in Gifford Woods State Park, Vermont in midsummer. The double white blazes tell the hiker to turn off the road and enter the forest.

Although MacKaye was the conceptual leader of the project, other conservationists, such as Myron Avery, provided general direction and coordination. Regional trail and hiking clubs selected and planned much of the specific routing. Some of these recreation-promoting organizations preceded the founding of the AT, while others were organized in response to the enterprise. The Appalachian Mountain Club and the Dartmouth Outing Club, for example, were founded in the nineteenth century, and cleared trails well before they pitched in on construction of the AT. Other clubs, like the Potomac Appalachian Trail Club, grew up with the trail. This analysis proposes that the segments in the different states and regions are based on common values and concepts, despite some differences among the clubs in maintenance principles and the specifics of design (fig. 1.2). The Appalachian Mountain Club built enclosed "huts" with food service in the White Mountains, while the Nantahala Hiking Club and the Georgia Appalachian Trail Club offer open-fronted shelters. The aesthetics expressed throughout the Appalachian Trail corridor, however, are rooted in landscape preferences originating in colonial European encounters with wild nature and evolving along with American concepts of nationhood through the twentieth century.

Though the Appalachian Trail has always had a recreational mission, the trail is also an idealization of human interaction with eastern deciduous forest environments. The AT is a conversation about colonization, settlement, capitalism, and industrialization, as well as about American identity. The concept of the trail partially owes its existence to nineteenth-century painters and authors, such as William Cullen Bryant, Thomas Cole, and Asher Durand, who saw God in the wild forests and waterfalls of the Catskills, the Berkshires, and the White Mountains.[8] The AT evokes the values of the transcendentalist essayists and novelists, including Ralph Waldo Emerson, Henry David Thoreau, Nathaniel Hawthorne, Herman Melville, and Louisa May Alcott.[9] One of the icons of the Appalachian Trail is a solo backpacker standing on a ridge, exposed against the sky; his self-confidence and individualism represent the essence of the adventure. He is a hiker with a heritage, imbedded in both American self-identity and beliefs about the land itself.

As environmental historian William Cronan has stressed, Americans perceive their terrains on a gradient from wilderness with little human intrusion to the natural resource–based farmsteads of the rural countryside, to the suburbs, and ultimately to the city. Americans have idealized the wilderness, and per-

Fig. 1.3. View from the Appalachian Trail toward Charlie's Bunion, Great Smoky Mountains. The Appalachian Trail is a ridgetop path with many sweeping views.

haps owing to the rise of a truly American art and literature during the romantic period, wildlands retain an association with the sublime. The wilderness is a locale to encounter God's grandeur and the essence of the original Creation. Americans also enjoy the rural countryside as beautiful and an expression of national values, such as hard work, and maintaining regional identities. As Cronan concludes, the city and the wilderness have a complex and intimate cultural relationship with each other, rather than representing two isolated poles. Often, in American politics, the rural counties and states, with their extractive economies, form one bloc, and the urban regions, in many cases with the wilderness in tow, form the opposing bloc.[10] Imbedded in this dialogue, Benton MacKaye's proposal for the Appalachian Trail is an intentional integration of populations from urban and industrial regions with untrammeled Eden. While weaving through the crowded east, the AT runs far from roads and seeks the heights (fig. 1.3). The AT remains a potent symbol of American beliefs about nature, and inherently, about the ideal human relationship to our environment.

THE APPALACHIAN TRAIL EXPERIENCE

Closed to mountain bikes and motorized vehicles, the AT is the domain of the foot-traveler (fig. 1.2). The various agencies managing the trail corridor allow horses on some sections, but many stretches are too rocky and steep for horses to climb. Most remain off-limits to equids to prevent damage. Although a majority of trail users are day hikers and backpackers out for a weekend, the through-hiker, or in AT jargon, thru-hiker, is the hero of the AT. Thru-hikers travel for weeks at a time, completing hundreds of consecutive miles. Attempting to finish the entire trail in one season, end-to-enders begin at either Springer Mountain in Georgia or on Mount Katahdin in Maine and trek to the opposite end of the trail within four to six months.

Of the hundreds starting in Georgia, usually between February and April, only a handful will reach Maine before the deposition of the deep winter snow-pack. Once hibernal conditions set in, the higher peaks of New England thwart even trained ice climbers and generate expensive rescues for poorly prepared hikers caught out in blizzards. Conversely, of the ambitious hikers departing Katahdin after snow melt in June, only a small group of survivors will cross the Great Smoky Mountains and head on to Georgia prior to the unrelenting wet snows of the southern Appalachian winter (fig. 1.4). Far fewer have completed the north to south journey than those traveling toward Maine with the early southern spring. Flip-flopping, beginning at one end and hiking to the middle, then traveling to the other end and heading back to the center—or beginning in the middle and traveling to one end, then returning to complete the remaining "half"—can optimize the weather, while reducing travel with the crowds leaving Springer around March. The flip-flop is thus becoming more common, especially for backpackers beginning during the summer and planning to finish in the fall. At the current time, about five hundred to six hundred hikers complete the entire 2,180 miles each year.[11]

Less focused than the end-to-enders are the section hikers who hike one ridgeline or a couple of states' worth at a time. Section hikers complete the AT in pieces, if they complete it at all. A notch below the thru-hikers in backpacker lore, they still wear the badge of the 2,000-milers, whether they finish in two or three years or if it takes them a lifetime. Many section hikers never give up and spend every vacation worming their way north or south until they have conquered the entire trail. Mixed with the long-distance walkers are day hikers, weekend

Fig. 1.4. A thru-hiker coming from Springer Mountain, now in the Great Smoky Mountains. He has just walked through deep snow even though the flowers are out in early April. The bright sun is an improvement.

backpackers, and the occasional organized youth group. While hiking the Appalachian Trail is a perennial wildland right of passage for recent college graduates and other athletic young adults, the ranks of successful thru-hikers include retired schoolteachers, businesspeople in the midst of a midlife career change, recently discharged military veterans, and individuals with disabilities, whose guide dogs become 2,000-milers too. Equally committed to the trail are the regional hiking clubs that perform most of its maintenance. These organizations form the Appalachian Trail Conservancy (formerly known as the Appalachian Trail Conference). Once managed entirely as a confederation of volunteer and nonprofessional bodies, the AT now falls under the watchful eyes (and bureaucracy) of the National Park Service, and of the ATC incorporated as a non-profit managed by professional staff, as well as by volunteers.

SPIRITUALITY ON THE TRAIL

Religious and sociological scholars have tested various indices of spirituality. Four academic lineages offer potential insights into defining and identifying the spiritual benefits of a national scenic trail. The first are the anthropologists and historians, such as Victor Turner and Peter Brown, who have analyzed the function and impacts of walking pilgrimages. These internationally known scholars have focused on symbol systems, the relationship between pilgrim and the sponsoring religious bodies, the evolution of pilgrimage through time, and economic and political interactions between locales sending the pilgrims and those receiving them.[12] Ethnographers often incorporate pilgrimages, walkabouts, and vision quests in their qualitative descriptions of regional religions.

The second, and very recent, source of academic models is the study of outdoor recreation as a form of religion. Joseph Price has argued that recreational activities can produce feelings associated with religion, such as a sense of awe, harmony, or even ecstasy. Recreationists may adopt religious language and metaphors.[13] Bron Taylor and his students from the University of Florida take this one step further and attempt to define aquatic nature religion as generated by aquatic sports, such as fly-fishing and kayaking. A. Whitney Sanford, for example, argues that while some kayakers do not associate their sport with religion, a subgroup of kayakers pursue their whitewater adventure as a form of mindfulness, similar to the Zen Buddhist concept. Sanford observes that whitewater paddlers enjoy "an intimate connection with immensity or perceiving something greater than the self, mindfulness, and finally risk and fear." The sport becomes "a ritual practice of an embodied encounter with the sacred, and the sacred encounter is mediated through the body's performance in the water."[14] Samuel Snyder, in discussion with fly-fishers, has found that they often describe their avocation with religious language, view their casts as a mediation between human beings and nature, and treat their rivers as sacred. For Taylor and his students, these mergers with the freshwater realm form "lived religion."[15]

Recreation and leisure sociologists who study the positive impacts of outdoor experiences are a third academic source. Paul Heintzman and Roger Mannell, for example, have investigated the effect of leisure on "ameliorating time pressure," and have found leisure does function as a buffer or coping strategy for the pressures of work, school, and even raising a family.[16] Heintzman concludes wilderness can stimulate spiritual growth and acts as a restorative environment—one that lacks the constraints of everyday life. Thus wilderness spirituality is not based on contact with nature alone, but in being away from home or having time for reflection.[17] Psychological research has found that contact with natural beauty generates feeling of awe, and thereby can generate virtues such as personal humility.

Approaches entirely based on religious participation, such as a majority of the studies of Christian pilgrimage, are not well-suited to the Appalachian Trail, because the trail population is very diverse in terms of beliefs and backgrounds. While opening new perspectives on the meaning of spending time in nature, the methods of Bron Taylor and his students do not compare Christian models with those of Eastern or alternative religions. Nor do their field studies consider the relationship of religious expression in outdoor activity to religious practice while on a river or trail. Leisure science studies frequently concern very short-term experiences, such as a day or a weekend fly-fishing jaunt, or center on guided trips, such as commercial river rafting adventures. Models aimed at leisure activities bring up the question of whether the AT thru-hike (or a walking pilgrimage) is leisure or not. Leisure usually implies a vacation from work or school. An AT end-to-end hike requires the better part of a year and is a completely lived-in experience. End-to-enders, in fact, take breaks from the trail, by visiting with their families or enjoying civilization for a few days. *Is it Leisure?*

Studies of the spiritual effectiveness of church activities, youth programs, and even long-term care options for the chronically ill offer a fourth source of academic models. These research projects overlap with attempts to define spiritual wellness in different cultural and economic settings, such as city versus country, or hospice versus resident care at home. John Fisher, Leslie Francis, and Peter Johnson developed the SH4DI, the Spiritual Health in Four Domains Index, for investigating questions such as how the spiritual wellness of teachers might influence interactions in an educational setting, or how urban adolescents fare in spiritual terms.[18] The SH4DI defines four spheres of spiritual interaction: personal, communal, environmental, and transcendent. While developing new questions for the trail survey and drawing on the leisure science findings, I utilized their strategy and methodology as a model, because SH4DI considers the environment as a critical pillar of spiritual formation. The SH4DI framework investigates interpersonal relationships, such as those with friends, family, and co-workers, environmental comfort and adaptation, physical and emotional health and wellness, and relationship with God or the forces of the universe outside the self. The AT study reaches far outside the constraints of organized religious ritual and uses variables such as comfort with the environment, improving relationships with a significant other, or feeling part of a helpful community as indices of spiritual wellness.

Two of these factors considered in the SH4DI, interpersonal and environmental interactions, change abruptly as the hiker leaves school, work, or home, enters a very mobile backpacker community, and sets out across an entire mountain range. A thru-hiker may be traveling with friends and family or may

Fig. 1.5. Winter conditions on the State Line Ridge, Great Smoky Mountains. Even in April, the weather can turn icy unexpectedly at the higher elevations.

be walking by herself, but on average brings only one or two established human relationships to the trail, if bringing any at all. AT hikers enter a beautiful, if sometimes stressful and unpredictable environment, where they camp or stay temporarily in shared and very basic accommodations (fig. 1.5). They face daily physical and logistic challenges, while being relieved of the demands of a paying job or the competitive pressures of the classroom.

The SH4DI concept is applicable to a spectrum of religious traditions, and the kinds of questions asked by SH4DI are also relevant to experiences not explicitly religious, such as building friendships while hiking. The AT hiker survey similarly had five sections, three of which utilized religious language:

1. Personal information and hiking schedule
2. Religious background
3. Ethical beliefs and environmental learning (some religious statements)
4. Significance of on-trail personal, communal, and environmental experience (no directly religious statements)
5. On-trail religious or spiritual experience

Although SH4DI does not necessarily include extensive exploration of ethics, "giving back" and practicing environmental care are both critical to the health of the AT itself.

Because the AT is historically a volunteer enterprise, the trail has generated a support network of volunteers and other individuals from surrounding communities who regularly offer assistance to hikers. Churches and retreat centers near the trail corridor sponsor hostels, and business managers go out of their way to help the thru- and section hikers. Spirituality is interactive and interconnected. Studies of wilderness or leisure spirituality usually concentrate on the recreationists, rather than on the people who provide services. This research incorporated interviews with support network individuals along the trail, including informants from both religious and nonreligious organizations. These extended conversations explored how individuals offering services to hikers became involved, whether they considered their activities to be ministry, what they believed they are offering hikers, and what benefits the AT hikers provided to them or to their home communities.

IS THE SPIRITUALITY OF LONG-DISTANCE HIKING RELATED TO PILGRIMAGE?

The walking pilgrimage, broadly defined, can follow prescribed rituals or it can be a search for personal meaning in a physical space. The fact that AT thru-hikers sometimes identify their journey as a pilgrimage, however, does not prove that the national scenic trail has evolved from religious rituals or that it is a replacement for overtly religious practice. A more valid academic approach is to ask if walking long distances has any inherent spiritual benefits, or whether the AT experience has anything in common with religious pilgrimage in terms of the motives of the participants or the outcomes they experience.

Historically, pilgrimage can be a requirement of community membership or it can be an option exercised to gain spiritual maturity or to address personal or family concerns. The best-known Christian examples are the network of roads leading to Rome, the track from London to Canterbury, now partially buried under asphalt, and the converging routes to the shrine of St. James the Greater (Santiago de Compostela), where a religious confraternity still maintains a foot and bicycle path through northern Spain. The routes to Jerusalem have attracted pilgrims since late antiquity, but the majority do not walk the entire way—they travel by sea or air to Palestine. The Hajj to Mecca is required of faithful Muslim men and unites a world religion by returning the pilgrim to a geographic source of his faith. These journeys have foundations in historic events, literature, art, and folklore, and they generate new traditions as the community of participants grows and reconstructs itself through time.[19]

Although pilgrimage roads are less common in the United States than in Europe,[20] both Roman Catholics and Native American religionists still honor distinctive montane examples.[21] The Hopi celebrate the seasonal arrival of the kachinas on Arizona's San Francisco Peaks. Roman Catholics believe the soil from a small, historic church, Santuario de Chimayo, in New Mexico has healing properties. Lenten penitents, carrying large wooden crosses, walk the upland road from Santa Fe to Santuario, demonstrating repentance and sharing in the sufferings of Christ. Asian forms of religious pilgrimage to holy mountains have also arrived in the United States. In 1965, for example, Gary Snyder, Allen Ginsberg, and Philip Whalen, all poets, circumambulated Mount Tamalpais, on the Pacific coast of California. They invoked the Asian practice of walking clockwise around the peak, which is a metaphor for the daily passage of the sun, and a form of veneration.[22] The contemplative circuit around Mount Tam has continued to the present, as have the recently established New Age and alternative religious pilgrimages to Mount Shasta, CA, and Sedona, AZ.[23]

Spiritual traditions concerning wilderness or long-distance walking fit roughly, with some overlap, into three major categories. The first is the wilderness sojourn, which often is stationary, once the practitioner has reached a suitable uninhabited sanctuary. In Asian religions, residence in the forest fosters enlightenment. Gautama Buddha left his family and sat under a bodhi tree, while seeking understanding of the cycles of life and death. Taoists established hermitages where immersion in isolated mountain landscapes, and meditation by foaming cascades, fostered simplicity and insight into the structure of the cosmos. In biblical terms, withdrawal into the wilderness was cathartic and purifying. The participants freed themselves from the sins of covetous civilization and encountered theophanies—appearances of angels or God. Moses viewed Yahweh (from behind) and received the Ten Commandments on a mountain far from the cities of oppressive Egypt. Wilderness provided stamina for difficult tasks, such as Elijah's return to Jerusalem to face Jezebel, after ravens fed the prophet in the desert. Spiritual disciplines, such as prayer, meditation, and fasting, are important preparation in both Eastern and Western wilderness traditions. One of my earlier books, *Christianity, Wilderness and Wildlife: The Original Desert Solitaire* and Belden Lane's *The Solace of Fierce Landscapes: Exploring Desert and Mountain Spirituality,* review traditions relevant to Christian wildland experience.[24]

Many regional religions prescribe extended wilderness solos, in the form of vision quests or walkabouts intended to build courage and self-confidence for warriors and hunters coming of age. The solo quest may be required of all young adult males or all shamans. In the world religions that have grown out of cultures with complex class structure, wilderness sojourns are more often the prerogative of religious professionals, such as monks and prophets. The first Christian ascetics believed entering into the wilderness without proper discipline to be dangerous, both in terms of physical risks and the possibility of being tempted by evil powers. Henry David Thoreau's extended withdrawal to a one-room cabin at Walden Pond has Christian precedents in its pursuit of simplicity, rejection of materialism, openness to nature's lessons, and search for cosmological insight.

The second historic form of religious travel seeks out a sacred locale, or passes through a sanctified landscape. Though wilderness residence may be solo, this type of outdoor or walking spirituality is often a group event, or a number of believers take to the road independently and form a temporary community as they meet each other along the way. The pilgrimage becomes a way of displaying commitment to God and a willingness to leave everyday occupations and devote one's self to God or to a saint for an extended period of time. Christian pilgrims may seek healing for themselves or for ill relatives left at home. The pilgrim may hope for a supernatural favor, such as a cure for a chronic disease, or may be seeking greater spiritual purity.[25]

Pilgrimage is also a historic form of penance—a way of saying you are sorry for harm caused to others, and that you are willing to make a greater effort to care for other people. Some cultures still send individuals who violate social norms on long walks or journeys, isolating them from their permanent abode. Natural environments create stress and increase the difficulty of the journey, or they symbolize the quest toward the righteous life. Climbing a mountain imitates the ascent to heaven or to entrance into the courts of the Lord. Circumambulating a peak is a common practice where single mountains are believed to be deities or sources of spiritual power.

The way the walker approaches a mountain can assist in developing a relationship with a religious community or landscape. An example is the climb up Croagh Patrick—St. Patrick's Mountain—on the west coast of Ireland (fig. 1.6). The path is steep and stony. Lenten pilgrims sometimes ascend on their knees and in bare feet, which are bruised and bloody by the time they reach the summit. A small chapel, which once contained relics of the saint, offers services on the peak. On a clear day, the pilgrim looks out over the lovely convoluted Atlantic shoreline below and enjoys the boundary between land and sea. The mountain is both Patrick himself and a microcosm of Ireland. Even the fog setting in is a part of Ireland's natural riches, as are the glistening lakes in the distant valley. (A number of pilgrims have been killed by lightning or by losing their way in the mist and stepping off the edge of the cliffs just below the peak.) The pilgrim, in the ascent, is uniting with Patrick and with the spirit of Erin. The strain and the danger seal the commitment and the belief in Ireland as a province of God.[26]

One-day or short term pilgrimages engage entire villages and participants of all ages. The extended journeys and more-strenuous tracks, especially those over mountain ranges or the open seas, draw adults who are very devout or who have specific needs or goals. A pilgrimage often begins in the wake of tragedy, such as losing a child or an estate, or may mark a life transition, such as entry into old age or widowhood. Devout Hindus may pursue a sannyasin phase, after they reach the end of child rearing and productive employment. A sannyasin

Fig. 1.6. The foot of Croagh Patrick, a holy mountain on the west
coast of Ireland. The mountain symbolizes St. Patrick, his journey, and the nation of Ireland as holy ground.

puts away material goods and family responsibilities and enters the forest to
dwell as an ascetic, or goes wandering without any means of support. Bishops,
abbots, confessors, or spiritual advisors may send a novice or a sinner on pilgrimage as a form of self-examination and atonement. The individual who has
asked God or a saint for a favor or blessing, such as healing a chronic illness, will
undertake pilgrimage as a form of repayment. Pilgrimage is assumed to reduce
or remove the distractions of family or business, and to allow time for prayer and
meditating on life's deeper meaning. Struggling along the sacred path is a form
of spiritual athleticism, a workout for body, mind, and soul (fig. 1.7).

The third form of spiritual trek is less programmed, and might be termed
immersion in nature. This genre of spiritual discipline does not require a wild
or isolated locale, and often consciously pursues aesthetics. Buddhists practice

Fig. 1.7. Climbing up the stony slope of Croagh Patrick, Republic of Ireland. The route is a penitential journey, simultaneously beautiful and difficult. Some pilgrims walk barefoot or ascend on their knees over the loose stones.

walking prayer on simple garden walkways or woods roads, and generate poems and paintings from visits to a quiet path, pond, or garden. In the wake of the Reformation, nonconformist Protestants jettisoned organized pilgrimage to shrines, while retaining the concept of a prayer-filled Sunday stroll in the countryside as a form of sanctified relaxation.[27] Contact with nature became instructional, providing insights into the character of the Creator. Thoreau's short and pithy treatise on walking describes the philosophical values of penetrating woodlots and exploring country lanes.[28] The late-twentieth-century revival of Celtic religious traditions has encouraged "walking the mist," a form of spirituality-attentive entry into natural settings.[29] Christians, Buddhists, and adherents of alternative religions are exploring mindful walking as a spiritual discipline.[30]

Even in the face of their international acceptance as legitimate spiritual practice, walking pilgrimage and withdrawal into the wilderness have detractors, including religious reformers. Protestant denominations have rejected pilgrimage to shrines as a self-centered waste of time and avoidance of household responsibilities. As medieval and Reformation critics have recorded, some Christian pilgrims were traveling more for entertainment than religious commitment, and engaging in drinking or even sexually unrestrained behavior while away from home. Geoffrey Chaucer's *Canterbury Tales* is a well-studied record of the aspects of pilgrimage not mandated by religious ritual.[31] Martin Luther discouraged pilgrimage, as did John Calvin. They also rejected monasticism, and with it, extended withdrawal from secular society to pursue prayer and contemplation. Although taking time out for a quiet stroll with God is fine, an extended wilderness sojourn is not, because it removes the Christian from his or her family and from direct service to other people. Even Roman Catholic bishops, who believed in the validity of pilgrimage to saints' wells and shrines, have been forced to legislate or discourage pilgrimage when it got out of hand. In the nineteenth century, Irish priests, for example, tried to reign in pattern days (celebrations of saints' days). The processions to holy wells and community masses were well ordered and brought villages together. The fairs, tippling, horse racing, and drunken fistfights detracted from the religious intent of the celebrations. Since the Reformation, Western theologians have argued over whether wilderness and walking pilgrimage experience is spiritually valuable or not.

Pilgrims on a National Trail?

What kind of spiritual experience might a national trail foster? And what environmental and spiritual values does a long-distance walk on a recreational trail teach? Since the 1960s, academic judgment has frequently found Christianity and environmental care at odds with each other. The creation of new "saints' trails," such as Cuthbert's Way on the Scottish border with Northumberland, and Declan's Way in Ireland, imply compatibility between more traditional Christianity and environmental yearnings.[32] Not only do these footpaths have published guides, but the revival of interest in Celtic spirituality has provided other historic materials, such as David Adam's *Fire of the North: The Illustrated Life of Cuthbert.*[33] While lacking saints' graves and priory ruins, the national trails in the United States are not without their religious and spiritual roots. Henry David Thoreau, the committed transcendentalist, trekked to Mount Katahdin, a rugged peak, now the northern terminus of the Appalachian Trail in Maine. He soared into a mystical experience during a sunrise on Mount Greylock, MA, also now on the AT.[34] John Muir, in his effuse praise of wandering the Yosemite Valley, invoked biblical imagery.

Geraldo Campo has argued that there are three kinds of pilgrimage land-scapes in the United States, those of

- organized religion, such as Santuario
- civil religion, which connect God and country, or patriotic events at such places as Gettysburg or Mount Rushmore (many of them supervised by the National Park Service)
- and cultural religion, which "involve ceremonial centers, ritualization, mythic figures, and journeys," such as Graceland Mansion.[35]

The Appalachian Trail, as an iconic destination, has elements of all of these cat-egories, and perhaps one of its attractions is the synthesis it presents among them. The vast majority of religious pilgrimages focus on a single religious struc-ture, holy city, mountain, lake, or spring. The AT is one long excursion through protected space exempt from economic productivity, where numerous natural features have exceptional symbolic or aesthetic value. After I had completed the fieldwork for this project, Kip Redick published a scholarly chapter identifying the Appalachian Trail hike as a "spiritual journey." Redick's analysis was based on observed integration of hikers into the landscape, rather than on interviews or questionnaires gathering user perceptions.[36] The essay, however, extends Campo's model of civil religion to a form of "civil spirituality."

In his original concept for the trail, Benton MacKaye did not mention re-ligion or spirituality, while being definite the intent was a series of linked com-munities that resided on the Appalachian heights. The ATC and the trail clubs, arising in the shadow of the transcendentalist and Christian belief that solitude in the mountains can bring one closer to God, have always accepted religious or spiritual experience as a legitimate individual goal for hiking on the Appalachian

Trail. John Hendee's and Chad Dawson's well-circulated textbook on wilderness management addresses spiritual development briefly as a common, if minority, motive for wilderness visitation.[37] The wilderness sojourner begins by observing the forces and extent of nature, which produces a sense of the insignificance of the individual. Ultimately, immersion in the wild causes a recognition of transcendence and a vision of wilderness as "Wholly Other,"[38] thus wild or protected nature is inherently sacred space.[39]

LAYERS OF MEANING

The AT presents several layers of spiritual meaning. At its most basic, the trail is the conglomeration of mountain ranges forming the Appalachians. Before the trail, there was line after line of ridges jutting up from the piedmont and the Atlantic flatlands, catching the clouds and absorbing the rains. The steep slopes embrace myriad small watersheds, flowing together to feed the great rivers, not just of the Atlantic rim but also of the Mississippi drainage. With the exceptions of a few peaks above timberline and the occasional plunging cliff, the Appalachians have been densely vegetated since the last retreat of glacial ice. Their thick forest is the perfect home for thrushes, warblers, and woodpeckers, while their acorns and blueberries sustain the "good life" for black bears. Clear rivers pour down from the well-watered highlands and form such ecologically productive watersheds as the Tennessee, the Housatonic, the Potomac, the Susquehanna, and even the Chesapeake Bay. The AT is a physical terrain and the center of the eastern deciduous forest biome (fig. 1.3).

At the human level, the AT crosses a political and residential territory. Formerly the secure home of the eastern woodland Indian confederations, the Appalachian ranges slowed the relentless advance of the early European colonists. Tales of the frontier, cultural conflict, and of European adaptation to the new land lace the mountains with myths of nation building and rugged American character. The establishment of villages, roads, and industry accompanied the formation of the new republic, as it rose from wobbly independence and took its place on the world scene. The Appalachians were an early recreational geography. The valleys had barely been cleared for livestock rearing when tourist hotels and spas began to spring up, particularly in the Hudson River Valley, Catskills, and Berkshires. The shaded, breezy hills have served as a relief from city life and from lowland summer heat and a magnet for the intelligentsia for more than two centuries. In books, essays, and paintings, the realm of the AT has been a metaphor for the character-building frontier experience and for the virtues of wildness.

On a third level, the trail and its protective corridor stand as public domain. The trail has no user fees or barriers to entry. It is a democratic enterprise, rooted in American volunteerism. A refuge for hikers, the AT gives them the legal right to pass through the heart of the eastern mountains unimpeded, via an intentional synthesis between the natural and the human.

On the fourth level, the trail is a human community, comprised not just of hikers but also of the people they encounter along the way. The trail is maintainers and trail clubs, hostel managers, outfitters, forest rangers, ridge runners, hut crews, and country store clerks. In the center is the hiker culture, sometimes entirely self-absorbed, sometimes strongly interactive with the business and organizations outside the official trail corridor. Today the trail has so much traffic, and such an extensive support network, that the human element frequently dominates over the natural in determining the spiritual and personal experience of the AT. Figure 1.8 shows the Founders Bridge and the recreational support facilities at Weser, NC, where the AT crosses the Nantahala River. One of many such connections between the trail and civilization, these nodes of development are a key component of the twenty-first-century AT experience.

On a final level, the Appalachian Trail is a state of being—a merger of ancient mountains, flowing rivers, caring companions, human endeavor, and individual growth and change. Nothing is merely human, and nothing is merely natural. The essence of both intertwines in a long thread, woven north to south, and back again.

Fig. 1.8. The Founder's footbridge, where the Appalachian Trail crosses the Nantahala River, North Carolina. The Nantahala flows into the Tennessee River. The trail connects the watersheds of notable East Coast rivers.

CHAPTER 2
THE TRAIL AS PHYSICAL AND SOCIAL ENVIRONMENT
TRAIL DESIGN

For the reader unfamiliar with the geography and construction of the Appalachian Trail, the AT is a footpath maintained at the width for one hiker, or about twelve to twenty-four inches of bare soil or treadway (about thirty to sixty cm), and a branch-free zone, just slightly greater, to about three feet (one meter). Many sections are wider owing to use of old roadbeds or the concentrated impacts of hikers and weekenders who trample the edges and widen the area of bare soil and rock on the sections connecting the most popular hiking destinations. The maintained width is usually the minimum needed to provide safe footing, while protecting adjoining vegetation. The trail is marked throughout with white linear blazes. A single blaze indicates walk straight ahead, and a double blaze indicates a turn. Although planners have considered other termini, and the AT formerly ended at Mount Oglethorpe in Georgia, the current trail extends from the summit of Springer Mountain, GA, to the summit of Mount Katahdin, ME. An extension to Canada is complete, and one south to Alabama and the very southern tip of the Appalachians is in process.

The trail preferentially follows the ridgetop—sometimes actually on the crest of the ridge, sometimes weaving just below the highest contour or switch-backing up a shoulder. This was the original concept of Benton MacKaye. The ATC trail manual, which sets design and construction standards, states: "the trail is primarily a ridgecrest track. It crosses a series of distinctive Appalachian summits, climbs countless rocky outcrops, and plunges into a seemingly endless number of gaps. It challenges hikers constantly with its bone-wearying ruggedness. . . . To this day, Appalachian Trail volunteers follow a simple guiding principle whenever they must relocate the trail: 'Put the land and mass below the hiker."'[1] Because of this principle, when topography forces the AT to descend into gaps and major river valleys, the trail usually seeks the shortest route back to the heights.

The ridgetop position does not always provide the best views or the greatest natural diversity while symbolizing the center or the pinnacle of the entire "Appalachian empire." Most of the route is heavily forested, and visibility off the ridge is limited in the summer months. Some sections are mile after mile of oaks and broad-leaved trees, while others are crowned with high-elevation spruce or fir forest (fig. 2.1). The effect is to be constantly above the surrounding geography and to descend only to cross major streams or to briefly parallel major river valleys such as the Potomac, Delaware, Nolichucky, and Housatonic.

While on trail, hikers usually stay at open-fronted shelters, in enclosed huts with food and bunks provided, or in primitive campsites (requiring a tent), usually with a nearby spring or stream as a water source. Thru-hikers share the simple, airy structures with overnighters and even day hikers dropping by to have lunch or just to see the shelter (fig. 2.2). The national parks along the route have es-

Fig. 2.1. View from the Appalachian Trail in the fall, Great Smoky Mountains National Park, looking out into North Carolina. The prevalence of national forest and national park lands in the southeast isolates the trail and provides views without proximate human development. The forest in the valley below is one of the most extensive tracts of old growth in the East.

tablished permit systems to reduce overcrowding, or in the case of Shenandoah have closed most of the shelters to overnight use, just allowing day hikers to visit the roofed structures. During the prime thru-hiking season, the shelters are often overfilled. Thru-hikers pitch tents around the shelter area, creating a high human-contact setting, even where the shelters are more than five miles from the nearest road. Thru-hikers are usually exempt from permit restrictions, so encountering twenty or more in or near a shelter has become a common experience, particularly in the southern states in midspring. Hikers traveling from north to south, beginning in June at Katahdin, ME, encounter fewer fellow thru-hikers, but walk through New England and the Middle Atlantic states at the height of the summer season, thus they maximize their encounters with day hikers and weekenders. Southbounders reach the Great Smokies and the Nantahalas during fall color season. While weekdays may be quiet and encounters with surviving thru-hikers relatively few, the October weekends are even more cluttered with day hikers than summer weekends are. Although current corridor management policy emphasizes the wilderness character of the trail, the majority of successful thru- and section hikers spend few nights alone if they chose to stay at official shelters and campsites.

Through the 1970s, the handful of thru-hikers attempting the trail each year usually packed several days' worth of food and resupplied at relatively long intervals. When off-trail they could either find a commercial campground or stay at a motel or hotel, the latter strategy considerably raising the expense of the trip. Thru-hiker traffic has increased steadily since the trail was established. From the 1930s through the 1960s, an estimated sixty-two intrepid, old-fashioned backpackers became 2,000-milers. During the 1970s, 753 reported finishing, and in the 1990s, 3,280 signed in as 2,000-milers.[2] Beginning in the 1970s, inexpensive hiker hostels began to appear along the trail, and municipalities responded to increased traffic by allowing hikers to use public parks or even police or fire station facilities to take a shower. The first operations were primarily volunteer or nonprofit—managed by churches, volunteer fire departments, and civic organizations. Some churches, for example, have built hostels, while others have allowed hikers to stay in a community room or parish hall. The steady increase in thru-hiker traffic through the 1980s and 1990s has supported establishment of commercial hiker hostels. Some motels and bed and breakfasts have added inexpensive hiker bunk rooms or a "hostel" within the context of their regular tourist-oriented operations. Overnight accommodations for hikers have emerged as a

Fig. 2.2. Backpackers and day hikers meet at Mount Collins Shelter, Great Smoky Mountains. Close interactions with new people and mixing with other hikers from different backgrounds characterize the Appalachian Trail.

mix of volunteer-run facilities, some of which are free or donation-based, and inexpensive bunk rooms, cabins, and even reduced-rate motel rooms. Figure 2.3 shows the living room at the Church of the Mountain hostel at Delaware Water Gap, PA, with its basic comforts and shared social space adjoining the bunk rooms. In 2008, this was still a donation-based hostel, and hikers could stay without paying if they were short of funds.

The first successful end-to-ender, Earl Schafer, who hiked the entire AT south to north in 1948, camped alone much of the time, and had no facilities available specifically for him when he came into towns. Today's hiker, in contrast, has a support network and knowledgeable guidance present along the entire route. Web sites, such as WhiteBlaze.net, and the published trail guides provide lists of overnight accommodations, directions to grocery stores, and even commentaries on which towns near the trail are the most hiker friendly. Unlike Earl Schaffer, the twenty-first-century hiker has a community of long-distance walkers who offer assistance to each other, such as lending moleskin to protect blistered feet or guarding a pack while someone walks into a village. The support network is

Fig. 2.3. The living room at Church of the Mountain hostel, run by the Presbyterian church at Delaware Water Gap, Pennsylvania.

now so well organized that shuttle operators offer "slack-packing"—a driver will take your pack to town so you can walk a section of the AT without carrying the weight of a full-sized backpack.

TRAIL REGIONS

THE SOUTHERN APPALACHIANS

In terms of environment and topography, the trail can be best understood by considering differences between the southern Appalachians, the Middle Atlantic states, and southern and northern New England. In the southern states, the Appalachian Trail largely traverses national forests (NF) and national parks (NP).[3] Backpackers most frequently begin in Amicalola Falls State Park, at the base of Springer Mountain, GA, and then follow the AT into the Chattahoochee NF. Although the initial elevations are moderate, thru-hikers initiating in Georgia encounter many tiring uphill and downhill pitches. Blisters and sprained ankles inhibit a confident stride within the first fifty miles. An estimated 30 to 40 percent of hikers starting the trail at Springer drop out before reaching Fontana Dam in southwestern North Carolina, the gateway to the Great Smoky Mountains.[4]

While the southern tip primarily traverses dense forest, Tray Mountain and Blood Mountain in Georgia offer sweeping views over blue-tinted ranges. Surrounded by national forest, the AT edges along the acrophobia-inducing cliffs at Standing Indian in North Carolina, and drops into steep-sided Nantahala Gorge, famous for whitewater kayaking. One of the most heavily utilized sections bisects Great Smoky Mountains NP from southwest to northeast along the Tennessee/North Carolina border and offers the highest elevations, but not the most extreme climate, on the AT. The honor of generating the most dangerous and swiftly changing weather goes to Mount Washington, NH.[5] Winds on the Presidential Peak have been clocked at a world record of 231 mph. Although the outliers of boreal spruce-fir forest on Clingman's Dome and Tricorner Knob are blanketed by deep snows in mid-winter, the highest promontories in the Southern Appalachians remain below timberline (fig. 2.1).

The AT bridges the French Broad River at Hot Springs, NC, and the Nolichucky River, near Erwin, TN, then climbs to the Roan Highlands State Park. The scenery here is spectacular, including both extensive grassy balds, with unrestricted views, and gorges with rapids or waterfalls. After traversing the Holston River, the trail rambles through the Mount Rogers National Recreation Area, where hikers can take a short side trail to the namesake summit, the highest elevation in VA. Once grazed by settler livestock, open grasslands grace the peak. Ponies still have the privilege of enjoying the cool summer and thick grasses on the broad crest. Remaining largely within national forest, the trail briefly intersects West Virginia, and winds back and forth across both the Blue Ridge Parkway and the Skyline Drive in Shenandoah NP. Heading toward the Mason-Dixon Line, the AT bridges the Potomac River at Harpers Ferry, WV, where the headquarters of the Appalachian Trail Conservancy is located.

When Benton MacKaye first suggested the route, very little of the current corridor was under federal or state management. In his 1921 proposal, MacKaye lamented the concentration of federally administered parks and forests in the West, while the bulk of the laboring population resided in the East. MacKaye spent his early professional career working for the U.S. Forest Service. He recognized the potential for establishing public wildlands in the East, yet his original proposal assumes the presence of permanent human communities along the backbone of the Appalachians. MacKaye believed that agriculture was necessary to self-sufficiency.[6] At the close of the First World War, the southern Appalachians were still the realm of small farms and logging camps. Herders' cabins and camps dotted the ridgetops and kept the rain off the guardians of the sheep and steers that summered in grassy patches at the high elevations. Today, south of the Potomac, a hiker feels surrounded by the feds (fig. 2.1). Though the lands here are public, they are also tightly regulated. MacKaye, in suggesting the AT as a barrier to the ills of industrialization, could not have known the future extent of public domain. The route MacKaye originally imagined would have accommodated orchards, wandering cattle, and moonshine stills adjoining a narrow hiker thoroughfare.

When the trail was first established, the route through the southern Appalachians had many sections that crossed high-elevation pastures or followed narrow roads through farming valleys. Hikers ran into southern highlanders out plowing with mules. Federal acquisition of much of the surrounding land and of the trail corridor itself has reduced hiker contact with agriculture and timber harvest. Removal of livestock from areas such as the Great Smoky Mountains NP, for example, eliminated the grazing pressure generated by sheep and cattle, and thereby the presence of open grassy balds, with their panoramic vistas. Today's hiker has less contact with rural Americana than AT walkers did for the first half century of the trail's existence.

Owing to the extent of public lands adjoining the corridor, today's thru-hikers generally walk or hitchhike several miles to towns and campgrounds. The first place, traveling northbound, to resupply on trail is Mountain Crossings at Neel's Gap, GA. The first genuine trail town, where the white blazes run right down the sidewalks, is Hot Springs, NC. The mineral baths established in the late eighteenth century are still in operation, albeit with renovated plumbing. Hot tubs on the French Broad River are available for a fee. The best-known southern trail town is Damascus, VA. Supporting the recreation based economy, hostels, campgrounds, ice cream shops, and outfitters line the main street and are available within a block or two of the trail (fig. 2.4). Damascus sponsors the best-attended annual hiker festival, Trail Days, in mid-May each year. Towns several miles off-trail, such as Franklin, NC, offer shuttles sponsored by motels and provide similar services for hikers.

Fig. 2.4. The main street through Damascus, Virginia. Damascus is nicknamed "The friendliest town on the Appalachian Trail" and also provides services for bicyclists.

The original trail planners ran the blazed route through incorporated municipalities from the beginning. Some of the deviations down sidewalks were necessary in the early days, because the towns have bridges across the deeper rivers. The trail has avoided larger cities, however, while treating the villages and small towns as healthy contact with the virtuous countryside. They have always provided access to groceries, hardware, fuel, churches, and bus or rail services. Benton MacKaye intended the AT to symbolize what is most worthy in terms of the culture of the "Appalachian empire," and the trail towns welcome the hiker into friendly and peaceful Americana. Today the trail could reroute around most of these towns, but tradition and hiker attachment resist the change.

THE MIDDLE ATLANTIC STATES

In the Middle Atlantic states—Maryland, Pennsylvania, New Jersey, and New York—the AT swings northeast across relatively low mountains settled by Europeans prior to the American Revolution. The historic villages near the AT have eighteenth-century churches to match the stolid, fieldstone farmhouses that sent men into battle formations, first at Monmouth and Valley Forge, then at Antietam and Gettysburg. Although upland dairying and truck patches filled the valleys between the ridges until recent decades, suburbanization has slowly pushed the agriculturalists out. For the observant, the abandoned pastures are marked by quaint stone walls adjoining the treadway and by rows of older trees along roads once used by horse-drawn wagons (fig. 2.5).

The AT passes a long-abandoned strip mine at Rausch Gap, PA, and a zinc mine dating from the early nineteenth century at Palmerton, PA. Also in this region, the trail intersects several relict canals, which once facilitated the shipment of manufactured goods and raw materials to a nation expanding westward. The ever-opportunistic trail briefly follows the C&O Canal and its towpath, along the Potomac River, providing views of the undammed waters churning around rocks and pouring unobstructed toward the nation's capitol. Once a mighty industrial artery, pumping goods and raw materials between the settled Atlantic coast and the midwestern frontier, the C&O is now a quaint bicycle adventure, distinguished by restored locks and canal boat rides for Washington tourists. The Potomac itself is symbolic of the country's political heritage, having once served as a vital transportation artery connecting the frontier to civilization, as well as being the brutally contested boundary between North and South during the Civil War. The uplands of the Middle Atlantic region have been at least moderately economically prosperous and accessible to nearby market towns and industrial cities since the Federalist period. The long-distance hiker will find that asphalt road crossings are relatively frequent.

In the Middle Atlantic, notably in Pennsylvania and New Jersey, the AT passes relatively close to some of the largest cities in the United States. The dense urbanization is one of the reasons the middle of the AT is to a greater extent on state forest, game, and parklands than it is in the South. State or municipal development of public parks and hunting lands began with such successful projects as Central Park in Manhattan and Harriman State Park along the Hudson. In Maryland, the AT passes through Washington Monument State Park while skirting the federal Catoctin Mountain Park, which encircles presidential Camp David. The exception is federally managed Delaware Water Gap National Recreation Area, bracketing the bridge across the Delaware River.

Through much of the Middle Atlantic, the mountains are low and relatively flat-topped, although the stony backbone of the Pennsylvania ridgetops is

Fig. 2.5. The Pinwheel view, Wawayanda Mountain, New Jersey. Despite the relatively low elevation of the Appalachian Trail there, the Middle Atlantic States still offer some spectacular vistas.

unforgiving in its impact on human heels, ankles, and knees. They still offer some stair-step–like climbs of more than one thousand feet and pleasing views of the surrounding countryside, dotted with farms or bedroom communities (fig. 2.5). The high interface of old open fields and residential lawns with deciduous forest, even into the Shawangunks and Hudson River Highlands of New York, make this region prime deer habitat and one of the worst areas for deer tick bites and therefore Lyme disease infection along the AT. Even with the suburban sprawl creeping around the trail corridor, these states can still produce both trip-stopping health issues and motivation lapses.

North of Delaware Water Gap, the AT reaches the first natural, glacier-carved water body on the route, Sunfish Pond, NJ. The Appalachian Trail generally does not follow rivers for long distances, nor does it seek out or circle lakes. Once the northbound thru-hiker reaches previously glaciated terrain, however, the AT allows a periodic glimpse of a lake or a stroll along an open shoreline. Under the influence of the National Park Service, the AT has become friendlier to valley bottom wetlands. Rerouting to avoid vehicle roads now incorporates substantial sections of boardwalk and puncheon in northern New Jersey (fig. 2.6).

Fig. 2.6. Appalachian Trail boardwalk in the wetland surrounding Pochuck Creek, New Jersey. This is a recently constructed section of the Appalachian Trail that eliminated a road walk. The choice of route and the expense of trail construction demonstrate the increased emphasis on incorporating diverse habitats and aquatic features.

NEW ENGLAND

In southern New England, through the Taconics and the Berkshires, the trail is village-friendly, skirting such historic hamlets as Shirley, CT, and North Adams, MA. The AT follows the Housatonic River, sometimes on the ridge above, sometimes low on the river floodplain. At Bulls Bridge and West Cornwall the trail provides easy side trips to covered bridges, remnants of rural architecture

Fig. 2.7. Great Falls on the Housatonic, Connecticut. Although hikers have to share the views with tourists from nearby parking areas, the Falls announces the northbound hikers' arrival back in increasingly elevated terrain after crossing the low point of the trail in the broad river valleys near the Atlantic coast.

that continue to be accessible into Vermont. The mountains are low and seventeenth- and eighteenth-century villages are always nearby. Although sub-urbanization has much reduced agricultural land, the AT still traverses pictur-esque valleys and looks down on fields divided by stone walls. Prior to the Civil War, the presence of water power and iron ore made southern New England a leader in industrialization. The trail passes abandoned ironworks and furnaces that supplied Lincoln's armies with cannons and, ultimately, a Union victory. As the AT follows the valley of Housatonic River and reaches Great Falls, it honors the colonial and nineteenth-century industrial heritage of the nation (fig. 2.7).

When the new republic began to form its own cultural identity, southern New England attracted painters and writers, who rented homes there and undertook extended stays at village inns. The valleys of the Hudson, Housatonic, and Connecticut Rivers were a nurturing ground for American romanticism. Washington Irving roamed the Hudson Highlands, as is evident in *Rip van Winkle*. Nathaniel Hawthorne took up residence in the Berkshires, as did Herman Melville, who could view Mount Greylock from Arrowwood, his rural residence near Pittsfield, MA. The hiker crossing Mount Greylock will have a premonition of the higher elevations to come. Coniferous forests dominated by spruces, missing since the southern Appalachians, once again crown the ridges.

Reaching Vermont and New Hampshire, a high proportion of the AT is in the Green Mountains and the White Mountains National Forests, while in Maine, state lands and the former properties of logging companies bracket the corridor. The AT ends at Mount Katahdin in the middle of Baxter State Park. In the north, the trail returns to very wild country and a region that remains sparsely occupied and primarily dependent on income from natural resource harvest. The White Mountains exceed five thousand feet and, along with Mount Katahdin in Maine, provide the only genuine tree lines and alpine meadows on the AT. The villages of southern New England fall away. Subtly, though, this portion of the trail is still protected by economies long rooted in tourist dollars. Where the AT descends to civilization in the White Mountains, for example, it either passes the campgrounds and facilities of the Appalachian Mountain Club or the U.S. Forest Service, or it enters towns such as Gorham, NH, where tourism is a predominant source of income. The hut system is an organized intrusion of this economy up to the highest ridges and, in fact, reflects the tastes of nineteenth-century tourists who traveled in horse-drawn coaches or by rail, and expected a bed and a meal to be provided at the inns they visited.

The full-service hut system (with indoor bed and meals) is confined to the White Mountains and ends at the New Hampshire–Maine border. Maine has historically been one of the most isolated legs of the AT journey, and still has some of the longest sections without easy access to supplies. The elevations in the middle of the Maine AT are not particularly high, but the ground is boggy and the original construction left treacherous river crossings unbridged. In the early twentieth century, Maine had fewer high-elevation residences and much less mountaintop agriculture than the southern Appalachians, so locals were

Fig. 2.8. Reaching the summit of Mount Washington via the Appalachian Trail, New Hampshire. The White Mountains are the second highest section of the Appalachian Trail. Here the trail runs above tree line for miles.

less present along the route, making it more difficult for travelers to round up some biscuits and gravy. The Hundred-Mile Wilderness can still leave incautious backpackers, who failed to stock up prior to entering this largely roadless area, hungry and short of necessities by the time they have slogged through. The final pitch from the south up Mount Katahdin is one of the most rugged and risky in the face of changing weather, not just on the AT but in the entire East. Katahdin has served as an icon of relict eastern wildness since Henry David Thoreau bushwhacked up its stream courses and through its evergreen skirts. This stoic pinnacle, rising out of dark-green coniferous forests and sparkling snowfields, accommodates today's automobile-borne tourists to its base (they still have to hike to the top) without losing its awe-generating grandeur.[7]

The White Mountains and Mount Katahdin offer some of the most dramatic scenery along the entire AT. The variety of the terrain in New England rewards the thru-hikers struggling up among the fir trees to alpine meadows and boulder fields above five thousand feet (fig. 2.8). Thru-hikers change back into cold-weather gear as they prepare for the notoriously variable weather. The terrain is steep and rocky, and injury-inducing falls are a major threat. Southbound hikers have to wait until snowmelt is complete, or nearly so, to start south from Katahdin and avoid plunging temperatures, high winds, and excessive ice on the rocky path.

THE HUMAN AND THE NATURAL

Although the AT is a unit of the National Park Service, an elected board representing the major stakeholders guides the management of the Appalachian Trail. A Stewardship Council oversees the practical side of conserving trail resources and providing standards for trail maintainers. The ATC, incorporating thirty-one member clubs, has about forty thousand members, the vast majority of whom are not end-to-enders.[8]

The Appalachian Trail offers a constant dialogue between the human and the "natural." Much of the route was previously disturbed by anthropogenic actions and economic exploitation, such as logging. Some of the most famous view points, particularly in the southern states, are the result of logging or agriculture, including grazing. Big Meadows in Shenandoah NP, for example, is an artifact of farming. Other spots have towers constructed to patrol for wildfire, or to provide views for tourists. Even the peaks in northern New England, which are naturally above tree line, harbor a collection of buildings, vehicle roads, ski areas, and the single-track cog railroad ascending Mount Washington. The trail clubs and conservation leaders who have designed and managed the AT have long engaged in dialogue about the wilderness nature of the trail. Protecting the corridor from intrusion and development is currently a primary objective of the ATC, as is maintaining the diversity of species and natural features along the corridor.

Today the ATC continues to work to maintain the wilderness nature of the corridor and its ridge crown location, goals that require extensive compromise concerning other trail values. Though the AT through the Great Smoky Mountains NP is out of earshot of roads for a majority of its length, it still ascends the highest peak on the entire trail to encounter a concrete tower, which looks like a giant snail rising above the fir trees (fig. 2.9). The AT sojourn is not on average an extended wilderness experience, as today's hikers spend many nights in town or in hostels or campsites with access to electricity. The human aspects of the trail add comfort to the hikes and provide views and landscape perspectives that would not otherwise be available, such as the walk up the tower on Clingman's Dome.

The position of the trail on the ridgetop sometimes compromises the wilderness ambience. This is most noticeable along the Blue Ridge Parkway and in

Fig. 2.9. Looking up at the concrete tower on Clingman's Dome, Tennessee, the highest point on the entire Appalachian Trail.

Shenandoah NP, where the trail shares the heights with scenic roads. The trail is so close to Skyline Drive, for example, that the hiker can repeatedly hear motorized vehicles. Trekkers must cross hardtop more than twenty times through the length of the national park. The AT also enters a number of cleared areas below the parking lots and overlooks constructed for the drive. These provide rare vistas in the density of summer foliage, while being direct encounters with automobile-based culture. The concrete posts, which have replaced wooden signs, reduce vandalism and sign theft, largely activities of automobile-based tourists. The concrete posts carry the white blaze of the Appalachian Trail, while announcing the conflict between the scenic drive and the footpath.

EVOLUTION OF THE TRAIL

The Appalachian Trail is constantly evolving. Both Appalachian economics and conscious management for wilderness values have greatly reduced hikers' direct contact with plowboys and woodcutters, as well as with the landscapes they create. The moonshiner, once a potential flesh and blood trail encounter, is fading into historic regional lore. The trail is in many ways undergoing a conversion from a gradient between a rural and a wilderness environment, as described by William Cronan, to a more abrupt transition between wilderness and urbanized areas. The countryside is disappearing from the route, and the influence of the small-town environment is diminishing. The trail experience is becoming a continual sequence of radical shifts between the wilderness corridor and hiker support facilities offering electricity, hot water, and Internet access. These changes are critical to how today's hikers experience the trail and what they learn about human and environmental values during their AT "residence."

The evolution of the trail as temporary human residence and as a social network greatly effects its spiritual ambiance. Though the AT corridor is better protected from intrusion of human developments, such as roads and power lines, than at any time in the past, the support network of hostels has become both better organized and increasingly commercial. Federal and state land management agencies have worried about overcrowding, yet the question remains: what impact does this have on the experiences of the hikers themselves? And what is the impact of trail towns and the care offered by their businesses, churches, and civic organizations? What makes the AT thru- and section hiking experience so memorable? And is it the natural or the social environment that generates the spirit of today's Appalachian Trail?

CHAPTER 3
TODAY'S HIKERS: GENDER, AGE, AND RELIGIOUS AFFILIATION
WHO ARE THE HIKERS?

Prior to introducing the volunteer support network and the question of hiker experience, it is important to consider who the hikers are. Is the iconic AT hiker—the young, muscular, white male, wearing loose rustic clothes and setting out happily by himself—still the typical Appalachian Trail thru-hiker? My AT questionnaire requested standard demographic information, such as age, gender, group size, and starting point for the current hike.[1] The hiker survey portion of this project began in the New York–New Jersey region of the Appalachian Trail in June 2007 and terminated the following May. The sampling area intersected thru-hikers in the middle of their journeys. In 2007, 1,334 would-be end-to-enders began at either Springer or Katahdin.[2]

Working with a field assistant, Robert Kent,[3] I quickly learned that sitting and waiting near a road crossing was not very efficient. The AT thru-hikers follow a variety of schedules—the ambitious start at dawn and the more relaxed amble out later in the morning.[4] The hiker schedules were so variable it was difficult to find a "best time" to contact the backpackers during the day, and very few were willing to stop while underway. We found that a drop box at a hostel was the easiest collection method to manage and had the best return rates. The second most effective was meeting with hikers just as they settled into camp in the evening, in off-trail camping areas.[5] In the end, the hostel drop box with donation was the least time-consuming method per return, and the best accepted by the hikers. Hostel managers were appreciative of the extra funds, and the hikers were very willing to contribute to the maintenance of overnight facilities. This form of survey collection also offers the advantages of being relatively anonymous and providing a relaxing indoor locale free from rain and bugs for survey completion.[6]

Field observations indicate that hikers who are trying to accomplish high-mileage days and those who are committed to a fast pace are less willing to complete a survey.[7] Further, because the survey handout openly announced the topic was spirituality and religion, hikers who had no religious engagement and those who considered religion irrelevant were potentially less likely to fill out a survey. Many nonreligious hikers did complete the survey, so the questionnaires incorporate the personal responses and beliefs of hikers lacking a spiritual self-identity. Owing to these factors, however, the results should not be read as an accurate cross-section of all hikers, but a representative subset. The methods potentially undersampled younger, very athletic, male and nonreligious hikers

That noted, the survey results indicated the largest group of respondents were males in their midtwenties, and that hikers filling out the survey incorporated a far higher portion of individuals who did not have a religious affiliation than the national average. Men comprised 78 percent of this AT survey cohort, thus they outnumbered women approximately four to one. The largest age group was eighteen- to twenty-seven-year-olds, with a strong peak of twenty-three- to twenty-five-year-olds (twenty-four was the mode, or the year with the most respondents).[8] Many of the AT hikers had just finished college and were taking a break before they began graduate study or took a full-time job. The median age, the age with half the hikers younger and half older, was twenty-nine. Put in other terms, just over half the hikers who answered the survey were under thirty (51 percent). These results were very similar to those of other studies of long-distance AT hikers. Gerard Kyle and his coauthors found that 65 percent of AT thru-hikers were thirty-five and younger.[9] Roland Mueser's analysis of 2,000-milers, with data collected during the 1990s, calculated an average age of twenty-nine, while reporting 72 percent males.[10]

For hikers older than thirty, the age distribution was relatively even, with hikers in their sixties as prevalent as hikers in their thirties. Although it might superficially seem that the number of hikers should decline steadily by age class, owing to increasing fitness limitations, hikers in their thirties and forties were more likely to be raising families or tied to jobs. Many senior hikers had recently retired and no longer had young children at home, thus they could more easily seek the freedom of the trail (fig. 3.1). The number of respondents declined sharply after age sixty-eight, and the oldest hiker who answered the survey was seventy-three. Hikers older than seventy-three have finished the entire AT in

Fig. 3.1. A thru-hiker and grandfather replenishing the fuel supply. His wife has stitched a plastic-coated picture of his grandchildren to his shirt. The Happy Hiker, Gatlinburg, Tennessee.

a single season, including trail pioneers Earl Shaffer and Ed Garvey, who both hiked the entire length more than once. Garvey was seventy-five when he began his final end-to-end ramble.[11] At the time of his second thru-hike, Shaffer was seventy-nine.[12] The rigors of the steep and rough footpath become a serious barrier for the truly elderly, and although many individuals in their seventies and older continue to visit the trail, the percent engaging in long-distance hiking is much reduced. For the survey respondents, gender was not correlated with age—the women were evenly represented among the age classes.

As one might expect for a younger population, a majority of the hikers were single and have never been married (61.5 percent). Only about one-quarter (24.4 percent) of the survey respondents reported they were currently married, while 14.1 percent described themselves as previously married (divorced or widowed). The trail culture was thus predominantly unmarried at the time of the trip, which influenced its interpersonal dynamics. The hikers were relatively well educated, despite the low median age. Only two respondents had not finished high school (both of them under twenty years old), and only one in ten had no college or university experience. Two-thirds (67 percent) had graduated from college and one in five (20.5 percent) had completed a graduate degree. Women and men on the AT had similar educational profiles. Because conversations with hikers indicated that many of the respondents lacking college education were from the skilled trades (landscapers, well riggers, military specialists) and a few had just finished high school and were hiking the AT prior to starting college, the hikers incorporated very low proportions of unskilled workers and wage labor from the assembly line. Benton MacKaye's original plan was intended to allow factory workers and city residents to escape to the fresh air and a healthy environment. The AT achieves this, but for the middle and professional classes.

In terms of region of origin (current residence), just over one-third (34 percent) were from the southeastern states (Virginia and Kentucky, through Texas). The northeast was the next most prevalent (25 percent), followed by the Midwest (12 percent). Though the AT is a national scenic trail with many international visitors, it really does serve the residents of the East Coast and the states adjoining the Appalachians. The 2007–2008 hiker survey collected no data on ethnicity. Field observations and conversations at hostels and campsites indicated, however, that African Americans and recent immigrants are less common as thru-hikers on the trail than in the general U.S. population, a phenomenon that is important to religious diversity. The survey respondents included hikers originating outside the United States, but all were from Canada, northern Europe, Australia, or New Zealand.[13] Discussions with informants also confirmed that thru-hikers who are not U.S. nationals were primarily from former British realms or from countries such as Germany, the Netherlands, and Japan, where cross-country trekking has long been a well-established avocation.

In terms of hiking goals, a surprising 81 percent of the survey respondents were thru-hikers attempting the entire length of the trail within a one- or two-year period. The remainder were section hikers, some of whom were attempting to complete the entire AT over a number of years. Of the thru-hikers, 78 percent were traveling from Springer Mountain northbound, 13 percent were traveling from Mount Katahdin southbound, and 9 percent were flip-flopping, a number of them starting at Harpers Ferry and heading toward Katahdin, then planning to return to the South for the fall season. The percentage of flip-floppers was higher than the percentage usually completing the trail each year because of the mid-trail location of the survey.[14] No day hikers or overnighters answered the survey. Because the hikers reported their starting points, it was possible to estimate how far they had walked on their current trip.[15]

Group Size and Composition

In terms of group composition, just over half the hikers considered themselves to be traveling alone (56 percent), while an additional 29 percent reported traveling with one other person. Only four respondents reported belonging to groups larger than four, and all of these were section hikers.[16] Mueser reported a higher percentage of soloists—66 percent. His sample, however, was entirely of 2,000-milers and did not include the section hikers present in this survey.[17] Just over one-quarter (26 percent) of the respondents to the 2007–2008 survey reported traveling with a family member or a significant other. A low percentage of the hikers were in a parent-child partnership (3 percent) or traveling with a sibling (2 percent) (fig. 3.2). More hikers responded that they were hiking with a boyfriend or girlfriend (11 percent) than reported hiking with a spouse (5 percent) or long-term partner (3 percent).[18] The remaining family partnerships were with in-laws, grandparents, or cousins. The typical long-distance hiker, therefore, is on his or her own, or is one-half of a pair.

Statistical analysis allows testing for significant differences between groups of hikers with different characteristics, such as married versus single hikers. A usual cutoff for determining whether a test is significant is p (probability)=.05, or one chance in twenty, that the difference is not real. A smaller p value infers a more significant result. P=.001, for example, implies there is a one in one thousand chance that another survey would have produced a different conclusion, rejecting a significant relationship between the variables.

Married hikers were more likely than average to travel with one other person, and divorced or widowed hikers more likely than expected to be traveling alone (p=.002).[19] Roughly one married hiker in five was traveling with his or her spouse. Conversations with hikers indicated that thru-hikers meeting family or friends along the trail was common, and family members sometimes joined briefly for short sections of a thru-hike. In some cases, a spouse or partner had begun the thru-hike and then dropped out, either as planned or because of injury.

Because the shelters and hostels are crowded during the main northbound season, the majority of soloists decide their own goals for the day, while frequently meeting other hikers they know along the way and staying with other

Fig. 3.2. Mother and son thru-hiking team, Franklin, North Carolina. Their permanent home is in the upper Midwest. This is an uncommon team composition.

hikers for the night. The low group size reported in the surveys implies that relatively few hikers started the trip with a team of friends and then stayed with them for the duration. The cheerful gatherings of three or four hikers congregating at country stores and hostels were primarily composed of acquaintances made along the trail. Because a majority of the hikers completing the survey had already tramped several hundred miles, it may be that the group composition of thru-hikers starting from Springer or Katahdin was different from those hikers responding to a survey in the middle of the trail—attrition reduced group size, or conversely, solo hikers entered new partnerships. Along the length of the AT, though, larger organized groups were either day hikers or short-duration backpackers, such as scout troops (fig. 3.3).

As a practical matter, teams hiking together have to keep a common pace, and require similar preferences for overnight accommodation to be compatible in the long haul. Groups of friends starting with differences in physical condition-

Fig. 3.3. Larger groups, such as this party descending Mount Washington, New Hampshire, are primarily day hikers and short-distance backpackers. Appalachian Trail long-distance backpackers are most likely to travel solo or in pairs.

ing or hiking styles are likely to lose members. Published trail journals confirm that hikers who began on their own or in twos made friends along the route and hiked with new pals for a day or two, and then moved ahead of or fell behind these temporary companions, catching up with them later. Field observations verified the ease of entering into conversations at shelters, campsites, and even road intersections. This pattern of solo and pairs of hikers entering repeatedly into a fluid dynamic of larger groups of individuals with compatible goals and interests was central to personal experience generated by an AT long-distance hike.

HOW DOES THE AT COMPARE TO DESIGNATED WILDERNESS AREAS?

Chad Dawson and John Hendee, in their text on wilderness management, calculated that a greater proportion of males than females use U.S.-designated wilderness, in the range of 70 to 85 percent.[20] Dawson and Hendee noted that: "The 56 years and older age groups are underrepresented among wilderness visitors as they are in all types of outdoor recreation."[21] The high percentage of men on the AT, which is not designated wilderness throughout its length, was thus similar to other protected backcountry areas, as was the predominance of young adults. In comparison with visitation in the majority of designated wilderness areas, the AT thru-hike favored seniors, perhaps because of the time required and the need for hikers to be at least temporarily free of employment. Recent studies have found that both female backpackers and those in their fifties and sixties have been increasing in relative prevalence in wilderness.[22] Nationally, about one-third to one-half of the parties entering wilderness included children under sixteen.[23] AT thru- and section hiking parties included few children,[24] which deviates from many other designated wilderness environments. Among adult wilderness visitors in general, 60 to 85 percent have attended college, while 20 to 40 percent have participated in graduate coursework.[25] The AT was thus analogous in the high level of educational achievement.

Typical group size for wilderness areas is two, three, or four.[26] In national terms, solo wilderness users are estimated to be fewer than 10 percent, although this varies by area, and conversely, groups larger than ten are fewer than 5 percent. The AT thru- and section hikers thus hiked in smaller parties than is typical of wilderness nationally. Recent studies have found solo hiking has been on the rise, which may have influenced the recent popularity of the AT.[27] The AT was also atypical in terms of the length of stay and season of use. John Hendee and Chad Dawson concluded that even for very large wilderness areas, such as the Bob Marshall or the Boundary Waters Canoe Area, fewer than 10 percent of trips lasted more than a week, and maximum use was in the summer. The AT long-distance hiker contingent was thus unusual in their multiweek trips and elevated numbers during the spring.[28] The small size of the backpacking parties, the relative absence of children, the length of the hikes, and the elevated presence of thru-hikers in their fifties and sixties on the AT could all potentially differentiate the AT spiritual experience from that prevalent in other wilderness areas. Studies of wilderness spirituality for organized groups, such as river rafting expeditions, differ demographically from the AT in terms of both party size and, in many cases, the lack of older participants.

Hiker Motivation

The survey asked hikers to outline the three most important motives for their hike in their own words. The statistics cited here concern just the surveys, while the quotes are extracted both from the surveys and from published trail journals and memoirs. The most frequent motive was adventure or challenge (37 percent), followed by the trail as lifetime dream or aspiration, and the trail as an accomplishment or a means to complete a project, such as writing a book. More than half the hikers self-reported a goal-oriented or adventure-based motive (table 3.1). M. E. "Postcard" Hughes comments, in his published journal, stating: "I've decided to seek out adventure, to vanquish the rut of just working and sitting around the house and then repeating the monotony of each day."[29]

Table 3.1

Motivations for undertaking an Appalachian Trail hike, percentage of the total respondents providing a genre of response

Motive	%	Motive	%
Challenge, accomplishment or goal oriented		*Interest and aesthetics*	
Adventure or challenge	37	Interest, see region, nature	24
Life dream, aspiration	27	Beauty, scenery	4
Accomplishment or project	13	*Social, contact with other people*	
Personal including dealing with change and reflecting on life		Meeting hikers or people along the trail	10
Taking a break from school, work, family, society, technology	25	Being with family or a significant other	12
Life transition, between school, work, military, retirement, and relationships	23	Being with friends	5
Self-exploration, reflection	21	Partying, having fun	5
Spiritual or religious	11	*Wellness*	
Appreciate life	6	Physical fitness	12
Simplicity	6	Weight control	4
Wilderness or solitude	7	Physical or emotional healing	2

The second most important class of motive was personal change. More than one-fifth of hikers identified that their hike came at a time of personal transition, such as finishing college, leaving military service, or entering retirement, or they were seeking time for self-exploration or reflection relative to their future goals. A twenty-five-year-old reported: "I ended a 4 year relationship and wanted to clear my head & find a center." A twenty-two-year-old noted: "Just graduated from college, needed a break before going to medical school." Another recent degree recipient stated: "I graduated from college and it seemed like if I didn't hike it now I'd settle into a career (or something else I couldn't leave) and never do it at all." A combat veteran listed his motives as:

- Adventure of a lifetime
- I just got back from the war, take a break between that and the next job
- Reconnect with America, haven't lived here in 5 years, but I love it

About one-quarter reported they needed a break or relief from their jobs, school, family, or society in general. A few were seeking greater simplicity. One hiker declared his goals were "To enjoy nature and get away from the rat race." Another said he was looking "For peace and tranquility—a break from the fast pace of civilization & city life." A forty-two-year-old female thru-hiker provided a list of burdens: "Mid life crisis, sick of employment, marriage & urban daily living hassles."

The published AT journals and memoirs also point to changing life direction as a common motive. Robert Rubin begins his account of his thru-hike: "About the time my job started to go bad a few years ago, I began collecting maps and considering places I would rather be. As the world closed in around me, as I learned to dread the work I'd once loved and to hide my heart from my friends, I would come home and reach for one of the maps stacked in the corners of my study."[30] David Miller also expressed dissatisfaction with his career: "Computer programming was the job I walked away from.... Would I continue reporting to a cube until retirement, with a few vacation days sprinkled in?"[31]

Slightly more than one in ten survey respondents cited a spiritual or religious motive for the hike (11 percent), or merely appreciating life. A Baptist thru-hiker noted he was looking "For a "fine tuning" of body, soul, and spirit."

A Catholic wanted to "connect to transcendent deity." A nondenominational Christian seeking God's guidance listed as his first motive: "Figure out where I am going, to seek the Lord's direction." A former Presbyterian with no current church ties felt: "The AT called me—it was a spiritual thing—I cannot explain." Hikers also considered self-development a major motive for undertaking an AT sojourn. A twenty-four-year-old wanted both to become "more in touch with nature" and she "wanted it to be a growing experience for me; I wanted to become a better person for it." Another hiker listed three straightforward goals: "Personal strength, growth, integrity."

A third common motive was interest, including a wish to see the East, wildlife, or the mountains (24 percent). One hiker merely stated: "I want to see a bear." J. R. "Model T" Tate, three-time end-to-ender, reflected in his journal on the draw to repeat the experience: "on balmy spring days when the awakening redbuds race March lilies onto Nature's canvas; when the first robins flutter across last fall's leaving of brown, now splotched with delicate green; I feel the Trail calling, and its echo haunts my soul."[32]

Fig. 3.4. Appalachian Trail hikers and highland residents who did not know each other prior to the Hiker Fest get together to play "Fire on the Mountain" and other songs most of them know, Franklin, North Carolina. New friendships appear all along the route.

The fourth most prominent goal was social contact, including generally meeting other hikers or people along the trail, accompanying family or a significant other, being with friends, or partying and having fun. One people-oriented thru-hiker wished: "To live ideally—to walk in harmony with nature, other hikers and the communities along the trail." A senior hiker's first goal was: "Enjoying the beauty of the trail with the companionship of my husband." A father intended "to take a thru hike with my son who just graduated from college." A twenty-five-year-old reported: "[My] girlfriend got me interested in it.... Missed [my] girlfriend—wanted to share [the] experience with her." Journal author Adrienne Hall concluded that her boyfriend asked her "on a date," albeit a lengthy one.[33] Another youthful hiker summarized his intentions in a single personal description: "I am a bad ass," while a second (from later in the season) concurred that his primary motive was: "Proving to everyone that I am a bad ass." Social contact overall greatly outstripped being in the wilderness or seeking solitude as motives (7 percent).[34] The AT, in fact, offers as many or more opportunities for conversation, partying, and getting to know new people off-trail as it does for solitude in the woods (fig. 3.4). A comparison of motives to the age, gender, and group structure of the hikers, and other social variables, produced no significant correlations other than a tendency for hikers traveling with a spouse to more likely report self-reflection as a motive than those traveling with a boyfriend or girlfriend or without such a relationship.

The last prominent motive was personal wellness, including pursuing physical fitness, losing weight, or seeking physical or emotional healing. A twenty-four-year-old recorded his primary motive as: "The challenge—had major knee surgery 3 years ago. This will complete my mental recovery." Individuals with disabilities and those hiking for charities promoting wellness or tackling chronic diseases have been prominent among the published journal authors. Jay Platt, diagnosed with von Hippel Lindau Syndrome and having lost one eye, raised $109,000 through his AT hike for the von Hippel Lindau Family Alliance.[35] Bill Irwin, one of the best-known end-to-enders, had completely lost his sight by the time he hiked the AT with his guide dog, "Orient." He had also wrestled with alcoholism and his family beginning to disintegrate under the stress of his disability.[36]

Of the hikers who answered the open-ended question about motives in the 2007–2008 survey, very few used specific vocabulary for natural features such as bears, trees, or flowers (eleven responses). And the number specifically mentioning beauty or scenery was also relatively low (five). More hikers mentioned nature or related terms (twenty-three) or the outdoors (eleven). A conclusion is that almost none of the respondents were seeking a specific natural history experience, such as accumulating a life list of birds or seeing rare plants, as a primary goal. On the religious end, specific vocabulary was also uncommon, with "God" mentioned five times, "spirit" or "spirituality" eleven times, and "pilgrimage" twice. A small subgroup of hikers were thus viewing their hike specifically as a religious or spiritual experience in the transcendent domain, while a larger number were intentionally seeking reflective time or a personal transition, or deeper self-actualization through the accomplishment of hiking the entire trail.

Bill Irwin wrote that when asked why he was walking the AT, "The easiest thing to say was that I was going because God had called me to do it. But that didn't seem enough as my purpose was to talk to people along the way and let them know what God had done in my life."[37] Harold Howell's journal, *Encountering God on the Appalachian Trail,* also treated more intimate contact with the divine as his basic purpose for the sojourn.[38] Some journals used the language of pilgrimage or inspiration, while religion was a minor component of the trip. Robert Rubin titled his memoirs *On the Beaten Path: An Appalachian Pilgrimage,* and he did attend services and pray during his walk. Rubin, in contrast to Irwin, did not present his walk as a direct outcome of his relationship with God. An even more critical difference is that Irwin considered his completion both a blessing from God and the fulfillment of a holy calling, while Rubin viewed his success, more typically, as a reorientation of his professional life. The majority of published journals incorporating religious language, such as "inspirational," in their titles did not report a directly religious basis for the decision to make the trip.[39]

These self-reported motivations correlate well with the observations of informants from the volunteer and support community, and indicate that the support network has an accurate understanding of why hikers undertake their quests. The results of the 2007–2008 survey are also consistent with a published qualitative study incorporating a high proportion of day hikers, which identified "environmental awareness, physical challenge, camaraderie, exercise and solitude" as consequences of an AT hike.[40] Mueser's survey of end-to-enders found that challenge was the dominant motive, while escape and simplicity were secondary. He reported a much lower level of social interest, 3 percent, than found by this study.[41] For a useful spiritual comparison, pilgrims to Santiago de

Compostela (in 1995) confessed that cultural exposure, such as learning Spanish or viewing art, was the primary motive for 73 percent, sports and physical activity such as cycling was the goal for 18 percent, and a mere 9 percent had religious interests[42]–compared with 11 percent of AT hikers who noted spiritual, religious, or introspective motives as one of the three goals for beginning a multiday hike.

RELIGIOUS AFFILIATION AND PRACTICE

My last demographic item was the religious membership of the hikers. The second section of the survey, on current religious practices and background, was based on questions utilized for a national religious survey organized by Rodney Stark and his coauthors from Baylor University. The AT version took less information on Christian denominational background, while allowing for a more refined response concerning alternative religions, such as New Age and Shamanism. The AT survey, which compared religious practices while at home and on trail,[43] found that 21 percent had no religious or consciously organized spiritual engagement on or off trail; 22 percent had a nominal tie, such as being raised a Catholic or Methodist, but at the time they responded to the survey, respondents were rarely praying or attending services. Just over half, 57 percent, had some continuing current engagement in religion or spiritual practice, such as attending services at least monthly, or praying at least weekly.[44]

The Baylor survey found that only 11 percent of adults in the United States had no religious affiliation;[45] therefore, fewer AT hikers had a religious affiliation than the average for U.S. adults. The AT situation was complicated, however, because nationally, eighteen- to thirty-year-olds were much less likely to belong to a church, synagogue, or other religious organization, and the Baylor project found that 19 percent aged thirty and under had no affiliation. Nationally, those under thirty who did attend services were as likely as those who were older to attend weekly, however. Across the United States, women (44 percent) were more likely than men (32 percent) to regularly attend religious services. Married people (44 percent) were more likely than those who were divorced (21 percent) or those living with an unmarried partner (10 percent) to regularly participate in a church or other religious organization. Families with children were also more likely to have religious affiliations.[46] Rather than consider the lack of religious ties particular to hikers or fans of the outdoors, national statistics predict the youthful, single, and predominantly male population on the AT should have fewer church members and regular participants in services than the U.S. adult average. The AT survey did find that older hikers were more likely to have a religious affiliation (p=.03).

The AT survey allowed for combinations of religious affiliations, such as a Christian practicing Buddhist meditation. The hiker respondents included 52.9 percent Christians and 4.4 percent Jewish, or 57.3 percent total, compared with the Baylor study's estimate of 84.3 percent Christians and Jews overall in the United States in 2006. Christians on the AT were well below national prevalence, while Jews were more frequent respondents to the survey than the expected national representation of 2.5 percent. A high 5.9 percent of AT hikers reported identification with Buddhism, often in combination with other religions, and an additional 2.9 percent reported affiliation with other world religions, particularly Taoism (fig. 3.6). A significant 8.3 percent provided profiles that might be classified as alternative religious interests, including Shamanism, Paganism, and New Age, often in combination with an Asian religion or a Christian background. The Baylor survey found that only 4.9 percent of U.S. residents belonged to religions other than Christianity and Judaism. Because the Baylor survey (for reasons not clear to me) included some denominations with Christian roots, such as Unitarianism and Greek and Russian Orthodox Christians, in the "other" group, the AT actually has nearly three times the national average of religious affiliations outside the Christian and Jewish mainstream. No Muslims or Hindus completed the AT survey, although hikers reporting multiple affiliations (usually an indicator of alternative religious interests) did check Islam or Hinduism, along with other religions such as Buddhism or Christianity.

The most common Christian denominational memberships for AT hikers were: Roman Catholic (9 percent), Methodist (6 percent), Baptist (6 percent), Anglican/Episcopal (4 percent), Presbyterian (4 percent), non- or interdenominational (3 percent), Lutheran (2 percent), Mennonite (2 percent), Pentecostal/ Charismatic (2 percent), and United Church of Christ (2 percent). The Baylor survey found 61 percent Protestants (including the 5 percent in African American denominations), compared to 21 percent Catholics nationally, while Catholics comprised 32 percent of the adults in the eastern United States. In response to the AT survey, Catholics were underrepresented, African American denominations

Fig. 3.5. Buddhist prayer flags fly across the ceiling of an outfitter, Tennessee.

were absent from the AT, or nearly so,[47] and although both "mainline" and evangelical Protestants were traveling the AT, more of the hikers who cited a specific Protestant subdenomination reported mainline rather than evangelical options.[48] A previous study of AT hiker motives, which included 65 percent weekenders and day hikers, included 98 percent Caucasians and only one African American, verifying that ethnic underrepresentation was likely influencing denominational prevalence.[49]

The trail poses a substantial economic filter. The cost of an end-to-end hike in 2007 was at least $3,000 to $4,000 dollars, and many thru-hikers drop out because of depleted funds (fig. 3.6). Family and cultural traditions, feelings of safety, and recreational preferences may also play a role. Studies of urban parks have shown that different ethnicities have different preferences for activities in the parks, and ethnicity influences participation in active recreation, such as long-distance walking.[50] The Baylor survey found that family income was correlated to religious affiliation, and that "Persons with household incomes of more than $100,000 a year are twice as likely to describe themselves as 'Theologically

Fig. 3.6. A line of vendors displaying lightweight tents, hammocks, and other backpacking gear, Trail Days, 2009, Damascus, Virginia. Such gear is expensive.

Liberal' than are persons with household incomes of $35,000 or less a year."[51] For the AT survey, the lower-than-national-average percentages of Roman Catholics, more conservative Protestant denominations, and African American denominations relative to mainline Protestants was potentially a by-product of both cultural and economic barriers to participation in thru- and section hiking.

Hikers preferring a mix of Christianity with other world religions and the prevalence of Buddhism both implied that a higher percentage of AT hikers than was nationally the case were seeking new religious options that may not have been part of their upbringing. Further, a majority of the respondents identifying with world religions self-reported low levels of ritual participation, which suggested that many of the hikers did not belong to or utilize a Buddhist temple or similar organization, and lacked family or ethnic ties to their stated religious preference. Though the sample size from the AT survey was too small to detect any overall patterns in terms of non-Christian religious affiliations, the results suggested a white middle class experimenting with new belief systems predominating over Asian heritage hikers.

Rodney Stark and his team concluded that Americans under thirty were more likely to identify themselves as spiritual rather than religious (18 percent, compared with 3 percent of Americans seventy and older). They also reasoned that well-educated elites who come from nonreligious family backgrounds are largely responsible for propagating New Age beliefs, synthesizing from a range of religious traditions. Individuals with graduate school experience were more likely to score high on a New Age index (29 percent) than those with only a high school education (8 percent).[52] Again, the age and the educational backgrounds of the AT hikers implied they should have more exposure to alternative religious views than the U.S. average.[53] Many hikers encountered a greater diversity of religious perspectives than they would in their home setting, and the roles of both doubt and of individual religious choice were likely greater. This may have led to difficulties identifying with other hikers' spiritual perspectives or, conversely, to exposure to new concepts and options. The dialogue, though, was very much internal to the established American middle class. It is tempting to compare the AT to a college campus in terms of contact with unfamiliar religious beliefs and the relative prevalence of individuals with no affiliation. The percentage of individuals over thirty was higher, however, than in the typical university dormitory, and many of the middle-aged and senior hikers on the AT were well settled in their religious preferences and had already raised children in a home church or denomination.

Hiker Religious and Spiritual Practice

Knowing the frequency of hiker engagement in religious activity prior to starting their Appalachian sojourn is critical toward determining the degree to which long-distance walking changed their routine. The AT hike provided a challenging environment for religious participation. Purposefully arriving at a church for a Sunday service required advance planning, to the point of laying over an extra day in town or making a conscious detour on Sunday. Attending weekly proved difficult. Hikers, facing rain and darkness in camp, did slip New Testaments and other inspirational volumes into their backpacks. Waterproof Bibles were available and stocked by outfitters, though remaining uncommon in the backcountry. Despite the difficulties of studying sacred texts by flashlight, the AT offered sites for isolated contemplation just about everywhere along the corridor.

Of the backpackers responding to the survey, two-thirds (67 percent) described themselves as attending services never or only occasionally (once or twice a year) prior to their AT hike. Just over one-quarter (27 percent) reported weekly attendance or greater when not on trail. Considering the youth of the AT hiker population, the overall profile was not too far from the national adult average—around 31 to 32 percent for all age groups.[54] The tendency for AT hikers to divide between those who hardly ever attend and those who attend at least weekly or more was rooted in the skewed age and gender composition. While on trail, participation in communitarian religious rituals, not surprisingly, declined radically. Individuals who would ordinarily attend once a week dropped to monthly. Only 4 percent reported attending services weekly or more frequently while on the Appalachian Trail (and, according to their margin notes, some of these respondents were considering the forest or wild nature as a site for worship). The questionnaire also inquired about participation in religious festivals and holidays while on the trail. The hiker surveys found that twenty-four of 205 respondents had or planned to celebrate Easter or Lent on the trail, and three, including one Christian, had celebrated Jewish holidays. Nationally, of course, participation in highly commercialized holidays, such as Easter, is much higher. Twelve, or about half the number celebrating Easter, planned to celebrate the summer solstice, including three who were celebrating both the solstices and the equinoxes, and one, self-identified as Pagan, who was celebrating all the astronomical observances.[55]

The AT hikers were more likely to pray or engage in contemplation (combined in the question format) than in religious services. Fewer than half (42 percent) reported never praying, or doing so only a few times a year, while 41 percent described themselves as praying or engaging in contemplation at least daily, or more frequently, when not on the trail. The percentage of those never or only occasionally praying was little changed by the AT (45 percent), while a slightly greater percentage (47 percent) reported praying at least daily or more frequently while on the AT. About even numbers thought their prayer or meditation had declined on the trip (16 percent), compared with those who thought it had increased (15 percent). The hikers who reported that they prayed only a few times a year and those who reported praying monthly decreased during the AT journey, indicating the respondents tended to move toward one end of the gradient or the other. In the Baylor national survey, about 60 percent of individuals resident in the United States *who were church members* prayed daily or more frequently. On average for all adults, 57 percent of women prayed once a day, while 40 percent of men did.[56] A fair conclusion, then, is given other factors such as the high percentage of men under thirty, AT hikers prayed as much or more than the national average relative to their age and gender.

Slightly fewer than two-thirds of hikers (62 percent) reported not reading sacred texts or reading them only a few times a year, while at home or prior to their long-distance hike. As is the case with service attendance, about one-quarter (25 percent) read sacred texts weekly or more frequently when not on trail. The national average for adult men of all ages is 24 percent.[57] Presumably, some of those reporting frequent reading did so during services, rather than on their own. On the trail, 17 percent of hikers reported reading sacred texts weekly or more frequently, while three-quarters (74 percent) reported reading sacred or spiritual texts very occasionally or not at all.

The American icons of wilderness, such as the whiskey-toting, unbaptized trapper, and the contemplative philosopher wandering the woods outside Concord, present a conflicted image of the backcountry traveler relative to religious confession. The soiled backpack and muddy boots of a thru-hiker announce that the wearer has probably missed a church service now and then. One suspects a mystic or two are wandering among the crags at Tinker Cliffs, or strolling over the alpine meadows of Mount Mousilauke, yet this is not who the AT hikers, on average, are. The hikers were less religious than the national adult average, but not less religious than the national profile for a youthful, predominantly male, and well-educated cohort. Though a notable portion of the hikers were intensely religious, the trail was not attracting a specific religious personality type. The range of religious backgrounds reflected the middle-class streams feeding the hiker contingents, which included evangelicals from the South and the Midwest, plus New Englanders from towns with a Congregationalist church bearing a historic marker, and stoic agnostics recently graduated from sequestered ivied halls.

CHAPTER 4
ANGELS AND VOLUNTEERS: THE HEART OF THE TRAIL
Informal Volunteerism

Much as the trail was originally the product of volunteers, one of the major expressions of the spirit of the Appalachian Trail has always been the people along the way who offer assistance to hikers without asking for compensation or, if running a business, who provide something extra for hikers at no cost. Today, hikers call those who just appear and offer a ride, or who leave bottles of water at undependable springs, "trail angels." Even highly practical and lightly packed end-to-enders identify these services as "trail magic"—those little acts of kindness that materialize at exactly the moment you need help. Although in AT jargon, hostel managers, café owners, and outfitters are not usually dubbed "angels," their often astonishing willingness to drive an injured rambler to a clinic or to search for a lost package at the post office belongs in the "guardian angel" category, and grades into the operations of the unseen helpers who deposit treats and necessities where hikers can find them.

The Appalachian Trail backpackers themselves form an informal network providing care and protection for its legitimate participants, and take seriously their responsibility to repay those who run hostels or allow no-cost camping in a back pasture. Hikers leave gifts and supplies for other hikers and stop to assist their comrades in trouble. Much as the historic pilgrimage routes of the world's religions have generated supportive hostelries, monastic houses, and confraternities to manage services for pilgrims, the Appalachian Trail has generated a complex matrix of helpers. This interactive constellation of nonprofits and businesses is formed not just from the trail clubs but from the people who live near

Fig. 4.1. Appalachian Trail section hiker trying to hitch a ride to Fontana Dam, North Carolina. Hikers depend on numerous small favors to handle the distance, lack of shelter, and necessity of resupply.

the AT. The trail has also spawned detractors—particularly neighboring property owners who believe the hikers disrupt their daily routines. The trail angels, in contrast, not only assist in providing for the backpackers' basic needs, they sometimes have negative experiences with hikers, yet they persist in offering favors, small and large, to help the struggling travelers on their way (fig. 4.1).

From May through July 2007 (working with an assistant, Robert Kent), and from June to August 2008 (working alone), I organized interviews of fifty-eight individuals or groups who either offered services for free or provided facilities or assistance above and beyond the usual offerings of their business or organization.[1] We concentrated on individuals offering food, accommodations, and supplies instead of on the volunteer maintainers, because the former had greater direct contact with long-distance walkers. The interviewees did incorporate loyal ATC members and residents of trail towns, who either assisted trail crews or served on them. In addition, I had multiple conversations with both helpers and hikers who were not formally interviewed. The informants included store owners, farmers who had faucets for hikers or permitted camping, managers of hiker hostels, and employees of municipalities that allow camping on public property. They incorporated the leaders or representatives of churches, other religious organizations, and integrative communities, as well as members of volunteer or civic organizations, such as small-town fire departments. When possible we met with interviewees at their place of business or the hostel, campground, or service they managed.[2]

We asked these trail "helpers" how they got involved and why they had decided to aid hikers.[3] Academic studies usually narrow their focus and assume that wilderness spirituality primarily concerns the "recreationists" and perhaps the professional leaders and guides. These interviews, in contrast, are based on a two-way model, which assumes the hikers can offer something to the volunteers and business owners as well as the angels providing for the hikers. A few responses varied from north to south, primarily as a function of differences in thru-hiker numbers along the route. The south-north gradient differed little in terms of the type of interviewees, with one exception—the southern volunteers representing religious organizations were more likely to be from denominations (such as Southern Baptist) emphasizing salvation or conversion than the northern contacts, who were more likely to be "mainline" (such as Presbyterian Church USA, Congregational). In the South as in the North, however, we spoke to individuals from a wide range of religious backgrounds, including evangelical and liberal Protestants, Roman Catholics, members of alternative religious communities, and the unaffiliated.

WHY HELP HIKERS?

As one might expect, a proportion of those who offered assistance were former end-to-enders or were committed section hikers. In 2007, Jim Murray, who completed the AT in 1989, was allowing thru-hikers no-cost use of a private cabin in New Jersey, referred to in trail slang as the "secret shelter," even though all long-distance hikers knew where to find it.[4] Among the interviewees, the owners and managers of recreationally oriented businesses and employees of parks were, not surprisingly, more likely to be hikers. All the outfitters reported hiring end-to-enders or section hikers. Thru-hikers often intentionally returned to work at hostels, outfitters, cafés, or motels near the trail. The staff at Mountain Crossings (Walasi-Yi Center) at Neel's Gap, GA, the first place where northbounders can easily replace badly fitting or inappropriate gear, were primarily 2,000-milers who wanted to work and live near the trail and lend a hand to others seeking a similar experience. Some business proprietors had never completed the entire AT but had a deep attachment either to a regional section of the trail or to one of the many Appalachian ranges. A restaurant owner, who provided shuttles and catered to AT hikers, described his first encounter with the AT as a ten-year-old who was roaming on his own with his dogs, above his grandfather's farm. A chance meeting with some long-distance hikers, settled at a campfire, made a lasting and positive impression. Kieran McGrath, owner of the Inn at the Long Trail, in Killington, VT, confirmed that he has hiked the Long Trail and walked or skied many wildland routes in Vermont.

The majority of store owners, municipal employees, and farmers who provided something extra, however, were not long-distance hikers, nor were the pastors or other "spiritual professionals" predominantly trail veterans. When asked if she was a hiker, one business owner responded: "I am a Holiday Inn kind of a girl myself" and elaborated that she had no interest in exploring the nearby trails, but "you have to admire somebody for doing something you can't do yourself." Another restaurant manager and her waitresses reported that they had never hiked on the trail, even for a few hundred yards, despite the fact the AT ran right by their parking area. A very committed unsalaried manager of a church-based hostel had a disability precluding long-distance walking. The founder of a very successful hostel had been drawn to his post through his service on a city council and his ties to the business community, rather than through prior involvement with the AT.

Often, conversations with business owners betrayed a longing for the freedom of the AT. The restaurant staff who had not tested the trail stated that they "envy" the hikers for their freedom. The owner of a bicycle shop and outfitters in New York confirmed that he had walked many of the local trails, and grew up hiking and hunting. He was running his business solo, though, and could not get away to complete a major portion of the AT. The businessman lamented that because he was usually alone in his shop, he could not always help thru-hikers who needed a shuttle, although he provided a ride when he was able. A country store owner, in contrast, explained that he only had time on Sundays to take a hike, but that he had been exploring the AT near his home with his daughter. The upland residents who go out of their way to assist hikers may actually be stay-at-homes, because they are running a shop or a farm alone or with their family. Often, outreach is multidirectional. Figure 4.2 shows a shuttle bus run by a motel owner who transported AT hikers to restaurants, grocery stores, and to other motels, as well as to his own establishment.

Most of the commercial enterprises identified in the *Thru-Hikers' Companion* (2006 through 2009)[5] as offering something extra for hikers were family- or individually owned small businesses, rather than national chains or corporate enterprises. The Toymakers Café in Falls Village, CT, was typical. The owners of the café cooked and waited on tables themselves. They knew many of their

Fig. 4.2. Bus stop in the sky, Winding Stair Gap, on the Appalachian Trail, North Carolina. A local motel and hostel provided a shuttle bus to more than one Appalachian Trail trailhead, and to Franklin, North Carolina. Here thru-hikers are unloading and heading over Wayah Bald toward Nantahala Gorge. This bus, with an experienced commercial driver, might make multiple runs and transport more than forty hikers on a busy day in the spring.

customers by name and stopped to chat while taking orders. Spending some time in conversation with hikers or helping them with a medical emergency was a natural fit in a community where friendliness and good conversation were still integral to business life.

About half of the religious communities or congregations we visited did have AT thru-hikers or trail club members among their members. Kesher Howes of the Twelve Tribes, which has sponsored a café and a hiker hostel in Rutland, VT, grew up in a hiking family, and has completed the Long Trail. Father David Raymond of St. Mary of the Assumption in Cheshire, MA, in contrast, reported that he did not have much time to hike, even though he and his parish often assisted AT travelers. The priest who preceded him at St. Mary, though, was a committed section hiker, temporarily escaping his ecclesiastical responsibilities under the trail name of Father Time. Father Time had first opened the parish hall to needy hikers more than twenty-five years previously. At the time of the interviews, a St. Mary's parishioner had recently completed the entire AT, and several others had walked portions of the AT in the Berkshires. A 2,000-miler among the interviewees helped to plan the hostel operation for St. Thomas Episcopal Church in Vernon, NJ.

When asked why individuals or organizations had become involved in assisting hikers, for most respondents it was not the result of a master plan, or even any initial intent to aid backpackers. In the case of fruit stands, organic farms, restaurants, and other small businesses, which were not specifically recreational, the hikers just kept coming by and they needed water, or it was late and they asked if they could camp. Many "angels" made statements such as, "I just like people," or "I am a people person." Others saw that the hikers had physical needs, and it seemed natural to assist. Even the service-oriented Franciscan friars of the Graymoor community at Garrison, NY, confessed "the hikers just kept coming by." Many of the angels were retirees or individuals already engaged in community service. They were likely to notice hikers coming through town, and took time to greet them. Long-term commitments resulted from these initial favorable encounters.

Gale Thomson of the Governor's Barn, NH, had a shock one evening when Emma "Granny" Gatewood, reputed to be the first female end-to-ender, knocked on the door. When offered pancakes, Granny, then sixty-seven years old, reached in her pocket and pulled out her false teeth. Gale reported that when Granny returned two years later, Gale and her husband took their first AT stopover to a country fair. Granny wore a corset, stockings, and a dress. Gale explained her motivation for assisting hikers for more than half a century as: "I just like doing it, I wanted to live in a house by the side of the road and be a friend to man." And, to Grannies. . . .

Interviewees were also likely to mention their personal feeling of belonging to a caring local community—this might consist of a religious congregation or integrative community, such as the Twelve Tribes, or it might be a village or township. They conceived themselves as extending the society, in which they felt at home or respected, to the hikers. "Angels" often mentioned receiving assistance from other residents of their town or from their base organization in aiding backpackers. A majority of the business owners noted that if they did not have time to help a hiker in trouble, one of their regular customers or a neighbor might. Leaders of churches or religious organizations described members simply stopping what they were doing to help a hiker, or relieving a hostel organizer who did not have time to handle a hiker emergency.

Trail towns often develop informal networks to offer support to thru-hikers. In Erwin, TN, for example, hostel staff shuttled hikers to town, and in 2008, Uncle Johnnie's Hostel even utilized school buses to give the midspring northbounders a lift. This transportation system clearly has not run on a Greyhound-like schedule, and included unplanned drop-offs for medical attention and other spur-of-the moment needs. When Miss Janet's Hostel was in operation in Erwin, (through 2007), she sometimes took hikers looking for a scenic dining experience to the River Side Restaurant, with its open deck and view up the Nolichucky River cliffs. Miss Janet even transported loads of hungry backpackers to monthly suppers at a local Methodist church.[6] Citizens of Bennington, VT, have organized a shared bicycle pool to allow both residents and visitors to shop without automobiles. Bennington business owners cheerfully assisted AT hikers in safely stowing their backpacks and borrowing the gold bikes to handle personal chores (fig. 4.3).

Those informants who intentionally created a commercial opportunity to assist AT hikers were usually 2,000-milers or dedicated outdoor recreationists. One hostel owner decided to give up his mainstream sales job and purchase a property near the corridor, after a life-changing end-to-end walk with his teenage son. Informants reported numerous instances of hikers stopping for longer

Fig. 4.3. Bicycles to borrow, Nature's Closet, Bennington, Vermont. This outfitter allowed hikers to leave their gear at the store, while they used the bikes to pick up supplies—at no cost to the hikers.

stays in communities along the trail, usually to work for funds to continue their trips. At the time of the interviews, Twelve Tribes had housed a number of hikers for extended stays and had welcomed one former end-to-ender back, an individual who had fully committed to living in the integrative community. This group constituted a small percentage of the hikers who have either dined or stayed at their facilities, however. Five of the interviewees were 2,000-milers who had developed a love for the Appalachians or the thru-hiker community and had left their original home area to settle or work closer to the trail.

If the angels frequently displayed a passion for community and an innate inclination to care for others, they were, in contrast, rarely formally trained to assist backpackers. The exceptions were the outfitters and their employees, many of whom were Wilderness First Responders or certified instructors of backcountry skills. The companies that manufacture and distribute backpacking equipment and hiking clothes have provided workshops for outfitters to teach them to fit gear properly and to demonstrate safe use. Only two religious professionals reported seminary coursework that provided any in-depth preparation for offering the social support or spiritual guidance relevant for hikers. When asked if he

Fig. 4.4. Bill Gautier with his dog Missy on the porch of Holy Family
Hostel, where he served as manager until his "retirement" in 2008.
Bill had retired from military service and brought organizational
skills to his volunteer post.

had any training to work with hikers, one pastor of a church that sponsors a hostel replied: "Absolutely not, when I was in seminary, I never would have imagined I would be doing anything like this." Aside from training by experience, leaders of successful volunteer hostels often had professional backgrounds in for-profit business, the military, educational institutions, or other organizations where they had acquired transferable managerial and communication skills (fig. 4.4).

In terms of potential societal origins of the helping response, several interviewees, ranging from country store managers to pastors, invoked the ethical concept, with its deep religious roots: "Do to others as you would have them do to you."[7] Trail angels both paraphrased or directly quoted the biblical text. A few interviewees were surprised to be asked why they helped hikers, and shrugged their shoulders and made replies such as: "Because they are hungry and tired and need food and a place to rest." One restaurant owner stated: "It is just the neighborly thing to do." Those with Christian orientation paraphrased biblical texts such as: "I was hungry and you fed me" Gary Poteat, of the Blueberry Patch near Hiawassee, GA, had Matthew 25:27–40 printed on envelopes for donations: "'Lord, when did we see you hungry and feed you, or thirsty and give you something to drink? When did we see you as a stranger and invite you in?' And the Lord answered, 'Inasmuch as you have done it to the least of these my brothers, you have done it unto me.'"[8] An ordained minister noted that she had thought about writing a book about some of her encounters, and she planned to title it "Angels unawares" from the passage in Hebrews encouraging the early Christians to take in and care for strangers, who might actually be angels.[9] A passage from the Book of Romans (12:13) also instructed the early Christians to extend hospitality to strangers. A hostel manager described the feeling he had about hikers as: "I've often wondered if one of them couldn't be Jesus Christ."

WHO JOINS THE HOST?

Aside from being people-oriented, the angels as the "heavenly host" had several common characteristics. First, in conversation, they either held a very positive view of their own home communities or volunteer organizations, or they had a strong attachment to the natural environment or to the regional human and natural landscape. Jeff Fife, a YMCA director from Waynesboro, VA, reported that he had grown up in the town. Several times during an interview he remarked on how friendly Waynesboro was. One of his motives for service to hikers was sharing his town and his affection for it with visitors. Winton Porter, owner of Mountain Crossings, lived at Neel's Gap, GA, when he first bought the outfitters and hostel. His feelings were rooted not just in the beauty of the natural surroundings but in a sense of the history of the Walasi-Yi Center, built by the Civilian Conservation Corps and situated between two summits prominent in Cherokee lore, Brasstown Bald (with a connecting trail to the AT) and Blood Mountain (on the AT), respectively the highest and second highest peaks in Georgia (fig. 4.5). The angels interviewed were those who could see good in the people around them, believed in their local communities, and who loved to share their social or natural milieu and connections with others.

Betraying their own basic character as "helpers," many trail angels praised the communitarian spirit the hikers themselves developed. Bill Gautier, care-

Fig. 4.5. Mountain Crossings, or the Walasi-Yi Center, Georgia. The white blazes take the Appalachian Trail straight through the building. Newly-started northbound thru-hikers lounge on the native stone patio and reorganize their often ill-planned gear.

taker of Holy Family Hostel (now retired from the position), admired the hikers for the care they show for each other, and was impressed that the hikers could (under most circumstances) safely leave their gear with each other (fig. 4.4). The angels respected the camaraderie and often described their engagement with the AT as if one community were flowing through another and merging with their hometown.

BENEFITS OFFERED BY HIKERS

The vast majority of informants had highly positive feelings toward hikers—only one informant was disparaging. Perhaps the three most common benefits the hikers offered the angels were interesting conversation and trail tales, assistance with mundane chores, and pitching in with larger or special projects. Reporting that the long-distance walkers bring a touch of excitement into the day-to-day lives of the angels, interviewees referred to the hikers as "fascinating" or "interesting," and made comments such as "I love their stories" or "I admire them for taking on the challenge." Father Jim Gardner of Graymoor described hiker contact as beneficial, because "Some of the people we have met are incredible." Stay-at-home small-business owners enmeshed in their financial ventures and hostel volunteers retired from full time jobs valued the adventure AT travelers added to village routines. When they located replacements for broken pack straps, or bought a pizza for some voracious twenty-three-year-olds, angels participated in the vigorous life of the trail.

Informant perception of economic benefits provided by end-to-enders varied from south to north. From Georgia through southern Virginia, AT long-distance hikers appeared in great enough numbers to provide significant spring income for businesses near the trail. In some areas, such as the Great Smokies, the AT attracted both long-distance hikers and weekenders, thus was considered a major factor in the flow of active recreationists, while the thru-hikers as a cohort were lost in the hordes of tourists. Because the hiker population was largest in the South, and attrition substantial, business owners, including outfitters, from mid-Virginia northward usually viewed AT end-to-end hikers as a minor component of their revenue. Owners of B&Bs and other businesses oriented to hikers and recreationists of all types mentioned, however, that AT hikers often returned to use their facilities at a later date. This positive economic effect remained substantial, even into New England, where informants at the Inn on the Long Trail verified the benefits of long-distance hikers who came back as guests after completing a thru-hike.

The attraction of clientele was especially important to towns such as Damascus, VA, where the intersection of three routes—the AT, the Virginia Creeper Trail, and the Transcontinental Bicycle Trail—has helped the town recover from the decline of a lumber- and agriculturally based economy and to enhance the tourist trade. Tom Haynes, a manager of The Place Hostel, indicated that the local Methodist Church continued to support the facility, at least partially to assist the town's residents in organizing the long-distance travelers, who had previously been arriving in town without any reserved accommodations. As a member of the town council, he also has been a leader in establishing the "Trail Days" event, which had not produced any profit for Damascus during the early years but had attracted trade for merchants. The past few celebrations had, however, produced a profit, and the income for 2008 was going to be invested in improving civic-run camping facilities—benefiting hikers, bicyclists, and the

Fig. 4.6. The municipal park open to thru-hiker camping in Unionville, New York. Civic officials often became engaged in organizing support for hikers because these efforts reduced illegal camping, encouraged tourism, and reduced conflicts with residents.

town's residents alike. Between 2007 and 2009, tourist-packed Gatlinburg, TN, in contrast, though providing friendly outfitters did not have a donation-based hostel or free camping.

Aside from members of religious organizations and a scattering of former 2,000-milers, the typical sponsors or managers of nonprofit hostels and campgrounds were fire chiefs, public park staff, mayors, and council representatives. The initial motivation often was maintaining public safety and social order (managing hikers so they stopped wandering around town and camping on lawns). This engagement often evolved into promoting town identity and attracting tourism. The incorporated village of Unionville, NY, for instance, allowed hikers to utilize municipal facilities, such as a small public park (fig. 4.6). The mayor and his staff monitored the hikers and maintained personal contact, which reduced conflicts with village residents and enhanced the village's reputation as friendly to recreationists.

Interviewees who served municipalities, such as the city manager of Palmerton, PA, were concerned that free or inexpensive accommodations or services not remove commerce from the for-profit enterprises forming their tax base. Several interviewees also expressed the belief that some towns catering to wealthier visitors, or the "country inn" trade, had given up on hostels because they did not want grubby hikers, hanging out and offending weekenders in oxford shirts and flimsy sandals. An informant from one of these "high-end" locales, Manchester Center, VT, indicated, however, that an incident concerning a hostel guest leaving his excrement all over the church building had condemned the volunteer enterprise. The informant, a shop owner, had been working with the hostel as a volunteer and had helped clean up the mess. An elite golfing destination, Manchester Center has cultivated a reputation as the home of a fly-fishing outfitter and sales outlet for casual clothes for the blue-blazer crowd.

Aside from their observation of the physical needs of hikers, "angels" were drawn by their perception of hiker motives and personal needs. The interviewees consistently characterized the AT thru-hikers as "seekers" or individuals with spiritual interests, who were pursuing challenges and tackling life transitions. They discussed individual hikers reprogramming their lives, such as soldiers returning from the Middle East, widowers still deeply missing a spouse, and computer programmers who lost their jobs in the "dot com" economic fizzle. Both religious and nonreligious "care givers" perceived a significant portion of the thru-hikers as searching for self-identity or a better future. This perception gave the angels' efforts greater meaning than merely distributing town maps or mopping up the suds underneath an overflowing washing machine. The angels believed themselves to be supporting and sharing the hikers' deeply consequential and transformative journeys.

WHAT CONSTITUTES SERVICE TO HIKERS?

The angels unilaterally believed that the first and most critical need of hikers was physical, and that the stress and forced simplicity of a thru-hike made hikers cognizant of their dependence on others. They described the extended trek as renewing enjoyment of the most basic underpinnings of existence. A number also mentioned the hikers' desire for simplicity, or attempt to reduce life to its most essential components. The angels believed this relief from materialism was beneficial and one of the central values of the AT sojourn. The asceticism of the AT thru-hikers was consistent with the religious background of many of

Fig. 4.7. Thru-hiker thankful for small blessings at a corner store
on the Appalachian Trail, Vermont. She paid for the popsicle,
while the store owner and local community provided the lawn
chairs and table.

the trail angels. It is in keeping with Christian principles to believe, for example, that fiscal wealth or an excess of material possessions inhibit spiritual and ethical understanding and discourage confirmation to God's will. Even nonreligious angels, however, valued hiker thankfulness for small blessings, such as a shower, a faucet with clean water, a chair, or even a place to enjoy a popsicle (fig. 4.7).

Following the publication of Bill Bryson's *A Walk in the Woods*,[10] hiker traffic so increased that many hostels filled during the prime hiking season for their region. Sheer numbers overwhelmed volunteers. One pastor interviewed complained that during the years of maximum traffic, in the 1990s, church members became unidentifiable in the flood. Hikers were in most instances tolerant of the crowds, but some became demanding or expressed disappointment at being turned away or jammed into limited space. Opportunities for quality assistance to hikers have fluctuated from not enough to too much, and then in some cases back to not enough, with concomitant degrees of strain placed on the volunteer and non-profit support matrix.

The municipalities that allowed camping or provided overnight accommodations, such as Palmerton, generally experienced limited tourist trade and wished to encourage more. Vacation hubs with massive and continual tourist traffic, such as Gatlinburg, and those that depended on high-end or "shi-shi" weekenders who frequent streets lined with boutiques and reservation-only eateries, were less interested in providing volunteer-run services for AT hikers. Although rock-weary AT veterans, with their wet and worn gear, would stand out from the weekenders almost anywhere, they become most conspicuous when loitering in front of an antique emporium, or a restaurant with a maître d. Delaware Water Gap went through a period of declining large hotels. In recent years, the town has experienced a moderate revival stimulated by the presence of the national recreation area and family-friendly sports, such as river rafting. The city government's willingness to assist the Church of the Mountain with a hostel was thus imbedded in an effort to remake the town's tourist economy. Some near-trail towns, with their tourist trade oriented toward professional and business-class visitation, such as Bennington, had, in contrast, remained hiker friendly because of their strong sense of community identity. Civic goals and economic need tended to fuse with neighborliness. The AT, as a democratic use of a public commons, continued to converge easily with small-town values—such as "everyone should be able to participate." The Trail Days parade in Damascus was reminiscent of the "Kids' Day" parade where I grew up on the Eastern Shore of Maryland (fig. 4.8). Any child could decorate a bicycle or walk in front of the volunteer firefighters as they drove a polished red pumper truck down Main Street. Trail Days festivities were also reminiscent of a Fourth of July celebration, where all sorts of organizations send representatives to march and a carnival staffed by nonprofits follows the diverse display of civic pride.

Prior to the 1970s, there were almost no services specifically oriented toward AT hikers along the route. Much camping away from the trail was informal,

Fig. 4.8. Trail Days parade, 2009, Damascus, Virginia. Events such as this advertise mountain towns as friendly and as nice places to visit. The event is also very democratic—everyone who wants to, wearing whatever, can march down Main Street.

in back pastures. The number of thru-hikers was too low for specialized facilities to develop. The Church of the Mountain Hostel opened in 1972, and The Place hostel, opened in 1976, have been assisting hikers since end-to-enders became a notable presence on the AT.[11] The current trend is toward an increasing number of commercial hostels and motels with hiker bunk rooms, and away from nonprofit options. Larger and more predictable AT hiker cohorts are more easily accommodated by small-business owners. The participation of fire departments and small churches and availability of city parks have always been unstable, and these organizations have increased or decreased their commitments dependent on their leadership. Although some of the better-organized projects, such as Church of the Mountain, are likely to still be conducting hiker outreach in 2020, a majority of the civic and nonprofit organizations contacted during the interviews in 2007–2008 will probably have abandoned their efforts by that point. For the thru-hikers, who are slowly becoming their own cultural entity and are turning increasingly to tourist-oriented infrastructure, the angels continue to offer access to regional culture and a touch of Americana genuinely rooted in the Appalachian landscape.

CHAPTER 5
RELIGIOUS ORGANIZATIONS AND SUPPORT FOR HIKERS
CHURCHES, RETREAT CENTERS, AND OUTREACH TO HIKERS

A unique feature of the Appalachian Trail is the involvement, along its length, of churches, retreat centers, and religious nonprofits in hiker care. The National Park Service has allowed a Christian nonprofit to recruit unsalaried, volunteer ministers, many of whom are seminary students. They organize worship services for national park campgrounds, at least during the summer vacation months. The ministers pursue seasonal paid employment to feed themselves, and find their own housing. Religious organizations' support for the Appalachian Trail, in contrast, has not been based in providing ritual opportunities for coreligionists, but offers housing, food, and guidance to the nearest sandwich shop or pharmacy. Further, no umbrella organization sets standards, provides oversight, advertises the availability of assistance, or solicits volunteers for ministries to the AT. The participating bodies look like a list of congregations and camps from the yellow pages in a small-town phone book. Independent good citizens, motivated to serve because of their religious beliefs, emerge as an eclectic collection of salespeople, schoolteachers, doctors, contractors, farmers, military veterans, engineers, and shop owners. They are the people next door, in the truest sense.

The religious organizations and churches reaching out to hikers generally have not been motivated by strategies to recruit new members from the AT to their home congregations. A mobile population such as the AT end-to-enders are not likely to join and remain with a church they encounter on the way. Kesher Howes reported that Twelve Tribes had already started a business in Rutland,

not just services & real charitable a.

VT, and they kept seeing hikers arriving in town, seeming lost and isolated because they did not know anyone. Their integrative community began by offering a friendly outreach and just trying to make hikers feel welcome in the city. A pastor confessed that he did not allow the first few hikers who arrived on the church lawn to go into the building complex, but permitted them to camp outside. Assisting hikers who needed medical attention—one of whom had symptoms of full-onset Lyme disease—encouraged him to allow hikers to use some of the church's indoor facilities. The director of a retreat center reported that an end-to-ender, whom she had offered a ride, suggested she offer assistance to AT users.[1] She decided to open a small hostel, away from her usual retreat participants. The well-known hostel The Place, operated by the United Methodist Church in Damascus, VA, originally catered to transcontinental bicyclists, and then began to absorb AT hikers as well.

A number of the religious organizations offered services to AT hikers that paralleled other charitable programs or shared the same space. One church used a common area as a hiker hostel for most of the year, while also closing the area to hikers for a few weeks annually and taking in families needing temporary housing as part of a diocese-based program. Retreat centers were already serving meals and providing housing or campsites for visitors. The managers and spiritual mentors confirmed that they had found that the AT hikers, owing to their individualized schedules, were better separated from their other guests. The exception was an integrative community where temporary residents usually camped. Some of the most stable volunteer-run overnight facilities were the hostels constructed specifically for one- or two-night stays by hikers and bicyclists, such as the quaint barnlike building that is a short walk from the Holy Family Roman Catholic Church parish hall in Pearisburg, VA (fig. 5.1).

HOSPITALITY AS MINISTRY

When we asked clergy or members of religious organizations if they considered their service to hikers as "ministry," all but one responded positively. The angels invoked two major concepts: (1) offering physical support to people in need is a core Christian principle; and (2) assisting others who are on a spiritual journey is ministry. Jeff Fife, a YMCA director, considered coordinating a campsite for hikers and allowing hiker use of the Y swimming pool as compatible with the Christian basis of the YMCA's mission. Fife immediately associated their simple

Fig. 5.1. The hostel built by Holy Family Catholic Church in Pearisburg, Virginia. The hostel diverts hikers from the parish hall, which reduces interference with masses and scheduled religious activities.

but effective program for hikers with "Christian values—caring and responsibility." He also related the YMCA's participation with the AT to the Y's desire to serve the greater community. The Christian director of an interreligious facility invoked biblical texts to provide for strangers and sojourners. The committed trail angels were sophisticated enough to distinguish among ministries serving the people in the congregation, parish, or town and those serving the greater good. A Baptist clergyman quoted Galatians 6:10: "We are to do good to all men." Further, these socially aware good citizens recognized that their organizations had diverse missions, including education and encouraging their home communities. Outreach to strangers and providing basic physical support was legitimate in the minds of the trail angels and did not need a formal or ritual religious context.

The pastor of a church that offered a very well-organized hostel articulated their ministry to hikers as one of hospitality. True hospitality was oriented toward the physical and emotional needs of those receiving it, and not toward receiving something in return. This religious professional, trained in counseling and spiritual guidance, described how the congregation managing the hostel had found that providing for basic physical needs, such as a bunk and a shower, was effective and appropriate, while they had concluded that providing rides to the mall actually degraded the trail experience and created strains for both the church members and the hikers. For this conscientious pastor, the practice of hospitality was a fully integrated part of the congregation's spiritual life, which encouraged the Christian membership to reach beyond themselves and actualize their faith by serving strangers. Respondents from other religious organizations, regardless of denominational affiliation, echoed this emphasis on hospitality as ministry. A Graymoor friar referenced their saintly mentor by noting: "St. Francis was very hospitable."

Hospitality is hard work. The volunteers ended up stacking toilet paper and worrying about soiled carpets. Figure 5.2 shows the manager of The Place loading a pick-up truck with trash after Boy Scouts had filled the hostel for the weekend. Hospitality to backpackers required an understanding that service to others is often a humble accomplishment of household chores. The AT hikers' needs were so elemental that any mature adult with patience and common sense had something to offer.

THE ROLE OF RELIGIOUS GUIDANCE

Although informants of all backgrounds described cases where they had provided social or emotion support to hikers, the pastors and religious leaders, such as elders, provided more reports than lay hostel managers or business and farm owners of assisting hikers by listening to their personal issues, guiding them in decision making, and providing general spiritual support, such as acting as a sounding board for someone confronting a major life transition. A minority of the conversations reported were about religious faith. Hikers, however, sometimes did inquire about Christianity or about specific denominations. Father Raymond noted that non-Catholics would occasionally ask for an explanation of Roman Catholic beliefs.

Long-distance walkers who had been seriously contemplating their own religious commitments or who had a numinous experience[2] while on the trail did pursue conversations with religious leaders who appeared to be trustworthy and nonintrusive. One pastor described hikers who had an experience with the

Fig. 5.2. Tom Haynes, manager of The Place hostel, cleans up trash after a large group of Scouts, Damascus, Virginia. Volunteers have to deal with mundane maintenance and repairs.

Greater Other, or an overwhelming feeling of a presence beyond the self, as quietly inquiring about what this encounter meant. Although conversations about religion or the meaning of life are common when hikers gather for the evening at shelters or in camp, discussion of intense or unexpected personal spiritual experience along the trail was more likely to generate a private than a group conversation. This type of interaction with the support network was relatively uncommon, and was preferentially directed toward someone who clearly had religious authority, knowledge, or training.

Discussions about religion were a two-way street. A Graymoor friar reported his most positive interactions were with hikers from another faith and with those who were Christians while being nominal in their practice. It was difficult for the friar, who had committed his life to Christian service, when a hiker sometimes expressed a thought like: "I don't like this Catholic thing." The patient brother added: "So you listen to them vent, it doesn't kill you."

A high proportion of interactions eliciting spiritual support concerned decision making about the trail adventure itself, or tackling life transitions, rather than making decisions about faith commitments. One pastor related that each year toward the end of the hiking season, she would offer a listening ear and consolation to hikers who were beginning to recognize they were not going to finish their planned journey before the Baxter State Park staff closed Mount Katahdin. She grasped that the feelings of personal defeat were both painful and conflicted for those stragglers who were going to terminate their walk without reaching their heart's desire. Another religious professional described encouraging a couple of runaway teenagers, who had no funds to accomplish an AT hike, to contact their families. The teens ultimately chose a more mature and sensible course of action, and requested a lift to the bus station so they could return home.

On numerous occasions, I observed hostel staff and other trail angels sitting down and chatting with hikers who were in deteriorating physical condition, had a chronic injury, or were running out of money and would not be able to continue their AT quest, at least in the immediate future. In some cases, a hostel manager offered aid to two or three hikers with different emergencies in a single evening. Far beyond a quick ride to the Amtrak station,[3] the assistance provided was laced with gentle affirmations that the adventure could be continued later, and the mountains would still be there after the ankle healed. The angels often just provided positive and friendly emotional support. Father Jim Gardner of Graymoor described his service to AT hikers as: "Making them feel welcome, affirming them, telling them it's a great thing. I pray daily for hikers' fulfillment and safety." Linda Austin, a Baptist, has addressed cross-country wanderers staying at her home, and simply said: "Have I told you how much I love you?" In terms of a venture as independent as the AT thru-hike, accepting the hikers on their own terms is necessary to accommodate both the array of walkers and the diversity of their immediate needs (fig. 5.3).

The hikers, of course, became their own support group in this culturally affirmed release from the preordained trudge through middle-class employment and achievement in an educational institution and the workplace. The angels offered a chance for hikers to talk to someone who had no immediate stake in whether one should switch from being a computer programmer to a high school teacher, or whether one should pursue a twenty-year stint in the Marines. From the perspective of the AT hikers, the archangels were care givers who enjoy the process of self-actualization of others, without believing that this eclectic troop of mud-spattered wanders would be best served by moving to the angel's hometown, adopting the angel's values, or joining the angel's denomination.

Fig. 5.3. Welcome sign for Trail Days, First Baptist Church, Damascus, Virginia.

EVANGELIZATION

The hikers differentiated between religious individuals or organizations that were offering services without expectation of recruitment and those openly focused on forwarding their own philosophy or theology. In the hiker surveys, respondents noted that religion is a common topic of discussion on the trail, and hostel logs, including those from hostels based in commercial or civic organizations, proved that hikers are sometimes reacting to religious outreach—both positively and negatively. The logs included both warnings about people trying to proselytize and rave reviews of stays at Christian hostels. These written accounts included descriptions of pleasant contact with people who shared their faith, and extremely negative impressions of both fellow hikers and volunteers with strongly articulated religious beliefs. On one hand, the AT trekkers believed they were "hiking their own hike" as they resisted the intrusion of external agendas. On the other, the backpackers, despite their independence, reacted positively to all the small favors and the kindness they receive along the way, including those offered by the churches and the integrative communities with a religious foundation.

The negative accounts in the logs usually concerned Christian "angels" who offered food or a place to stay for the purpose of offering tracts or religious reading materials, or having a chance to openly proselytize during a hiker's visit. Hikers also reacted to other hikers, not because they were on a religious journey but because their religious self-expression became demanding or projected personal religious expectations on others. These encounters were remembered and recounted far from the original locale. Hikers who had reached New England were still telling stories about the characters they met in Georgia and North Carolina (religious and not). Some of the best-known figures had acquired trail names (not all of them complimentary) and hikers shared their impressions freely in the closed and cozy realm of the end-to-enders. Several of the interviewed pastors and hostel managers were also negative about the occasional "John in the wilderness" calling others to God. They perceived the intentional evangelist as corralling or exploiting the hikers—taking advantage of the hikers' need for food and shelter or the close quarters in the shelters to gain an audience.

Both evangelical Christians and leaders of alternative religious retreats or integrative communities were, in contrast, convinced they had something essential or life-saving to offer. A Baptist pastor was definite: "Our primary motive is not just to provide a social gospel, but is to provide the Gospel of Christ." Evangelicals, particularly in the South, considered Jesus to be a best friend and an immediate presence. Nonreligious hikers from outside the region had difficulty grasping the concept of God as sitting at the same table at a covered-dish supper. The more sensitive angels understood this cross-cultural gap. One astute volunteer described preparing mountains of food for a hiker dinner. She attributed the hiker longings for the AT and personal change not to the church or human ministry but to "the Holy Spirit." This volunteer believed the hikers "just recognize His work and His stirring." She also described her struggles with welcoming stinky, ill-kempt nonlocals: "I just started praying that God would

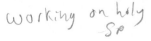

allow me to see people through his eyes. I never would have thought I could love people the way I do." Some Christians reached out by just being themselves. Dave Mertens of St. Thomas Episcopal Church in Vernon, NJ, commented that their volunteers did offer spiritual assistance: "but we don't push it on the hikers. Some of them seem a little surprised that we are here for them, twenty-four hours a day, 365 days a year. . . . We try to anticipate what they need."

Christian hostels left Bibles and other reading material out for hikers. At least a few hikers were happy to have these options, and some materials were well-thumbed. Those who were not interested could ignore the opportunity. No one reported serious problems with having bookshelves disturbed or vandalized. On a random visit to The Place, I found a Bible sitting out on the living room table, as if awaiting a willing reader. Hostels may actually be distributing less material than the hikers would like to have available, because it often is not clear if the hikers may take the Scriptures and pamphlets with them. Some volunteers stocking reading materials considered the specific needs of hikers (including for fiction) in determining the selection, while others just borrowed from the church supplies. The book rack in The Place hostel, for example, offered tracts, Gospels, and entire New Testaments. This system was strictly take-it-or-leave-it, which suited the hikers and bicyclists who stayed overnight.

The hiker perception of religious outreach was complex, because many backpackers viewed organizations that happily share their beliefs with others and recruit new members, such as Twelve Tribes in Rutland, VT, as an interesting trail stopover. Informants indicated that a few AT hikers openly avoided any direct religious contact and skipped visiting hostels with religious foundations. On average, however, the informal communication network along the trail has recommended the Twelve Tribes hostel because the restaurant offered good food at a fair price, hikers could stay more than one night if they need to, and the hikers found the encounter with the alternative integrative community culturally intriguing. Twelve Tribes, unlike many of the church hostels, had enforced strict separation of men and women in the bunk rooms, which was a matter of much commentary along the AT. Thru-hikers from previous years who were walking the trail again and section hikers already familiar with the various trail segments provided a detailed critique of facilities along the trail, forming an orally transmitted travel guide. Shuttle operators and hostel volunteers as far south as Georgia were familiar with Twelve Tribes. Thus long-distance hikers knew something about the facilities in Rutland before they arrived, and were not surprised by the hostel regulations. On their part, Twelve Tribes was very oriented toward meeting hiker needs and allowing hikers their own space, as long they did not violate the rules of the community. By their own report, the integrative community rarely had difficulties with hiker behavior, and mutual respect was the norm. They did invite overnighters to join their religious celebrations, which included dances, with men, women, and children all participating together.

Although the majority of hikers did not realize it, buying food from an alternative religious community with a communitarian structure, strict rules about sexuality or family composition, and a membership who resided together and operated commonly-owned businesses is a New England tradition going back to the eighteenth-century Shakers, and before. Even the emphasis on dance to celebrate the divine or enhance religious experience has historic precursors. The same hikers who camped overnight at a Shaker campsite, established on a former Shaker farm in Massachusetts, could reside for an evening or two with today's religious utopians, striving for purity and godliness by welcoming strangers.

Gentle evangelical outreach was often carefully integrated with hospitality, including giving hikers an opportunity to socialize. The First Baptist Church of Franklin, NC, for example, provided a pancake breakfast during a trail festival. AT Servants, a ministry to hikers that supports Christian laity or pastors on long-distance hikes, has operated out of First Baptist, Franklin. Volunteers concentrated on offering hot, home-cooked food. Other than a prayer before the meal, the hikers did not have to engage in any religious rituals. The church left free books and materials out for the hikers, and ministers were available if anyone wanted to talk. Hikers did take the reading material, having a preference for authors such as C. S. Lewis, who could provide both entertainment and spiritual reinforcement for the difficult climbs ahead.

The First Baptist Church of Damascus, VA, similarly assisted with Trail Days (fig. 5.4). Linda Austin, a volunteer operating under the trail name Sonshine, described the wrong approach to assisting AT hikers, from the hikers' point of view: "We get there and we're tired and thirsty. A church van pulls up and they get in your face." She believed that "God's imbedded in us that [service] has to be relational. We provide food, medical attention, clothes. . . . We're fulfilling Scripture and doing what Jesus told us to do. . . . We always tell the hikers we are thankful they are spending time with us." She was open with AT hikers about her

Fig. 5.4. The medical team from Appalachian Trails Days 2009, Damascus, Virginia. These friendly Southern Baptists have driven up to Virginia, from Alabama, to care for hiker feet, knees, and spirits.

dependence on Christ, while holding that caring for hikers does require practice: "We've gotten better at it, . . . we've finally almost gotten good at it."

HIKER PARTICIPATION IN WORSHIP AND RELIGIOUS SERVICES

Using low-key methods such as posted notices, the religious organizations assisting hikers all invited hikers to participate in worship, prayer, covered-dish suppers, and other events planned for the local membership. Conflicts sometimes occurred, however, not because hikers did not participate in services, but because they did not remove themselves and their gear from spaces needed for Sunday school, children's activities, or church meetings. Hikers would oversleep or simply ignore requests to clear out between 9:30 and 12:30 on Sunday morning. The hikers encountered during this project did not complain about coercion to join religious events while staying at hostels, and no one mentioned regarding as offensive the presence of religious readings in the stacks of books left out for hikers in church common rooms. The vast majority of backpackers were aware that they had choices concerning where they stayed overnight or resupplied, and understood the church-sponsored hostels had their own missions and identity.

All interviews conducted at churches or Christian hostels produced reports of long-distance hikers attending services. The managers of the Blueberry Patch hostel took anyone who was interested to either Sunday or midweek services at their home church. Ministers, hostel managers, logs, and the hikers themselves all described the attempts of Christian hikers to arrive at a specific trail town in time for Sunday worship. David Raymond, of St. Mary of the Assumption Church, in Cheshire, MA, noted that some Catholics scheduled their stop so they could attend Mass, while other hikers who were not Catholic also sometimes attended, perhaps out of respect for the parish that opened their doors, or just to see what the service was like. Hostel logs contained comments about the effort some hikers have made to reach a particular church on Sunday. The Church of the Mountain has regularly welcomed hikers who participate in Sunday worship, and purposefully scheduled a supper once a week where hikers mix with the congregation. This public-spirited body has sponsored summer concerts in Delaware Water Gap, and although these have been staged primarily for the town folk and their visitors, the AT hikers have joined in. Several informants, including those from outside Delaware Water Gap, suggested that hikers liked to hit the Water Gap on a weekend because of the musical performances and other opportunities to socialize.

The interviews and hiker surveys identified only a handful of cases of a religious conversion generated by the AT experience. Both current and former thruhikers attending Trail Days in Damascus have made new or renewed commitments to Christ. An informant reported at least six such decisions in 2008, which were discussed with Christians assisting with the event. The recruitment of new members for small-town churches directly from the AT hiker cohort, however, has been a rare event. If they wished to enhance their own membership, the congregations engaged in hiker outreach would find that the time dedicated to assisting muddy itinerants was better spent in recreational outreach to local soccer moms and scout troops. The transience of the hikers has made them exceptionally poor candidates for filling the pews, at least in the congregations hikers visit along the trail. Several Christian informants valued the hiker ministry specifically because it was not a self-serving form of recruitment, but was a form of outreach with minimal expectation of a direct return.

The attraction and interest of the AT ministry activity itself was more likely to draw new members already resident near the AT than the return of walkers originating outside the region of the church. One pastor noted that people had joined the congregation because they liked working with the hostel and participating in suppers and other events attended by hikers. Informants, not just from church-based hostels but also from activities such as Trail Days, reported that interaction with hikers benefited their churches by drawing the members outside their immediate social sphere and encouraging the congregation to interact with people who were different from themselves. Christian respondents often articulated a deep personal benefit in being able to share Christ with others, even in nonobvious ways, such as finding a first-aid kit or serving stacks of hamburgers without asking for payment. Southern Baptists and individuals from evangelical backgrounds were more likely to directly quote Scripture or to describe Jesus or the Holy Spirit as present in their AT-related activities or church events. Yet, even reserved Yankees mentioned Jesus directly as the ultimate source of their outreach.

ALTERNATIVE AND INTERRELIGIOUS OUTREACH

The informants included directors of interdenominational or of alternative religious retreat centers as well as church-based hostels or shelters. A trustee of Enota Retreat Center, GA, explained that the locale itself, with its forests, trails, and waterfalls, below Brasstown Bald, provided spiritual support to hikers. She enthusiastically described how Enota "just feels sacred, even to the most uninformed." Guests from mainstream America were experiencing "profound isolation, disconnection, and emptiness." Enota facilitated developing respect for trees, getting in tune with the seasons, and getting "in touch with animals." The Enota staff provided good food made from fresh ingredients, a sweat lodge, conversation, and a listening ear to hikers who needed help. According to the trustee, Enota's "fundamental mission is to allow people to get in touch with themselves, nature and God." AT hikers impressed with the lifestyle and nature-oriented values have returned to volunteer.

At another retreat center adjoining the trail, hikers participated in interfaith services. One noted in the log: "Enjoyed the book *The Wisdom of Zen.*" Another described a pleasant visit as: "A wonderful day of rest from us—experiencing the Monday night Buddhist Service . . . a lazy afternoon of spiritual & native reading—just lovely." A third wrote, in alternative religion terms: "I feel a surge of Power now. I'm off. This place is powerful."

SERVICE AND IDENTITY

Businesspeople as well as representatives of religious organizations believed the end-to-end hike was a time when the participants were close to God because they were living in nature. Interestingly, this belief was consistent from Christians with an emphasis on salvation and conversion as central, to Christians from more liberal denominational backgrounds, to relatively nonreligious respondents and those who had pantheistic or New Age beliefs. Brother John Hildreth of Graymoor related the hikers' experience in nature to his own: "When I see a lake, or a river, or a mountain, it's almost like an orchestration of music, it's a joy and Francis had that same joy. . . . There is a benefit for anyone to get out into creation." Gale Thomson, with Mount Cube, NH, rising above her farm and sugar house, commented: "It is hard to look out this window and not think: 'I will lift up mine eyes to the hills, from whence cometh my strength. My strength cometh from the Lord.'"[4] A Baptist minister observed of the end-to-enders: "their minds are uncluttered, being away is making a difference. . . . They have been immersed in this creation. Who did this? Why did He do it?" This pastor believed sharing the natural revelation so evident in the Appalachians was a step toward sharing the "special revelation" of Christ's life. For these informants, the natural environment combined with the human ministry to provide an overall impression of what is important about Christianity or religion in general, and to offer spiritual enrichment to those hikers who were interested in absorbing it.

Many hikers found that hostels, retreat centers, and camps with a religious basis fit their personal journeys or immediate spiritual needs. One hiker log entry at a retreat stated: "I wished to have a place for Pentecost, where I can just be and enjoy nature. I can hardly believe it, this is really a great place, exactly the place." Another quoted Psalm 8, and then noted: "This is truly an ordained retreat." A third hiker encountered just the right combination of support: "A won-

Fig. 5.5. View from the hill adjoining the Baptist hiker hostel at Troutdale, Virginia. The setting is peaceful and combines Christian symbols with mountain scenery.

derful sanctuary for both the Body (shower, laundry and bed) and the Mind (library, beautiful setting, nice people)." A weary hiker was grateful for "everything you did to rejuvenate me & make me spiritually ready to return to the trail."

Overall, hiker logs contained hundreds of friendly comments about religious organizations offering assistance. Repeatedly, hikers thanked church-based hostels by writing "God bless" or "what a blessing this place is." Or they described a carpeted floor with shower as "a hiker's heaven," "the rainbow after the storm," "like home," or "a piece of heaven" (fig. 5.5). In concert, the hikers identified managers and pastors as gracious, hospitable, caring, kind, warm, and friendly. Just prior to my interview, Dave Mertens, manager of St. Thomas Episcopal hostel, received a thank-you note, which read: "God bless you Dave, for everything you do for us. You help us find our way when we are lost." Few hikers who stayed at this hostel realized, though, that the congregation actually planned their own communal space to also provide for "strangers," and the architect designed the church undercroft so it could serve as temporary housing.

Father David Raymond remarked that one of the values of assisting hikers was that freely given aid encouraged them to abandon negative impressions of

Roman Catholics. Within the context of the village parish, where members prepared common meals and genuinely wanted the hikers to join them for dinner, the hikers could see Christians for who they really are. Participation in communal life helps hikers to understand what the church is really supposed to be. Volunteers from other denominations concurred that at least some hikers came away with a more accurate perspective on Christianity or spirituality. A Baptist verified: "I think we are showing [the hikers] what Christians are really like. So many have had bad encounters with the organized church; they have been treated badly by Christians." Dave Mertens hoped the hikers would "see this [hostel] is the outreach of a church, that we are trying to be more than place for them to flop."

The interviewees reported differential interest among church membership in offering services to hikers. On one end are churches, such as Presbyterian Church of the Mountain at Delaware Water Gap, where the congregation overwhelmingly identified with the hiker ministry. This church draws members from surrounding communities who have joined because they wish to participate in the AT activities. Some congregations were more skeptical. One southern pastor thought that contact with hikers was assisting his congregation in developing acceptance and tolerance of outsiders, and thus helping them to grow. He quoted the Apostle Paul, who said: "He had become all things to all men." For a small and relatively isolated mountain community, the AT was the whole world walking to their doorstep.

The Church of the Mountain outlined ministry to hikers in the job description of their pastor, and their recent searches for a minister covered hiker support in the interviews. This both integrated the hiker activities and aligned accountability for hiker engagement with accountability for other congregational events and the management of church buildings and offices. Not every seminary graduate has the patience or the identification with the needs of others necessary to effectively oversee a hostel, thus the selection of the professional staff has had a major impact on the success of ministry to hikers. At the other end of the gradient are churches that participated briefly and gave up the effort because it was in conflict with other activities, or required too much work or organizational skill to sustain. Interviewees believed that a change in leadership had caused more than one church-based hostel to close its doors. Some operations, such as Holy Family Hostel and The Place, have survived the arrival of a new priest or pastor, owing to the presence of capable lay managers. If a very active volunteer steps down from a managerial post, though, the shoes may be difficult to fill. Religious organizations where the professionals and laity cooperate fluidly with each other, and concur in the belief that service to hikers is ministry, have been the most likely to remain engaged over a decade or more.

A second factor leading to longevity was the degree to which the religious organization believed itself to serve the needs of the greater non-AT community. Pastors who were able to work happily with the city government, and church hostel managers who knew the local police chief, were better equipped to handle problems, from hiker overflows to backed-up sewer lines. Further, if the hikers precipitated an unpleasant incident, the concept that the hostel, campsite, or festival was also supporting the local economy provided additional motivation to continue to serve wandering backpackers. In figure 5.4, the smiling medical team[5] for Trail Days was finishing up a day of inspecting knees and heels. They had driven up to Virginia from a Southern Baptist church in Alabama. Their very effective presence represented not only cooperation among congregations but with the town council, the chamber of commerce, and the trail clubs.

CHAPTER 6
HIKER ETHICS: INTERACTIONS WITH THE SUPPORT NETWORK AND VOLUNTEERS
POSITIVE PERSPECTIVES ON HIKERS

This project tapped five sources of information on the ethics of Appalachian Trail hikers, the hikers themselves, the support community, environmental and trail professionals, journals published by 2,000-milers, and personal observation. The comments of hostel managers and owners of trailside businesses reflected the perceptions of hiker-friendly communities and organizations, who while loving the hikers also bore the brunt of any disrespect AT users showed for people living along the trail corridor. The informants for this project represented the tolerant end of the spectrum. They mentioned numerous situations where they had served as peacekeepers, calming irate neighbors or providing a safe place for hikers to stay where they could avoid conflicts with the permanent residents of the Appalachians. The vast majority of interviewees had highly positive feelings toward hikers and noted what good people hikers were. Kesher Howes remarked that it was one in fifty who would not help with chores at the Rutland hikers' hostel. One business owner said that some hikers took getting used to, but he had never met one who was not basically a good person. Gary Poteat commented that of the approximately five thousand hikers who had visited the Blueberry Patch, he had only told one "to leave and never come back." *generally*

Bill Gautier of Holy Family Hostel in Pearisburg, VA, took me outside to show me an area of property that the church had acquired adjoining the hostel. The hikers had helped clear the overgrown area and build a fence. More than one informant reported hikers who were landscapers or painters who had stayed for an extra day or two to install larger decorative planters, to renovate a lawn area, or to repaint a bathroom with a peeling ceiling. Although some chores were

hikers help make place better

closed to hikers, owing to insurance regulations concerning use of motorized equipment or other risks, the vast majority of hikers had a sense of giving back to the communities supporting them. If a hostel manager walked in asking for help moving some supplies or cleaning a shower, the hikers responded.

Many of the informants considered the hikers as a group to be honest and willing to care for their trail companions. Gautier remarked: "Hikers do not steal from each other." He verified his view with the fact that he could not remember hikers ever taking anything from the hostel, and that on one occasion, when gear went missing, the hiker who had accidentally packed someone else's backpacking stove with his own gear called back a couple of days later to report that he had it, and tried to determine who it belonged to. Another hostel manager admiringly described a hiker who, on finding another hiker's poles on the trail, went to look for him by hitchhiking north, and then walked the trail south until he found the owner. Multiple informants described the trail as encouraging simplicity and appreciating the basics in life—central hiker virtues.

Negative Perspectives on Hikers

When asked if the hikers ever caused any problems, the respondents fell into categories based on whether their organization was directly recreationally oriented or not and whether it was indoors and in confined space or outdoors and allowing people to move freely in the open. The perceptions of representatives of religious and nonreligious organizations were very similar, with one surprising exception, discussed below. Among the businesses where hikers contact other customers indoors, the consistent concern was hygiene—particularly intense body odor owing to lack of access to showers. The owners or managers of enterprises, such as organic farms, where close contact between AT hikers and other customers was a minimal concern generally did not mention the AT trekkers' accumulation of dirt and unique aroma. Reports of odor increased from south to north. This may be coincidence, but could also be because of aging gear, soaked and soiled repeatedly, inviting microorganisms. Long-distance hikers may become adjusted to their own pungent body scents and those of their companions, and thus less concerned about the perceptions of onlookers, or onsmellers. Leaving backpacks outside does help to reduce affronts to the nonacclimated. The problem is not just skin bacteria and fungi, but gear and clothing

Fig. 6.1. Laying out gear on a hostel lawn, Pennsylvania. Keeping gear clean and as dry as possible reduces odor, as does leaving packs outdoors. This hiker had received a package at a mail pick-up, and was reorganizing his pack.

also become rank (fig. 6.1). The bartender at Inn at the Long Trail kept a bottle of clothing deodorant (Fabreeze) under the counter, and cleansed "ripe" hikers who wanted to chug a pint prior to going to their rooms to take a shower.

The business owners also described scattered damaging incidents, usually no more than one or two per interviewee. Most of them concerned money. One country store proprietor mentioned a single case, over more than a decade, of a wallet disappearing when hikers were present. A café owner said only once in five years had a hiker "stiffed" her (not paid for his food), and that he had left her a flower as an apology. Outfitters mentioned situations where thru-hikers stole gear, although all indicated it was a sporadic and infrequent problem. Because the outfitters allowed hikers to hang around their shops or provided other services, such as shuttles or gear repair, the need to keep an eye out for petty theft was an added burden. The AT hiker shoplifting has generated considerable extra work for store staff, despite their kindness to thru-hikers. One outfitter reported having facilitated two thru-hikers by leaving the store open after-hours for them. The dishonest backpackers stole several items while he was on the phone. The outfitter heard later that other walkers had seen the thieves with the missing merchandise, but he could not prove they had stolen it.

A second group of informants noting problems were those managing hostels or others allowing hikers to stay in civic or church facilities. These spatial stewards consistently reported having difficulties once or twice a year with hikers who were loud, rowdy, intoxicated, disruptive, or disrespectful of others. Although vandalism and physical violence were not common, interviewees did recount some disturbing incidents. The managers confirmed these nasty encounters involved a very small percentage of the hikers they assisted. Individuals supervising indoor accommodations frequently attributed their worst headaches to visitors who were not "genuine" long-distance hikers. The troublemakers were either transients not actually hiking the trail or were weekenders or overnighters with vehicle support.

One clergyman provided a case that would dissuade most pastors from ever allowing hikers on church property again. A small group (he thought weekenders) arrived at the church and then went carousing in the village. Their raucous behavior apparently upset multiple local residents. The troublesome cadre talked a long-distance hiker into keeping the door to the sleeping area open for them after the official closing hour. When the clergyman went to prepare for vacation Bible school in the morning, the "hikers" were hung over and had not gotten up by the mandated hour. He asked them to depart, because he was expecting children to arrive shortly. Just after he left them alone to pack their gear, he heard loud crashing sounds. When he returned to the room where the "hikers" had stayed, he found they had broken two of the tables by smashing the furniture against the wall. To the credit of the church and their village, they still welcomed hikers, despite such disruptions, and continued to offer their time to those who truly needed their services.

In another even more dismal confrontation a number of years ago, an AT hiker shot someone inside a church building. When the pastor called the congregation together to deal with the legal, safety, and public relations crisis, an elderly woman, who had been a member for many years, asked if they were not all called to take risks when serving Christ. This church, also to the great credit of its congregation, decided to continue their hostel operation. The understanding that any outreach has inherent dangers, considering that human behavior can be unpredictable and unstable, indicates the community has gone beyond the superficial and is willing to struggle with the negative side of human nature.

Kesher Howes identified long-distance AT hikers as occasionally becoming rowdy when off-trail. He expressed tolerance, however, when he noted that each year, "one or two groups of six or eight" long-distance hikers would form who would seek opportunities for "revelry" when in town. In my own observation, the hard partiers among the thru-hikers formed a small, if very evident, subculture. I did encounter hikers returning drunk to camp during 2007 and 2008, and a twenty-one-year-old wrote profanities all over a survey form. The Back Home Again Café and hostel, run by Twelve Tribes, has been a well-organized operation, with adults continually around the premises. They make an effort to greet each hiker and be certain everyone is properly settled in. They have been better able than more informally structured teams to handle trail youth displaying "shelter fever" on returning to civilization. At establishments where drinking alcohol was part of the commercial operation, such as some of the country inns, and at commercial campsites that were also open to vehicle-supported hunters and other guests likely to guzzle a few beers, reports of out-of-control drinking by AT hikers were minimal. Experienced bartenders and campground managers responded to deportment lapses quickly and, relatively speaking, have seen much worse than most trail-weary thru- and section hikers can dish out.

Graymoor friars reported difficulties with hikers violating the rules during the period when they allowed hikers to stay indoors. Hikers were out of sync with the strict schedule of the Franciscans, which was necessary for serving sit-down meals and holding worship services for the entire community. The hikers also conflicted with institutional norms establishing behavioral boundaries in a Christian milieu. Allowing hikers to camp at an open shelter and providing a menu so they could call for take-out food has resolved most of the issues. A supervisor of a hostel, with retreat facilities adjoining, confirmed that even legitimate trail users were inclined to violate quiet hours. She noted that groups of younger hikers, especially those recently beginning their trips, had more inclination to keep others awake (including herself). A rebellious hiker resisted the concept of shared social order via a note in a log: "Not much of a retreat. Cannot relax when I get constantly asked to move my shit and be quiet." Ironically, noise after hours has also been a source of interpersonal conflict in the shelters and camps of the trail corridor. Thru-hikers are often tired and tied to a solar clock.

noise disrupting sleep

Weekenders, large youth groups, and short-term hikers tend to stay up later and, in the process, disrupt everyone else present.

The informants concurred that the bane of the donation-based hostels has been "yellow blazing"—the practice of using automobiles to follow the end-to-enders along the trail. Informants believed that yellow blazers did occasionally amble out on the AT, while skipping difficult or longer sections. Yellow blazers were drawn to the "spring break"–like aspects of trail life and had limited interested in the natural aspects. The informants viewed yellow blazing as an abuse of donation-based facilities, because the faux end-to-enders had continually available vehicle transportation and were better able to stay in commercial campgrounds and motels than genuine thru-hikers. Hostel managers thought the vehicle support encouraged alcohol and drug abuse and disrespect of trail support facilities.

Unrealistic Expectations and an Attitude of Entitlement

The one common concern was that hikers sometimes had unrealistic expectations of volunteers or commercial operations offering their services. These irritating attitudes might be called the "McTrail" mentality, which expects any needed service to be available immediately, at the whim of the hiker. One fruitstand and farm owner remembered offering a hiker a plate of cookies. He proceeded to eat all the cookies, leaving none for anyone else. Hikers sometimes treated volunteer-staffed hostels like they were commercial motels, and assumed someone should be ready to assist them at any time of day or night. An owner of a bed and breakfast, which had an attached hiker hostel, described a hiking couple who demanded a private room, even though all private rooms were full when they arrived. The self-oriented pair then dominated computer and Internet access, staying up half the night, blocking everyone else from using e-mail. A rural restaurant owner expressed dismay that hikers would approach him and ask for a nonemergency ride to town in midafternoon, when he was exceptionally busy with food preparation for dinner. Several other business owners said hikers asking staff for rides during normal business hours was a distraction and led to tensions between their employees and hikers. Offering rides is a liability-insurance issue for a business, and owners were often reluctant to assist because they could lose coverage if there were an accident not covered by their policy. Some businesses, particularly inns and outfitters, had shuttle services available, although rarely "on demand." So, patience on the part of the ride-seekers was necessary to prevent disrupting business chores and personal schedules.

If volunteer services were listed in a trail guide, even an out-of-date guide, hikers sometimes became upset if the facilities were either temporarily or permanently unavailable. In rare instances, a hiker argued about leaving a donation or paying for laundry. One of the best things hikers could do for the angels was to understand that they were not a commercial hotel chain or a recreational club where the hikers were official and privileged members. The angels did not regard themselves as night clerks for a 2,200-mile-long motel. The friendly locals assumed any gifts or services offered would be shared considerately with other hikers.

Most hikers displayed consistent gratitude for the fact that there were any support services available along the trail at all. A few grouched about churches requesting a ten-dollar donation, holding this to be too expensive. One note in a log complained: "No clean sheets, no ride to town, give a $ again—2 more $s—then be quiet." At the time of the interviews, the minimum cost of a commercial hostel night was about fifteen dollars, but twenty to thirty was more usual. I encountered hikers who, having stayed at one church-run hostel for free, criticized other church hostels that asked for small donations to cover expenses. The hikers were unaware that the "free" hostel was subsidized by the municipality, who provided garbage pick-up, water, and sewage without charging. The pastor responsible for the "free" hostel did need donations and confirmed that the hostel would be forced to change its fiscal policies if the subsidy from the town government disappeared. The detractors did not realize that other hikers often did leave donations at the "free" hostel, or sent a check after they arrived back home.

The total cost of running a hostel includes electricity and air conditioning, cleaning, toilet paper, water, garbage disposal, and, of course, liability and fire insurance. A commercial hostel has to pay its staff. Although the actual cost per hiker-night circa 2007–2009 varied with the region, ten dollars was almost certainly below cost for most hostels, even those entirely run by volunteers. One of the reasons churches have found it easier to become involved in hiker support than many other types of volunteer organizations is that they carry insurance, which allows use of the site for meetings and events incorporating nonmembers.

Some interviewees, most notably public officials, did express concerns over insurance and its expense, and mentioned that it affected the question of using municipal properties for camping. AT hikers sometimes had difficulty recognizing that the peace of the forest and the beauty of the vistas were free, but maintenance of the trail, and the water and electricity for a washing machine, were not (fig. 6.2).

The degree of difficulty with this sense of "entitlement" varied with geography and the type of business. Outfitters sometimes had trouble communicating with hikers who were building confidence and trail time. One noted: "you have people who progress through and become more relaxed, then there are those who progress through and become entitled, and then there are even a few who progress through and become righteous." Winton Porter reasoned that at Mountain Crossings, at Neel's Gap, GA, thru-hikers were still humble and willing to take advice. He rarely had the experience of outfitters a few hundred miles north, who encountered hikers with a state or two to their credit. Some hikers believed they knew more about backpacking than anyone else, and would not listen to the suggestion of an experienced salesperson. Outfitters, particularly from the middle sections of the trail, mentioned spending extra time waiting on hikers making unreasonable demands, such as expecting a pair of boots to last 1,200 miles without resoling. They often ended up negotiating over warranties for gear they did not sell. Outfitters near the northern terminus of the AT experienced declining arrogance, as the surviving end-to-enders were fully settled in their journey and expecting most of their gear to last to Katahdin.

Distance influenced financial resources. Trail supporters from all locales described hikers offering to work for food or replacement equipment. Younger hikers, starting in Georgia on a few hundred dollars, reached Virginia with empty pockets. They struggled on until the more isolated stretches past Damascus or Pearisburg, where offering to work for food became impractical. Stopping for temporary employment caused delays that put Katahdin farther and farther away in terms of arrival dates. Owners of small businesses were concerned about expectations of obtaining gear or food without paying or other behaviors rooted in financial naïveté or irresponsibility. Informants also thought hikers who engaged in frequent partying often depleted their funds quickly, were more likely to make excessive demands on available resources, and end up terminating their trips. Hikers sometimes attempted to use overdrafted or expired credit

Partying

Fig. 6.2. Hostel donation box, Damascus, Virginia. The request is only four dollars in 2009.

cards, and pizza delivery services were (rightfully) suspicious of orders delivered to vehicle-accessible shelters and camps.[1]

CONFLICTS WITH RELIGIOUS AND VILLAGE ETHOS

The attitudes of the hikers themselves, including disobedience of the simple rules for maintaining cleanliness, quiet, and order, clearly caused repeated strains

Fig. 6.3. The bunk room under the municipal hall in Palmerton, Pennsylvania. Keeping the bunks basic, without mattresses, keeps hiker impacts down and discourages longer stays.

with volunteer-based support operations. End-to-ender Robert Rubin, in his published journal, described a stay in a church in Manchester, VT, where a disobedient thru-hiker snuck his dog into the sleeping area, breaking the church's rule against bringing pets indoors. The dog, no better disciplined than his master, relieved himself fully in the playroom. The inconsiderate hiker and pooch had already left when the church secretary discovered the mess. She, very appropriately, made the hikers, specifically Rubin, clean it up. As he describes: "There, surrounded by alphabet blocks and rubber balls, in solitary splendor dead center on the wooden nursery room floor, reposes Tagalong's [the dog's] fresh, warm turd."[2] Although Rubin presented the incident as amusing, the church staffers were stuck for hours with the rancid, musty smell, while he and the other hikers headed back out into the refreshing atmosphere of the trail. The *Thru-Hikers' Companion* no longer lists this church as providing services to hikers.

Problems with alcohol and drug abuse and sexual conduct have strained relationships with the angels, particularly the municipal and ecclesiastical. The city of Palmerton, PA, has allowed hikers to stay overnight in the basement of the municipal building. The project began at the suggestion of a city employee who was also a long-distance hiker. Initially, the hikers kept the peace, perhaps because of the presence of the police department and all-night law enforcement staffing in the same building. After the police department moved out, binge drinking became so common among the overnighters that thru-hikers coined the expression "getting Palmerized" to denote a full emotional release from the trail, with blood alcohol elevated until unconsciousness set in. A tavern owner, with a fondness for hikers, was offering discounted beers at a nearby bar, exacerbating the disorderly behaviors. City employees checking on the hostel were finding hikers passed out on the floor, too groggy to get up and get back on the trail. City employees experienced more than one instance when a hostel resident had been vomiting, and the entire bunk room cadre was too intoxicated to clean up the mess, so the fermenting stomach contents remained scattered among the toilets or the bunks in the morning. The hikers' concept of a good time had clearly exceeded municipal hospitality.

The city manager also reported increasing safety concerns for blitzed twenty-something hikers with little discretion, who were wandering the streets after dark or, in the worst case, lying down on the railroad tracks, still open at all hours to freight trains. Palmerton is a Pennsylvania mining town, where a couple of beers after work is an acceptable way to transition from labor to relaxation. Public drunkenness and sheer stupidity are, however, a serious threat to civic order and the industrial economy of the municipality. Palmerton has found that setting firm rules and advertising them in shelters on the approach to the town has helped to curtail disrespect of their generosity. Planners have kept the bunk room simple and without mattresses (fig. 6.3). They also have adopted a no-tolerance policy concerning disorderly behavior and hikers sneaking back for multiple-night stays.

The angels were highly concerned about the potential for hikers to offend congregants, village residents, or visiting tourists. One business owner wryly described a nude AT hiker sauntering down the center street of a New England hamlet. He frightened a staid, ninety-year-old woman whose front porch faced the thoroughfare. Church hostel managers felt frustrated when they discovered they needed to monitor free computers to thwart hikers from accessing pornography on the Internet. The managers made it clear their congregations were not amused. Considering the shared nature of showers and sleeping areas, embarrassing encounters between fully dressed congregants and partially dressed hikers were surprisingly rare. The angels' acceptance of couples was practical and nonjudg-mental. The volunteer and civic organizations have understood that hikers are living out of their packs, and therefore extend toleration. The occasional parade of hikers who are flaunting it as they stroll into the village is, however, remembered for years among farm-country Yankees.[3]

The one distinctive difference between volunteer- and church-operated hostels and camps and their commercial equivalent was that the churches and volunteer-run establishments reported more incidents of disrespect and actual physical damage than the commercial operations. A church hostel reported a case, for example, where two hikers broke into a church office. Then there are the violent incidents such as the shooting and the retaliatory furniture dam-age. The sample size was not large enough to statistically test this differential between volunteer and commercial services; however, hikers and other service users did appear to approach volunteer and free or inexpensive services differ-ently. Free services were more likely to attract transients or nonhikers than paid services, and volunteer-operated facilities often had unpredictable staffing and less supervision. In addition, troublemakers may have believed volunteers and pastors were less likely to call for law enforcement or charge them for damages.

Hostels with several committed mature staffers, executing management plans and schedules, did better than those based in more informal organiza-tional structures. Because Twelve Tribes was composed of multiple families who work in a commonly owned business complex comprising a bakery, restaurant, and shop, responsible adults familiar with the hostel operation were continually available. Authority and decision making were consistently aligned. The family-operated Blueberry Patch rarely had difficulties, owing to the close proximity of managers to the hostel and bans on alcohol and drugs. Palmerton has found that once they established absolute regulations about alcohol and the number of nights hikers could stay, campers began to sober up and the conflicts receded. As of 2007, after Palmerton advertised the regulations in nearby AT shelters so the hikers would become aware of the behavioral boundaries before they ar-rived, visitors could find someplace else to stay if they found the new rules too restrictive. In 2007, the city manager reported that the municipal government was no longer considering closing the hostel area, although any such arrange-ment that extended the role of city into caretaker for out-of-town visitors always remained tentative.

The communitarian spirit led to internal patrol of the trail and enforcement of the common values of respect and mutual assistance. Five different hostel or business managers in this series of interviews reported problems with a single hiker who was stealing from other hikers and from businesses along the way. The informal communication network among the hostels tracked the culprit north. One interviewee from Virginia reported denying the troublemaker admission to a hostel. Other interviewees described his apprehension owing to the vigilance of a village mayor, well north of the Mason-Dixon Line.

CARE OF THE TRAIL AND ON-TRAIL FACILITIES

The support community had few concerns about thru-hikers and other experienced walkers purposefully damaging the trail. Hostel managers and outfitters made it clear that they instructed inexperienced hikers in leave-no-trace camping. The outfitters typically stocked gear that was both lightweight and low impact, and did what they could to guide hikers in appropriate use and disposal. Vandalism or property damage caused by thru-hikers was uncommon, but writing on shelter walls and souvenir collecting did occur. The staff of the Inn at the Long Trail reported that about once a year, a group of hikers staying at the inn damaged furniture or carved their trail names on a wooden surface. The informants and the hikers themselves attributed most of the serious vandalism along the Trail to local residents and to vehicle-supported overnight partiers. My own observations, particularly of trail users in the Great Smoky region, find that most incidents of backcountry campers leaving piles of trash or dismantling signs involved weekend or inexperienced backpackers. Vehicle-supported overnighters who pack in alcoholic beverages are particularly destructive. Over the years, vandals have purposefully burned shelters and destroyed other trail structures. The guilty parties are often unsupervised adolescents from nearby communities or residents of the local region who perceive the trail or federal land ownership as an intrusion.

Since they meet each other repeatedly, thru-hikers display a communitarian and protective attitude toward campsites, springs, and shelters. They are very aware that if they leave garbage it attracts bears, skunks, and mice. The biggest problem has often been unburned food wrappers in the fire pit, which tempts wildlife to visit. The trail clubs and public land managers leave brooms and other cleaning tools at the shelters (fig. 6.4). Human waste, unfortunately, has often intruded around heavily used campsites. In an unpublished survey I supervised during the 1980s, we found more than thirty piles of human excrement or toilet paper on the surface within the trampled zone around a heavily used AT shelter that did not have a privy at the time. Shelters used primarily by long-distance backpackers did not exhibit this level of sanitary disregard, and some shelter grounds at less heavily trafficked sites were largely clear of obvious human waste. Typically, however, we would find scattered, used toilet paper near shelters, and occasionally, right behind the shelter.[4] The responsible land management agency, incidentally, has since reinstalled a privy at the waste-littered shelter. Inadequate cleanup of food and human waste remains a threat to hiker safety on the AT, because scraps attract mice, which carry illnesses such as hantavirus and Lyme disease, and human waste contains microorganisms that can cause intestinal disruption and even skin infections such as staphylococcus. The issue of whether shelters and campsites need privies has been one of the long arguments among maintainers in regard to managing for wilderness ambiance.

Hikers just beginning an AT hike often have difficulties with their gear and sometimes simply abandon a dysfunctional stove or a leaky jacket they do not need. I have seen full, high-end frame packs jettisoned at shelters or trail intersections by hikers who were giving up and quitting early. Bill Bryson's *A Walk in the Woods* is self-effacing about his own overpacking, and droll concerning the equipment wastage of would-be end-to-enders abandoning the enterprise. As long-distance walkers adapt to the rigors of the AT, they usually adjust their clothes, portable shelter, and diet to the ambient conditions. Experienced AT hikers are, with few exceptions, tidy and self-contained.

TRAIL MAGIC—GRAY OR WHITE

At the time of this study, the support network was engaging in an interstate conversation concerning "trail magic"—the practice of providing free services and treats for AT hikers. These include both meeting the need for basic provisions, such as giving a hiker with a damaged ankle a vehicle ride to the emergency room, and gifts of items difficult to find on-trail, such as soft drinks left cooling

Fig. 6.4. Appalachian Trail shelter broom closet in New Jersey has one implement. Hikers should be carrying trowels for burying waste. This shelter is well swept, free of trash, and in good condition. Graffiti is beginning to appear on the new wall surface.

in a mountain creek. Some informants expressed a subtle cynicism and viewed the "cute" forms of "trail magic" as either superficial on the part of the angels or self-serving on the part of the hikers. Although veterans of years of interaction with hikers universally respected the "angels" who hauled plastic jugs of water to a trail intersection near a dry spring, they also expressed a concern that leaving

Fig. 6.5. Building and conserving sections of the Appalachian Trail requires a large and committed cadre of volunteer maintainers. Here a large bridge crosses a wetland in New Jersey. Such efforts require raising funds and/or volunteer time.

small gifts might be replacing the more time-consuming and critical forms of service, such as repairing damaged trail beds and refurbishing aging shelters. Angels who managed hostels individually contributed hundreds of hours annually, as did the committed leaders of volunteer trail crews. Figure 6.5 displays a complex trail management task, the construction of a bridge, which required both acquisition of funds and continued maintenance. Although the AT has had far more thru-hikers in the past two decades than at any time previously, the Appalachian Trail Conservancy and many of the clubs have been having difficulty recruiting enough volunteers to keep the treadway clear of brush, to patrol shelters and check on hikers (ridge running), and to monitor wildlife habitat. The informants also expressed doubts over the availability of "mobile magic," such as rides to the mall and other gifts that, even though well meant, might detract from the trail experience.

Trail families, loose confederations of hikers who walk together and meet at shelters and hostels, improve safety. They check up on friends who have fallen behind and provide assistance to comrades with injuries or damaged gear. They can become self-absorbed, sponsoring barbeques and reunions for their "family members," while showing little interest in caring for the trail itself. From the early days of the trail through the 1960s, the hiking clubs and their events dominated AT society. Today, owing to the increase in mega-hiking, thru-hikers generate a peripatetic, seasonal society that may only have occasional contact with club or official ATC functions.

As a second ethical conflict, most forms of trail magic concern the provision of civilized assistance—such as leaving bottles of soda or offering rides to town. The magic either materializes as a minor intrusion into the wilderness ambiance, or the magic is an alternative to remaining on foot or camping on-trail. The use of cell phones, including calls for shuttles, has arisen as an ethical issue. Cell phones improve response time in case of injuries and facilitate family contact and meeting shuttles. The ATC has not encouraged cell phones because the fees one pays are used to build additional intrusive cell towers, which have become ever more visible to hikers. By 2007, however, the cell connection was pervasive throughout the corridor, despite efforts from the ATC. Other signs of industrialization, such as power lines, gas line rights of ways, and radar towers have intruded into vistas or cut across the AT itself. A tower complex has marred the view from Highpoint in New Jersey, a short hike from the AT, and a garish red and white[5] metal monster has loomed up over the corridor, just to the south of Delaware Water Gap and next to some lovely views of farms and barns in the valley below (fig. 6.6). Towers have sprung up through the trees hither and yon along the Blue Ridge Parkway and Skyline Drive, where the AT has long been wrestling with civilization in the form of scenic highways.

While trail magic has become a potent symbol of hiker society and of the communitarian values of an AT hike, it is in fact industrialization as a form of freely given gift. The more venerable hostels, such as Church of the Mountain, have taken positions against offering rides or vehicle support, except in the case of injured hikers. The ATC has posted guidelines differentiating appropriate from inappropriate trail magic. National Park Service authority only extends to the boundaries of the trail corridor, and much trail magic and angelic outreach blossoms miles away from the Park Service's domain. The NPS has focused on trail magic that might attract wildlife, damage flora and soils, or leave trash at campsites. As of this writing, the NPS suggests that magic follow "leave no trace" practices, and that angels watch food "magic" and not leave it untended (at

Fig. 6.6. Towers visible from the highest elevation in New Jersey at High Point State Park. Such visual clutter has become an increasing threat to the Appalachian Trail and adjoining scenic areas.

which juncture it becomes trash). Event planning should avoid trampling fragile sites, seek out durable surfaces, offer inclusive activities for all hikers, and also program a thorough and restorative cleanup.[6]

Though the presence of full-service huts and even the open shelters within the trail corridor has generated periodic controversy as potential intrusions into wilderness,[7] the ATC has never taken a strong stance against hikers staying off-trail overnight. Having no legal mandate to worry about what hikers are up to when they head to town, ATC staff nonetheless stay in contact with the hostels catering to hikers. Outside the activities of the AMC, the clubs have avoided offering supplies or hot showers on corridor. Although the AT has never been a typical wilderness, the experience has evolved into an alternation between mountains and town—an alternation ironically facilitated by the actions of trail angels.

An advantage of trail magic and events, such as Trail Days or Trail Fest, is that they have encouraged permanent residents of trail towns and people residing near the trail to identify with thru-hikers. The process has also generated hiker advocates who remain in contact with chambers of commerce and village churches. Trail magic thus has helped to keep the peace and reduce conflicts between hikers and residents along the corridor. The ATC has inadequate resources to offer much of what the angels provide, so the informal relationships have become critical to the smooth and normative functioning of the trail.

A last ethical property of trail magic, and a very positive one, is that trail magic has been a major influence in convincing hikers that human beings can be kind to each other. Assistance offered with no expectation of reciprocity is an argument that people can care about each other in a nonmercantile way. Relationships do not have to be bought and sold. An expression of old-fashioned neighborliness, trail magic has emerged as a statement that other people are valuable, just as they are. The hiker surveys, numerous comments in trail logs, and interviews with volunteers all indicate that trail magic encourages hikers to believe that people can treat each other well, and is thus an important generator of "the spirit of the Appalachian Trail" and of positive hiker experience. Is trail magic good for the AT environment or not? Or, perhaps, better stated: What forms of trail magic are good for the AT and which are not? Where should technology stop and the trail begin?

Common humans

CHAPTER 7

ENVIRONMENTAL VALUES AND LEARNING ON THE TRAIL

The Hiker Survey—Ethics Sections

The second major source of information on hiker ethics was the self-reported perspectives of the AT hikers themselves. My hiker survey incorporated sixteen questions concerning ethical values, with an emphasis on environmental ethics and care for other people; and thirteen questions concerning how the AT trip had influenced the hikers' ethics. In other words, the questionnaire first asked what the hikers considered to be important ethical issues, and second, if the AT hiking experience had taught them anything about environmental care or motivated them to act on behalf of the environment or people in need. Hikers could score each question from "not at all true" to "very true" on a five-point scale. The questionnaire utilized three negative statements about environmentalism in the first set of sixteen questions, and one negative statement about the value of the trail as learning environment in the second set of thirteen. These "reverse" questions made certain that respondents were really reading the sentences and were not randomly circling one number. Reversals also reduced political bias, by allowing someone who was skeptical about the importance of environmental issues to score a more neutral statement as "very true."[1]

The AT survey addressed frequent points of discussion in academic environmental ethics, including whether people can be simultaneously oriented toward care of human beings and the natural environment. The process of trail corridor preservation itself excludes forms of human use that compete with recreational activities.[2] Environmental ethicists have contrasted anthropocentric (human-centered) and ecocentric (oriented toward all living creatures and ecological processes) ethics. Thomas Vale, in his review of the meaning of American wilderness, proposes that wilderness can serve as "a vision of moral philosophy," or an ethical stage of human development. On one side are the biocentrists or ecocentrists, who believe they can defend exploited nature from big business, capitalism, and the materialistic middle class. On the other side are the anthropocentrists, who recognize care for nature "as a uniquely human trait," or who embrace "an active role for people in the transformation of nature."[3] Considering that surveys have concluded wilderness users are well-educated and economically privileged, a second question is: Are AT hikers a snobby elite with little interest in the recreational and environmental needs of people who do not have the freedom to take to the woods? Thomas Vale termed this negative interpretation "wilderness as aristocratic castle."[4]

A third question, with a substantial academic literature, concerns how people develop in-depth knowledge of environmental problems and solutions within their home region and the habitats they depend on for food, water, and energy. The bioregional movement has encouraged people to recognize the species present where they live and to become familiar with ecosystem protection issues near their residence and employment. Because visitors to the AT are largely from the eastern and midwestern states, they should be encountering many environmental problems during their hikes, such as noticeable air pollution, that also concern their home counties and cities. The survey compared hiker concern for wilderness protection to concern for conserving the rural and historic landscapes, also subject to encroachment by development pressures in the populated East.[5]

INTERPRETING THE SURVEY RESPONSES

Hikers rated the ethical statements from 1 to 5, with 1 as "not at all true," 3 as "somewhat true," and 5 as "very true."[6] The mean is the average response, and the median is the response falling in the middle of all the replies—half will be higher and half will be lower. The mode is the most common response overall, the value selected by the highest percentage of respondents. Many of the strongly positive responses to environmental ethical values also had relatively low variation—that is, a majority of the AT hikers agreed that pollution and wildlife protection were important. In contrast, hiker responses to a question about the spiritual or religious value of nature often display high variance, indicating a wider range of perspectives and individual experience. The analysis utilized both parametric and nonparametric statistical tests. Often, with this type of data, nonparametric tests find a greater number of significant relationships between variables (factors). To avoid cluttering the text, I distinguished nonparametric results as NP. The bulk of the numerical results are tucked away in the tables, appendices, and footnotes (where academic readers may peruse the specifics).[7]

ENVIRONMENTAL VALUES

Although the public often view long-distance AT hikers as exceptionally committed to nature, the hiker surveys provided little evidence of radical environmental views. The AT hikers overall, however, had a very strong concern for the impacts of pollution and for protection of biodiversity and of wildlife and habitats (appendix I.1). The hikers gave the statement: "Proper waste management is a responsibility of all good citizens" an average rating of 4.6 (mode=5) or "very true." The ratings given to "Humans should do more to protect wildlife and their habitats" were 4.5 on average—also "very true." The survey respondents awarded minimal ratings to statements casting environmental values as extreme or as financially wasteful. The trail had only low levels of trash, although there are some eyesores along the route. Figure 7.1 displays debris including logs, old tires, styrofoam, and plastic bottles on the shore of Fontana Lake as viewed from the Appalachian Trail crossing Fontana Dam, in North Carolina. This visual disaster was not the result of hiker behaviors, but other recreationists, such as boaters, did contribute to the mess.

A commonly held and unfounded criticism of environmentalists and of wilderness recreationists is that they do not care about people, only about nature. The hikers did give a slightly higher rating to the statement "Care for nature should be an integral part of my life" (mean=4.3) than they did to the statement "Service to other people should be an integral part of my life" (mean=4.1), but the difference was not statistically significant. Further, the hikers believed that caring for the world's needy people (mean=3.9) is nearly as important as caring for nature, while not at the same time believing that money committed to environmental care should be diverted to assist needy people (mean=2.1). The AT hikers did not concur, however, that poverty prevented recreational access

care for nature v oth

Fig. 7.1. Piles of trash viewed from the Appalachian Trail on the shore of Fontana Lake, North Carolina. The trail had little trash, but there are exceptions.

(mean=2.6) (appendix I.1). The ratings hikers gave to environmental and human care statements were positively correlated (cc=.30, p=.000), suggesting that hikers who give care and service a high priority were likely to do so concerning both the environment and human beings. The respondents who believed care for nature was highly important, however, were more likely to score higher on other questions directly concerning environmental care than those who gave higher ratings to human service. AT hikers who placed an emphasis on service to people were less likely to believe human population growth is an environmental threat and more likely to believe that money used for environmental care should be diverted to serve needy human beings.

WALKING FOR OTHERS

One of the themes in the published AT journals, and an accepted practice on the trail, is to "hike for someone else." An example is Buddy Newell's *You Won't Get to Maine Unless You Walk in the Rain.*[8] Newell's son had multiple sclerosis, so Newell and his daughter hiked the trail for him. Jeff Alt hiked to raise money for the Sunshine House, where his brother Aaron, who suffered from cerebral palsy and mental retardation, was a resident. Jeff raised $16,000 and his AT effort inspired an annual walk in Ohio.[9] Alt's *A Walk for Sunshine: A 2,160 Mile Expedition for Charity on the Appalachian Trail* described a very normative Springer to Katahdin trek, with the usual problems with blisters, snow, and his companions quitting. Jeff integrated his fund raising for his brother's long-term facility with his AT mission, primarily by sending newsletters to his sponsors. The hike was an extended athletic event, with the spectators participating through giving. The end-to-end adventure was similar to walks or runs held by cities or towns to raise money to fight breast cancer or heart disease. Jeff Alt brought his personal service objective to the trail, which provided an attractive venue for sponsors, who could follow the adventurous walk for charity on a Web site. During 2009, a thru-hiker was conducting a hike for the autistic child of a friend, and was donating the funds to a state society for autistic children. The hiker was also managing a Web site providing information about autism and leaving cards at hostels. Informants described end-to-enders who were hiking for a deceased spouse or child. Although these hikes-for-others were rarities, they have become entrenched in trail lore and have gained acceptance by other members of the AT community.

Hikes for others were also examples of bringing family and friendship ties and the concerns of home to the trail and attempting to improve them through walking. Christianity has long accepted the practices of walking for someone else, and entering the pilgrim's vocation in response to the illness or death of a loved one. The pilgrim may visit a healing spring and return home with a bottle of the empowered waters, or actually bathe in holy waters in place of a sick parent or child.[10] In the days when extended stays in purgatory were a Christian concern, a widow on pilgrimage prayed for the soul of her husband and for a speedy release to heaven. The AT does not offer a formal system of credit for effort, although the concept of raising money through miles walked for charity is analogous, as is the belief that a deceased love one or a friend who is incapacitated by an injury also participates in the hike.

The examples I have encountered of individuals walking the trail to raise funds for charity were human health or pet/domestic animal care–oriented rather than environmentally or wildlife-oriented. One informant did report a case of two supposed thru-hikers who fraudulently collected money for a non-existent nonprofit and were arrested in a trail town. Although I did not conduct any monitoring of these walks for the benefit of others, there were fewer reports in the northern reaches of the corridor, probably because the fund raisers had dropped out.

CHANGING BEHAVIORS

Personal ethics

The second ethics section in the questionnaire concerned the hikers' perceptions of their own personal ethical formation and learning responses to the AT trip. How much does the extended trail experience influence hiker behavior and values? In general, these scores were lower than they were in the sections concerning ethical beliefs. The hikers were already convinced that controlling pollution is the responsibility of all good citizens and human beings should act to prevent biodiversity loss. They universally affirmed the concept, however, that experiencing natural beauty was a key motivator to environmental care (mean=4.3) (appendix I.2) The respondents believed that spiritual or religious experience was less important on average to encouraging environmental care (mean=3.3). Here, however, the mode was 5—"very true." The variance was high. Hikers who had a religious or spiritual identify viewed environmental care through a spiritual lens, while other hikers rejected completely the idea of spirituality as an environmental motivator. Overall, 81 percent of hikers reported that it was true or very true that natural beauty prompted them to environmental care, while 48 percent gave the two highest scores to spiritual experience in nature promoting environmental action.

An unexpected outcome was the degree to which hikers reported their trip as fostering ethical self-reflection or self-awareness. The questionnaire used tandem questions. One asked if the AT experience increased awareness of how personal behaviors or ethics can affect the environment. The other asked if the experience increased awareness of how personal behavior or ethics can affect other people. I had expected the AT experience to have a greater impact on environmental values than on interpersonal relationships, yet the means, respectively (3.7 and 3.6), were not significantly different, and the responses were strongly correlated (cc=.71, p=.000).[11] Individual hikers who perceived themselves as developing greater ethical self-understanding did so simultaneously in the environmental and communal domains. Just more than half of hikers reported that it was true to very true they had a growing awareness of the effects of their own behavior: 57 percent in terms of the environment and 53 percent in terms of their impacts on other people.

The AT experience was more equivocal in terms of influencing hikers to either join environmental organizations or to take political action concerning the environment (mean and mode=3). Just more than one-quarter, 26 percent, rated as true or very true the statement that the trip was encouraging them to greater political action concerning the environment. Although the hikers rated service to others as an important ethical value, they reported that it was equivocal to somewhat untrue that the AT experience had motivated them to join humanitarian or human service organizations. Comparing hiker motivation to join environmental organizations (mean=3.2) with hiker motivation to join social service organizations (mean=2.8), the difference was significant (p=.000). The AT long-distance hike was, therefore, a moderate to neutral motivator when it came to joining organizations oriented toward achieving the greater good—serving either the degraded natural environment or people in need.

ENVIRONMENTAL EDUCATION

Although hikers unilaterally rejected the idea that they had learned nothing about environmental care on the trip (mean=1.7), the scores for the impact of environmental education or learning experienced were low—below 3.0. Hikers reported that it was somewhat untrue (mean=2.7) that exposure to educational materials or programs about the AT had increased their interest in environmental care. Interestingly, the long-distance hikers filling out the survey were not resoundingly positive about the need for additional environmental education along the AT. In response to the statement "I would like to have more access to printed or educational materials concerning environmental issues along this trail," the average score was 3.0; only 27 percent, or about one-quarter, rated this statement as true or very true. Considering the possible prejudice against more athletic and goal-oriented thru-hikers when distributing the survey forms, the survey method was likely to overreport interest in educational access, rather than to underreport hikers' felt need for greater environmental and, presumably, natural history education. Henry David Thoreau, a highly competent field naturalist, would be very grouchy about this outcome. The AT offered very few points, relative to its mileage, where interpretive materials were available on-trail. Such access was often tied to structures and developments with dual purposes, such as the combination with a bench in figure 7.2 or monuments marking summits. Educational displays are intrusions in wilderness, thus they conflict with other trail values.

In reading contemporary AT journals, I have been struck by the relative dearth of ecological commentary and the authors' variable interest in natural history, from almost none at all to genuine excitement in encountering new habitats or ecosystems. Personal achievement–oriented hikers logged the landscape so generally that if the Appalachian place names were not in the text, the peaks and rippling streams could just as easily be in the English Lake District or the Tyrol. The challenge-driven hikers were inclined to provide step by step descriptions of dealing with injuries and organizing a lightweight pack and almost no detail concerning geology or flora. Buddy Newell's hike with his daughter was a series of small crises, such as stepping over rattlesnakes and searching for hot meals. Although the diary's natural history was suspect, the family team enjoyed its encounters with wildlife, such as white-tailed deer and the ponies on Mount Rogers, VA. The descriptions were of the obvious and more easily identified species. Newell's perceptions and interests appeared to be typical for the majority of thru-hikers.

Jeff Alt, in one of the few natural history discourses in his journal, did provide a brief overview of the vegetation on Roan Mountain and nearby grassy balds: "Beneath the snow blanket, Roan Mountain is covered with rhododendrons and mountain laurel. Off the trail, there are whole mountainsides with nothing but rhododendrons and tall grass. Tourists come from all over when the rhododendrons bloom with pink flowers. It was too early in the season to witness the pink beauty. A drastic descent off Roan Mountain, opened up to Carvers Gap, which

Fig. 7.2. Interpretive display adjoining the Appalachian Trail in Walkill Wildlife Refuge, New Jersey. Appalachian Trail backpackers have very low access to materials conveying information about nature or environmental issues while on trail.

is a series of bald mountains. I could see for miles across the mountain peaks and down into valleys dotted with farms and cleared fields, surrounded by forest."[12] Although Alt was impressed by the Roan area, he articulated little interest in why the mountaintops were treeless, nor was he aware that he was walking through one of the most spectacular biodiversity hotspots in the southeast. In contrast, the author provided a detailed description of his dinner at a gourmet restaurant in Charlottesville, VA (which was well off-trail). Aside from the list of entrees, he recounted trips to an ice cream shop flavor by flavor and the acquisition of boxed donuts the next morning.[13] The excessive chow-down verified the rigors of the walk, and characterized the genuine 2,000-miler. The emphasis was athletic rather than on absorbing the natural milieu.

The purpose of this comparison is not to critique thru-hikers for their perpetual calorie shortage and weight loss but is to point out that many skilled and thoughtful AT hikers have little basic idea what they are striding through. They are not fully reading the AT landscape in environmental and ecological terms. The journals demonstrated that would-be end-to-enders were more likely to prepare by gaining incrementally increasing distances with a rock-filled pack than by reading books about the ecological richness they were about to experience along the way, such as the spruce-fir forest or the plethora of oaks. The thru-hikers frequently observe interesting animals and spectacular plants like the umbrella leaf in figure 7.3, which is only found in the southern Appalachians. AT hikers would like to know more about these species, but do not have an easy way to look them up. Other hikers have sometimes asked me about plants like umbrella leaf when they have encountered me botanizing along the trail. The hikers' descriptions of natural objects were, more often than not, accurate enough to identify what they had observed, so they were absorbing their surroundings. The practice of very lightweight backpacking has discouraged bringing scientific guides, including volumes on Appalachian natural history, such as *Mountains of the Heart*,[14] or even very easily stowed pocket books, such as the *AMC Field Guide to the New England Alpine Summits*.[15] Hikers belonging to regional trail clubs or repeatedly day or weekend hiking in a particular mountain range are usually better informed, because they own bioregional reference volumes, attend educational events, and follow local environmental news.

When Bill Bryson was tromping through the Great Smokies (more or less) he hoped to see salamanders but did not find any. The salamanders were all around him (probably laughing their red-cheeked heads off). He walked by hundreds. Bryson needed to stop stumbling onward over tree roots and instead snoop in a few wet patches around cascades or fallen logs. Although thru-hikers were penetrating an enticing and interest-generating terrain, on average, they lacked the training and the time to locate amusing amphibians. The wilderness ambience and inaccessible nature of the trail inhibit environmental outreach by the agencies and clubs managing the corridor. The great variation in flora and fauna along the trail is also a barrier to casually studying the array of species and habitats. Hundreds of wildflower species flourish in the corridor, not just dozens. The dense foliage adds to the challenge, particularly in observing wildlife. When the hiker stops and immerses himself in his surroundings, he develops greater sensory acuity and natural perception.

AT hikers expressed a strong contrast between increasing their appreciation of the value of wild or undeveloped lands (mean=3.7, mode=5) and becoming more aware of environmental concerns in their hometown or region (mean=2.7, mode=3). The hikers perceived the trail as a particular landscape, with issues that did not overlap with more-developed and residential locales. This finding

not overall environmental aware

Fig. 7.3. Umbrella leaf, southern Appalachian endemic, along the Appalachian Trail, Georgia. Hikers often do not have the background to identify regional specialties or unusual species.

was ironic, considering the impact of air pollution generated by urban and suburban areas on the Appalachian Trail corridor. The higher-elevation forests in the southern Appalachians have experienced devastating die-back of species such as red spruce, which are potentially pollution related (fig. 7.4).

Blue Ridge 2020: An Owner's Manual has outlined the major threats to the southern Appalachians.[16] Both Great Smoky Mountains and Shenandoah National Parks have posted ozone warnings for hikers, runners, and bicyclists to ensure they protect themselves from the health effects of this subtle hazard. A solid 57 percent of hikers responded that it was true or very true that the AT experience was increasing their awareness of how their own behavior could affect the natural environment. In contrast, 26 percent gave similar ratings to becoming more aware

Fig. 7.4. The die-back of both Frasier fir and red spruce in the Great Smokies are the result of human activity. The nonnative balsam woolly adelgid has attacked the fir, and the spruce has been in decline, probably because of air pollution.

of environmental concerns in their home region, about half of hikers who were gaining environmental wisdom were not consciously transferring what they had learned to other terrains. The surveys implied that many AT hikers did not glean an in-depth understanding of environmental cause and effect while trekking, and treated the immediate AT landscape as unique and disconnected from the greater Appalachian ecosystem.

RELIGIOUS ENGAGEMENT AND AT ETHICS

Some studies of American Christians have found that evangelicals are more conservative in their political views and, depending on their denominational background, may consider the environment to be a lower priority than personal morality (particularly sexual and family values) or economic development. Strong belief in the authority of the Bible, frequency of church attendance, and fundamentalist theology generate opposition to government funding for the environment, or lowered environmental priorities.[17] Douglas Eckberg and T. Jean Blocker, in contrast, found that a proenvironmental effect correlated with religious participation,[18] while Justin Longnecker and colleagues found a higher level of ethical judgment among religious people, including evangelicals.[19] Environmental ethicists and Christian theologians, from evangelicals to liberal Protestants, have responded to environmental ethical deficiencies within their own religious denominations with biblically and philosophically based arguments for increased Christian environmental care.[20] Buddhists, Jews, and leaders from many other religions have constructed environmental ethical strategies consistent with their own traditions.[21]

Whether an AT survey respondent had a religious affiliation or not, or belonged to a particular belief system, did not have a major influence on ethical responses in the AT survey. In fact, comparing the Abrahamic faiths[22] with all other religious backgrounds produced no significant differences between the two major religious categories for either ethics section.[23] Comparing hikers with religious affiliations to those without indicated that religious hikers were less likely to consider industrialization a threat (p=.005) and more likely to believe that service to other people should be an integral part of their lives (p=.007). While hikers with religious affiliations were less likely to give a high priority to integrating care for nature into their lives than other hikers (p=.035), they were much more likely to affirm the concept that spiritual or religious experience with nature increased their motivation to environmental care (p=.000). Hikers with religious affiliations gave both more "very true" and "somewhat untrue" ratings to the AT's impact on their perceptions of wildlands (p=.028), suggesting a liberal to conservative split. A nonparametric test found that hikers with a religious identity were more likely to believe environmentalists exaggerated the issues (p=.027).

A better means of evaluating the impact of religion on ethical beliefs is correlating the level of religious practice to the hiker responses, because it corrects for nominal religious participation. As a general pattern, hikers with higher levels of religious practice were more moderate in their environmental beliefs and more likely to believe service to other people was important.[24] Involvement in religious activities, such as prayer, may also reflect personality types and, in a deeper sense, perception of people and nature, even among major religious traditions such as Christianity and Buddhism. Table 7.1 indicates that different frequencies of personal religious activity were correlated to ethical values. Hikers with higher levels of pre-AT service attendance, for example, were significantly less likely to believe human developments and industrialization damage the environment, and were also less concerned about caring for nature or for wildlife and its habitats. They were more likely to believe environmentalists exaggerate the critical nature of environmental issues. The degree of off-trail engagement in religious or spiritual practice was (fortunately) significantly positively correlated to the belief that care for other people should be an integral part of the hiker's life.[25]

Religious practice did not influence all ethical perspectives, however. The hikers with higher intentional religious and spiritual activity were similar to other respondents concerning the impacts of human population, prevention of loss of the rural scene, believing that care for the environment did not harm human economic interests, and identifying proper waste management as good citizenship. Interestingly, hikers with high levels of service attendance or other religious practice did not differ from other hikers in believing that caring for the environment was important in caring for the world's needy people (table 7.1).

The levels of religious practice or engagement *had no significant correlations* to scores concerning the impact of AT experience on increasing or influencing ethical motivation or on providing environmental learning, with the exception of two statements. Hikers with higher levels of prayer, service attendance, and reading sacred texts were all more likely to consider spiritual experience with nature as an important motivator in terms of care for the environment. The amount of time spent in prayer or meditation while on the AT presented the highest correlation, cc=.456 (p=.000). An interesting negative correlation appeared among hikers who had increased or maintained their levels of reading religious texts, or of service attendance while on the AT. They were less likely to believe experience with nature increased their commitment to the environment.[26] In studying visitors to Mount Shasta, CA, Lynn Huntsinger and Maria Fernandez-Gimenez found no differences in perception of environmental degradation, erosion, or overcrowding between visitors with a religious motivation

Table 7.1

The correlation between the level of pre-trail and on-trail religious practice and ethical beliefs

Ethical beliefs	Pre service	AT service	Pre pray	AT pray	Pre read	AT read
Negative correlations						
Human developments, such as roads and buildings, are damaging our parks and hiking trails	-.234**	-.099	-.159*	-.198**	-.099	-.035
Care for nature should be an integral part of my life	-.166*	-.085	-.137	-.171*	-.154*	-.083
Environmental degradation could result in the disappearance of humanity from the earth	-.162*	-.031	-.095	-.116	-.180*	-.161*
Humans should do more to protect wildlife and their habitats	-.151**	-.098	-.146*	-.188**	-.164*	-.088
We should preserve as many of the earth's wild plant and animal species as possible	-.061	-.035	-.188**	-.183**	-.178*	-.144*
Caring for the environment is important to caring for the world's needy people	-.099	-.154*	-.064	-.084	.095	-.065
Positive correlations						
Environmentalists often exaggerate or make issues seem worse than they are	.183**	.128	.082	.116	.103	.143*
Service to other people should be an integral part of my life	.191**	.120	.262**	.222**	.146*	.131

NOTE: Hikers with more frequent service or ritual attendance and more frequent engagement in prayer and meditation were less likely to give care for nature a high priority. Pre are off-trail or pre-trail levels of religious practice, including "service" or ritual attendance, "pray(er)" and meditation, and "read(ing)" sacred texts. One * indicates p=.05; and two** indicates p=.01 or better.

(pilgrims) and those without.[27] These results parallel the AT hiker responses, considering that AT hikers with and without religious backgrounds experienced similar increases in motivation to environmental care (or lack thereof).

MILEAGE, PREVIOUS HIKING EXPERIENCE, AND PERSONAL BACKGROUND

Gender and age did have significant relationships to hiker ethical beliefs. Women gave higher ratings to the concepts that air and water pollution are threats to human health, people who are poor do not have enough access to outdoor recreation, industrialized culture is a threat to the Earth's environment, and care for the environment should be an integral part of their lives. Men were more likely than women to believe environmentalists exaggerate issues. Women were more likely to rank the trail experience as a motivation to join environmental organizations, join humanitarian organizations, or to vote concerning environmental issues.[28] Female hikers, therefore, awarded greater importance to organizational responses to social issues.

Though there were no differences by age group concerning care for wildlife, older hikers were less likely to think increasing human population was a major threat, air and water pollution are threats to human health, money for the environment should be directed to needy people, caring for the environment is important to the world's needy people, and that human developments are damaging parks and hiking trails. Older AT travelers were also less likely to believe care for nature should be an integral part of their lives. The more senior backpackers therefore were both less likely to perceive human beings as a threat to the environment and less likely to perceive human needs and environmental care as integrally linked. In terms of ethical change generated by the AT experience, age made less difference, with two exceptions: younger hikers were much more likely to report increasing awareness of environmental concerns in their hometown and were somewhat more likely to desire greater access to educational materials concerning environmental issues along the trail.[29] These results could arise from the younger generation's greater exposure to environmental education in school and through the media. Level of education similarly produced only one significant relationship concerning ethical beliefs: hikers with higher levels of education were more likely to believe proper waste management is the responsibility of all good citizens (p=.029). Hikers with higher levels of education were more likely to report that the AT hike encouraged them to take political action for the environment (p=.052), or the hike had made them more aware of how their behavior could influence the natural environment (p=.001).[30]

Only two statements from the first ethics section were significantly related to mileage completed, while none from the second ethics section were. This outcome was a shock to this investigator. AT hikers who had traveled greater distances were *less likely* to believe industrialized culture is a threat to the Earth's environments, and that environmental degradation could result in the disappearance of humanity from the Earth![31] It is important to note, the survey could not distinguish cause and effect. Hikers who had more tolerance for development may have been more likely to survive for 1,400 miles. However, it is clear that longer-distance AT hikers did not have a declining belief that human beings and nature are compatible.

Because the ATC is continually trying to maintain the natural qualities of the trail corridor, the data suggesting longer-distance hikers were less concerned about industrialization was puzzling. The trail itself often strikes a compromise with roads and other products of industrialization, by bridging major interstate highways and weaving over scenic drives. The quick passage over I-64 as northbound thru-hikers enter Shenandoah NP, for example, implies that real wilderness experience can coexist with multilane highways (fig. 7.5). The speedy trail crossing does not convey the extent to which I-64 generates air pollution or serves as a barrier to wildlife. Today's hikers make liberal use of cell phones and vehicle shuttles. The ideal lightweight AT walk is hybrid mix of high-technology gear, in-town support, and a protected natural corridor. The end-to-end walk itself is an extended compromise between the forested slopes and anthropogenic infrastructure.

Interestingly, the amount of previous hiking experience, and whether hikers were traveling with a significant other or family members, did not significantly influence ethical beliefs, at least concerning environmental values and commitment to service to other people. The surveys inferred that spending months on the AT did not turn hikers into antisocial environmental radicals who dislike people and treat humanity as if we are ruining the planet. Nor did it greatly increase their motivation to environmental care. In other words, the strong environmental values of the hikers were largely in place before the hike started,

Fig. 7.5. View from the Appalachian Trail, Rockfish Gap, as it crosses the bridge over I-64, Virginia. Transportation, energy transmission, and communication corridors are major intrusions into the trail corridor.

and a longer AT sojourn produced a compromise between human development and resource use and wild nature, rather than an infusion of radical "wilderness only" environmentalism.

PARTICIPATION IN TRAIL CLUBS AND ENVIRONMENTAL ORGANIZATIONS

Consistent with moderate responses concerning the importance of environmental politics, only one hiker reported belonging to Earth First!, and only two reported belonging to Greenpeace (which is on the soft side of radical these days). Overall, about 6 percent reported belonging to environmental organizations (including the Sierra Club) that might be considered "activist," while an overlapping 6 percent reported belonging to an organization, such as the Nature Conservancy or the National Audubon Society, that has a mission primarily in ecosystem or species conservation. The profile was of a higher commitment to environmental organizations than one would find among the general public, while slightly more than one hiker in twenty had a membership in an organization that would provide education in species identification or protection of biodiversity. These findings are further evidence that the average AT thru- or section hiker was not likely to be well-versed in natural history or in Appalachian ecology.

The surveys indicated that younger hikers were significantly less likely to belong to the ATC (Appalachian Trail Conservancy) or AMC (Appalachian Mountain Club). Of hikers under thirty years old, 21 percent were members, while 43 percent of hikers from thirty to forty-nine belonged, and 50 percent of hikers fifty and older belonged to either the ATC or AMC (p=.001). Older hikers were also more likely to belong to multiple regional trail clubs (AT and other trail systems) or to multiple trail-related organizations. Though hikers fifty and older constituted 24 percent of the respondents, they accounted for 53 percent of the regional trail club memberships (some belonging to two or more) (p=.001). This age-related trend was also evident in the case of conservation organizations, where hikers fifty and older were twice as likely to report an environmental membership as hikers under thirty. Hikers who belonged to the ATC or AMC were twice as likely to belong to an environmental organization as those hikers who did not belong to a national trails organization (p=.0001). Although more-mature hikers were less likely to be concerned about environmental issues, they were far more likely to participate in nonprofits offering constructive responses.

Some members may have neglected to report their club-based activities, but the data from the surveys suggested an evolving displacement of the hikers from the regional trail organizations, which provide a locus for volunteer efforts. Youthful hikers were more likely to lack these ties, even though they accounted for a majority of the long-distance AT hikers. If one were hiring a trail crew, hikers in their twenties would be desirable candidates. The clubs have established a presence at hiker-oriented events such as Trail Days, which helps them to contact the geographically diverse thru-hikers who would like to give back to the trail. Figure 7.6 shows a ridge runner and a trail crew manager distributing information at a hiker festival.

The public tend to think of trail and footpath management as being inherently the same as environmental advocacy, and a few NGOs,[32] such as the Sierra Club, serve both roles. Dual identities go back to the nineteenth century. John Muir advocated for national park establishment and protection and also led

Fig. 7.6. Nantahala Hiking Club leaders establish a public presence at a hiker festival, Franklin, North Carolina.

Sierra Club members on wilderness excursions.[33] For the survey, though, hikers who were members of environmental organizations gave more "true" or "very true" scores to statements concerning the importance of care for human beings or nature than did other hikers, including the concept that service to both other people and nature should be an integral part of their lives, and that caring for the environment is important to caring for the world's needy people.[34] Members of clubs with a major investment in trail management did not, in contrast, respond differently than non–trail club members concerning the potential for people to damage wilderness and backcountry areas.[35] Members of trail organizations (a majority from the ATC and AMC) were less likely than other hikers to think of human population and air and water pollution as threats, and there was a trend toward trail club members being *less likely* to believe human beings should preserve as many of the Earth's wild plants and animals as possible.[36] Ironically, the ATC has had an increasing focus on conserving biodiversity in recent years.

Planning documents for the Appalachian Trail now include inventories of rare, endangered, and endemic (regionally restricted) species found along the trail.

In terms of learning from the AT walk, members of environmental organizations were significantly more likely than other hikers to desire more access to environmental educational materials and to find the journey had inspired them to vote on environmental issues. There were trends toward members of conservation organizations finding they had not learned anything new about the environment, being more motivated to join environmental organizations, and finding that exposure to environmental educational had increased their interest in environmental care.[37] Members of trail organizations, in contrast, *were not* significantly different from other hikers in their level of ethical response to their journey or in terms of their desire for environmental education. This result may originate in the social goals of hiking a very well-used path, such as the AT. That the Appalachian Trail offers such beauty and diversity of natural habitats in the center of the industrialized East Coast may also have convinced thru-hikers that human beings can strike a healthy compromise between environmental use and conserving natural values. Some AT ramblers presumably joined the ATC or member clubs to facilitate a thru-hike or to receive discounts on maps and gear, not because they were concerned about species or habitat conservation on the trail corridor.

Giving Back to the Trail

As thru-hikers have expanded in number, and long-distance hikers have become increasingly identified by trail names, rather than by club membership, the long-distance hikers have formed a self-organized, alternative community—which has, more often than not, functioned independently of the regional trail clubs. The majority of AT thru-hikers did not have a permanent residence close to the trail, and participants in end-to-end hikes were frequently in a transitional life phase, having just graduated from college, changed jobs, or retired. The reorganization of the AT under the National Park Service may also have influenced hiker attitudes, as federal administration suggests a tax-funded service offered to the public, rather than an opportunity provided by hikers working together to steward an ideal hiking route. Interviewees who had a superior knowledge of the organization of trail maintenance, or the volunteer nature of the enterprise, lamented that hikers who had finished the entire AT or substantial sections might return for Trail Days or a reunion dinner, but not to assist with erosion control or building a reroute.

In a study of the ATC, Teresa Martinez and Steve McMullin found that "increasing awareness of volunteer programs, ensuring the programs provide results of which the individuals are proud, requesting participation of individuals on both local and national levels, and recognizing volunteers for their contributions" all enhance volunteer recruitment and retention.[38] Reading through the published trail journals and memoirs ascertained that stopping for service to the trail during the journey has not been an established component of the expected "end-to-end hiking experience," while trying to eat a half gallon of ice cream in one sitting has emerged as a well-entrenched rite of passage.[39] Informants indicated that the Hard Rock crew, which conducts projects during Trail Days at Damascus, VA, has drawn a very good turnout, perhaps even more help than was needed. Providing additional events of this type, astutely aligned with thru-hiking seasonal timing, could attract more new club members and provide labor for trail maintenance and special projects. A possibility is to organize work events that parallel the thru-hiking season, especially northbound. The increasing number of trail festivals and reunions could also serve as sources for recruiting skilled maintainers.

The titles and advertisements for the published trail journals often distinguish the author in terms of personal characteristics or mission. The outdoor writer has self-identified as a senior, single woman, military veteran, or as physically disabled. A number emphasized the author's life phase or finding a significant other. The journals, many of them self-published, represented a very democratic array of trail ventures. Hikers sometimes call the AT "the great equalizer." Father Jim Gardner summarized: "The Trail is a great leveler. You can have a PhD or not be able to read, and have a similar experience. It doesn't matter who you are when you start, or what region you come from, it is how you handle the adventure that matters." The trail itself is also free—there are no admission fees, and the emphasis is on public ownership and use. The trail and related events have an "everyone belongs" atmosphere, which is in itself an ethical statement. Because of relatively low ethnic and socioeconomic diversity on the trail, however, this democracy and openness to others operates within a largely white middle- and professional-class framework. Intended as a respite for urban residents and industrial laborers, today's trail is, if anything, less accessible by public transportation than it was immediately following World War II, when most medium-sized Appalachian towns still had daily bus or rail service. Although many AT thru-hikers consider themselves to be of limited means, and some borrow money to make the trip, the majority are financially buffered by generous parents, a retirement account, savings from a well-paying job, or college-age exemption from fiscal obligations. Several weaknesses in hiker ethics, including the McTrail sense of entitlement, ingratitude for free or inexpensive services, and a limited understanding of the barriers to recreational access imposed by poverty arise from the middle-class nature of the venture. Studies of recreational preferences in other locales, such as urban park systems, have found that ethnic minorities, unlike AT thru-hikers, were concerned about a lack of recreational access for the economically disadvantaged. The sense of entitlement, unfortunately, extended to trail maintenance. The question of how a hiker should give back to the AT is perhaps best answered by: "directly"—by caring for the trail itself (fig. 7.7).

Fig. 7.7. Ruts and water bars washed loose on the Appalachian Trail, Great Smoky Mountains. The trail is fragile and requires repeated maintenance to prevent erosion and damage.

The trail clubs have made a great effort to build and stabilize the trail-bed and to secure the corridor. Their public information efforts have focused on guides, maps, and signage. Though the clubs have produced high-quality educational publications (the AMC is particularly prolific), the clubs have never sponsored a coordinated environmental or cultural educational program accessible along the trail. Thru-hikers enter national parks and state forests via the AT corridor, and have to divert off-corridor to find visitor centers, interpretive exhibits, and museums. The evolution of the Appalachian Trail Conservancy has stimulated a greater emphasis on environmental education and on biodiversity conservation, yet the ATC has put much of its effort into its magazine—an effective tool for reaching ATC members, but a less effective means of informing a thru-hike. The hikers responding to the survey were equivocal about the need for more written educational materials, perhaps because such items are difficult to use on the trail corridor itself. The lack of environmental educational impact may be linked to club difficulties in recruiting new members, a connection that deserves further study.

The weakness of the bioregional connection suggests that the city-to-wilderness model dominates on the corridor, and that hikers undergo a radical shift from their lived-in home environment to nature under preservation and have difficulty perceiving the linkages between the two. Hikers were thus under-informed about the roots of ongoing environmental issues such as deterioration of air quality, which has degraded views and threatened the health of active recreationists. Figure 7.8 presents a vista from the AT overlooking the Shenandoah Valley one spring day after a rain, with a particulate (brown) layer of haze already developing on the horizon. The problem has become so serious that, four or five days after rain, the first ridge across the valley would be obscured. The photo also displays the spreading residential development, which has been displacing agriculture and changing valley environments, as well as creeping up toward the AT.

A study conducted on Mount Washington, NH, has shown that hikers who had a medical history of wheezing or asthma had a four-times greater response to elevated ozone levels than other hikers. In addition, elevated levels of ozone, acidic aerosols (a source of acid rain), and fine particulate matter all caused declines in pulmonary function in healthy hikers. A parallel study of day hikers walking the AT to Charlie's Bunion in Great Smokies did not find that air

Fig. 7.8. Haze develops over the spreading residential development in the Shenandoah Valley, below the Appalachian Trail, Virginia, one day after rain. Within four to five days, the ridge across the valley will be almost completely obscured.

pollution had a significant impact on pulmonary function. The Smokies air was relatively clean, and the levels of ozone and fine particulates were safely below federal cut-offs.[40] Better hiker grasp of environmental degradation in the Appalachians could improve individual trail experience and protect personal health. Much of what AT hikers were learning in environmental terms, they were not applying on-trail or taking home with them when they finished. The AT could provide a deeper environmental ethical experience if hikers had more educational bridges to help them link issues like ozone and haze sites to the rest of the Appalachian empire.

ETHICAL FORMATION

Ethical review of wilderness experience, long-distance walking, or pilgrimage on foot can easily descend into invalid preconceptions. The first of these is to believe that individual journeys are a social panacea and should build character or encourage spirituality in all personal spheres. This misconception can lead to devaluing the experience if it does not meet every possible societal goal for constructing good citizens or if it does not adhere to the ideal religious formula for producing perfect saints. The second misconception is to mythologize the experience or to assume it unilaterally meets historic ideals. In the case of the Appalachian Trail, the public and even the trail angels have viewed the thru-hike as thoroughly Thoreauvian, though if Henry David were to botanize his way along today's AT, he might be skeptical. Thoreau possessed an insatiable desire to study natural objects, and acquired an in-depth knowledge of New England's natural history. The average AT hiker lacks this scientific passion and affection for nature at all scales.[41] Further, the third mistake is to assume that all withdrawal into the wilderness or mega-hiking has the same outcomes. The experience of the solo AT hiker, setting his own pace and drifting in an out of various trail "families," is a priori different from participation in a guided, short-term wilderness expedition.

A historic criticism of religious pilgrimage and wilderness experience is that the journey is self-serving and divorces the pilgrim from the home community. The AT, as a "pilgrimage" without a formal religious framework, indeed provides more care-giving opportunities for the angels and volunteers than it does for the hikers. Individual hikers, conscious of societal or family needs, have, however, turned the thru-hike into an act of outreach. Though the frequency of hiker religious or spiritual practice produced negative correlations to several of the environmental ethical statements, this outcome likely originated in pre-trail experiences. Religious hikers reported environmental learning and ethical formation as a result of their AT hike at the same level as nonreligious hikers. The AT gave religious hikers an opportunity to see God or spirit at work in nature, which encouraged them to further develop environmental values, even if they were not fully absorbing the ethical lessons available along the trail.

CHAPTER 8
BUILDING FRIENDSHIPS, DISCOVERING SELF, ENJOYING TERRAINS
EVALUATING PERSONAL EXPERIENCE

The AT survey quantified hiker perceptions of the impact of their journey on personal outcomes such as forming friendships, improving physical fitness, and experiencing inner harmony. The questions were an amalgam, primarily derived from the original applications of the Spiritual Health in Four Domains Index (SH4DI).[1] The format drew statements from other surveys intended to determine spiritual wellness, including an instrument the World Health Organization had developed for application internationally in a range of socioeconomic settings and in regions where religions other than Christianity are dominant.[2] I added statements that reflected historic beliefs about the outcomes of the long-distance walking pilgrimage and the value of the American wilderness experience.[3] In reading the survey results, it is important to remember that the respondents were predominantly successful hikers who completed major sections of the AT. The outcomes might be different if the survey had been conducted with day hikers, weekenders, or hikers just starting from Springer or Katahdin. The attitudes recorded may not be entirely the result of the thru- or section hike. Hikers who were in good health when they began were better conditioned to survive the rigors of the ridgetops and less prone to drop out because of fatigue or injury. A predisposition to the casual and oft-instant friendships the AT generates may have assisted a hiker in finding comfortable social and physical surroundings through the mud, rocks, and drizzle. Those who had backgrounds similar to other hikers may have negotiated easier entry into hiking partnerships or "trail families" comprised of kindred spirits. A degree of spiritual well-being at the beginning of the walk should help the would-be 2,000-milers survive the trail.

ENVIRONMENTAL EXPERIENCE

The hiker response to the trail environment provided some of the highest personal experience scores overall. (Appendix II.1 displays the fifteen personal experience statements with the highest average ratings, or in the case of negative statements, the lowest ratings.) The hikers thought "the natural environment on this trip is pleasing" (mean=4.5) and "the trip has produced many interesting events and experiences" (mean=4.7). The AT hikers reported low rates of boredom despite some long plods through relatively unchanging blocks of forest. In response to: "I often feel bored on the trail" (mean=2.0), a mere 13 percent found this to be true to very true. The hikers gave the AT trip a high rating, though, as "a learning experience" (mean=4.5), in concert with the high level of interesting personal experiences. This learning appeared to be largely informal, arising from interactions with other hikers and from the Appalachian landscape itself.

An unavoidable part of the AT is the heavy precipitation and the frequent patches of muck. End-to-enders mutter "you can't get to Maine if you don't hike in the rain" (fig. 8.1). Hikers taken by surprise have to back down off the ridge when caught in a May ice storm. Raiding bears trap weary backpackers in shelters. Granola-seeking mice run across packs and jump out of the pockets (which I personally leave open so ambitious rodents do not have to chew their way in). One of my field assistants woke up one night at Derrick Knob shelter to find a skunk sitting on his chest. He had difficulty finding a polite way to ask the skunk to leave, so he lay awake for quite some time just wishing the skunk would depart. Youth groups sometimes stay up most of the night in camp, and make certain everyone else does too. Out for a spring ramble, I once arrived at an undistinguished shelter in late afternoon to find that more than thirty thru-hikers, including Dan Wingfoot Bruce, author of more than one AT handbook, had gotten there before me (bunks for ten). Survey respondents reported, however, they were not bothered by the continual dampness, crowding, and primitive overnight facilities. They rated the statement "Environmental or weather conditions have been unpleasant or uncomfortable" as somewhat untrue (mean=2.4). These stoic wanderers were even less concerned about sleeping on the ground or bunks, and rated "Overnight accommodations have been unpleasant or uncomfortable" as untrue (mean=1.9). A mere 4.5 percent whined about the hostels and pavilions by deeming this sentence true or very true (appendix II.1).

The surveys proved that for successful thru- and section hikers, the degree of environmental acclimation is high, and the hikers were not trading perceived

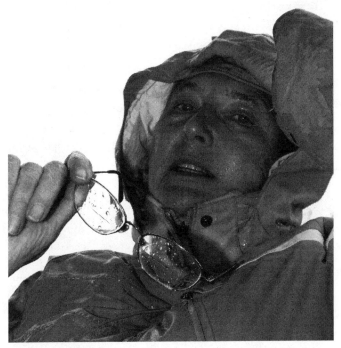

Fig. 8.1. Getting soaked is part of trail life. Some days are simply difficult.

discomfort in some circumstances for postcard-worthy vistas and sunlight in others. End-to-enders in New England suggested I go out of my way to have dinner at the Home Place Restaurant near Catawba, VA. Hikers recommended places to stay hundreds of miles in advance. Finding a floor to sleep on became a multidimensional escapade, where the friendliness of the hostel volunteers, access to a washing machine, and a great view of a sunset all matter. Hikers accepted the simplicity and tolerated the odor of molding cotton permeating the bunk rooms.

Communal Relationships

A second and very consistent result was the trail-generated friendships. Field observations and conversations with hikers confirmed that these friendships may last for the duration of the end-to-end venture, and former thru-hikers go out of their way to meet AT buddies at Trail Days or reunite for a few days of nostalgic tramping. The trail provided a shared focus, making it easy to start a conversation and to find a common platform for relating to others. Merged with other parties in cramped overnight accommodations, the hikers formed peer groups, based on life phase, physical ability, and personality. During the project, I chatted with more than one temporarily structured squad attempting to walk New Jersey as an overnight, which required two dawn-to-dusk days of approximately forty miles. Although these temporary teams were not originally hiking together, the participants enjoyed the sheer exertion and the element of contest.[4] Similar alliances formed to visit town, help the injured, and chat over hot sandwiches at a country market. The dominant topic of conversation was the trail.

The AT sojourners solidly affirmed the statement "I have made new friends on this trip" (mean=4.5). One hiker, in describing his spiritual experience on the trail, concluded: "The world is a different place on the trail. I've been able to view how unconditional personal relationships should be. Doesn't matter [what] your name, job, money [is]. Everyone is your friend." Hikers rated a second parallel survey statement: "I have strengthened old friendships on this trip" with more equivocal responses (mean=3.0). In the case of improving old friendships, there were three peaks, at ratings 1, 3, and 5 (tri-modal), indicating that hikers were dividing into three groups. Some hikers had little contact with buddies from off-trail life, some hikers felt pre-trail relationships were unaffected, and some were experiencing further development of well-established social bonds, including those hiking with friends (fig. 8.2). Whether the hiker was traveling solo did not significantly influence ratings of this statement, so factors other than group size must have driven the high variance in perceptions. An important element of communal ethical formation is the recognition of the impacts we have on other people and our environment. The hikers strongly scored the statement "This trip has given me time to think about my relationships to other people" as true or very true (mean=4.4). One of the surprises of the survey was the relatively large percentage of hikers (82 percent) who were contemplating their impacts on or relationships with others.

AT journals and memoirs also recorded instance after instance of successful thru-hikers building lasting or personally enriching friendships while on the AT. In fact, major themes of the journals were keeping in touch with other hikers met along the route, and the joy of encountering trail acquaintances not seen for a week or two. These accounts of thru-hikes favored trail names, rather than

Fig. 8.2. Walking together on a rainy day, Damascus, Virginia. Long-distance hiking partnerships usually consist of one to three hikers, although groups may combine and temporarily walk together. Appalachian Trail hiking builds relationships within and between hiking parties.

their given names, as symbols of community belonging. Trail names both acknowledged the individuality of other hikers and created a sense of intimacy in a community where all greetings and introductions use locale-generated nicknames, rather than the officially sanctioned social security card or passport epithet. The practice is similar to that of sports teams or military units, while far more all-encompassing. Religious orders and societies use renaming to mark the acceptance of a new identity or superior life path. A trail name such as Achilles conveyed a statement of character, while Golden Sun became a statement of individual worth. Nomad served as accurate descriptor. An informant who assisted with managing a hostel said that when she began the trail, she was Aimless. Her trail name, though, was Aimlee, verifying how the trail gave her direction in life. Humorous trail names, such as Straight Jacket or Monkey Butt, were common and accepted by the hikers who bore them.[5] They announced the openness of the trail to good fun and the self-effacing nature of wearing fungus-encrusted socks and torn, damp T-shirts, for days on end.

Hostel staff used trail names to address hikers, and the hikers have awarded trail names to a number of the most notable characters who own businesses or assist along the route. Even without trail names, the AT community preferred nicknames and first names. Father David Raymond was not Father Raymond but was Father Dave, just as his pastoral predecessor, an AT section hiker, was known as Father Time. Naming a hostel "Miss Janet's" or "Uncle Johnnies" implied the social intimacy and hominess of the small-town South, where a title of respect still became attached to a first name.

Lynn Setzer's journalistic account *A Season on the Appalachian Trail* provides a portrait of accumulated friendships as she reached Katahdin. Setzer was not an end-to-ender but a section hiker, who did not complete the entire AT, as she composed her easy-going narrative. She tracked the fortunes of more than a dozen of her fellow travelers, including Nu-Tek the dog, as they tackled the Hundred-Mile Wilderness. According to Monsoon, Allgood passed a kidney stone but did not quit. "Raindrop and Hibird became engaged on the top of Saddle Back Mountain." Six Pack and Will-Make-It had serious problems fording Big Wilson Stream. A half-dozen other hikers, including the dog, sunk into difficulties with rain or high water. A honeymooning couple stopped for good just seven miles from the end because of Mrs. Honeymooner's sprained ankle, while Ester of Poly-Ester fell and broke her arm. Setzer herself decided to hike nude to White Cap Peak to cheer an exhausted Cygnus Swan.[6] The ragtag band kept regrouping, stopping at a last store and then passing each other as they climbed the highest mountain in Maine. Setzer's photo of victory counted eight hikers around the wooden sign marking the northern terminus.[7] The photo was typical of so many others sent back to angels met along the way and posted on inn and hostel walls. Some of these proudly-dispatched pictures verify one conqueror. Others document twos, threes, fours, and more who have ascended together. Such trophies, also characteristic of religious pilgrimage, corroborate the successful transition into a higher spiritual state, and the elevation not just to the apex of the Appalachians but in community standing.

Both the published journals and field observations verified that couples formed on the trail, some lasting for a section or two and others ending in marriage. Because men greatly outnumbered women, especially among the higher-speed and more challenge-oriented contingents who reach Katahdin in midsummer, the opportunity for trail-based "dating" was not equitable, and inhibited higher levels of forming male-female partnerships. As previously noted, a majority of the hikers traveling in pairs, and about one in five hikers answering the survey (19.5 percent), were hiking with a spouse, long-term partner, boyfriend, or girlfriend. The survey respondents on average did not report an improvement in their relationship with their significant other (mean=2.6). Several respondents wrote NA or penciled in a comment that the question was not applicable. For many single and solo walkers the question seemed irrelevant. On the other hand, 27 percent rated the statement "This trip has improved the relationship with my significant other (spouse, partner, boyfriend or girlfriend)" as 4 or 5—true to very true. Looking at just the hikers traveling with a significant other, this percentage rose to 71 percent! (p=.000). Rather than feeling extra stresses and strains, couples felt the trail was helping them develop a deeper relationship. Only 6.6 percent of those traveling in couples, in the midst of all the physical stresses, felt it was untrue that the trail had improved their relationship.

The hikers' mean response to "This trip has strengthened or improved my relationships with my family" was higher (3.0)[8] than that for building relationships with a significant other, despite the fact that very few AT hikers were traveling with parents, children, siblings, or in-laws. The hikers were strongly split over whether the trail was building family relationships—30 percent reported the statement was true or very true, and a similar number, 32 percent, reported the statement was untrue to very true. Looking at just those hikers traveling with family members (other than spouses), 50 percent thought it was true or very true that the trail was improving their family relationships, while 30 percent of hikers traveling without any family members at all, and 18 percent of hikers traveling with a significant other, thought so (p=.014). Clearly, both in the case of couples and of families, hiking together was better for relationships than being at a distance. The elevated reports of improved relationships for significant others hiking together, as opposed to family members as a team, may have resulted from greater intimacy for couples. Different generations had a greater potential to be mismatched in terms of hiking ability and preferred spare-time activities. Respondents traveling with family or a significant other were less likely than hikers traveling without family to believe that the large number of hikers on the trail interfered with their trail experience (p=.032).

The survey question on family relationships did not distinguish whether some hikers were experiencing strains with their families at home, while others were merely not experiencing meaningful family interactions. Hikers, however, strongly rejected the concept that "Being away from home has harmed my relationships with my family or friends" (mean=1.6). Only nine respondents, 4.4 percent, marked this statement as true or very true (appendix II.1). The AT trip improved family relationships for about 30 percent, while being a neutral factor in terms of family relationships for the majority of others. The majority perception of the hikers, therefore, was that their lengthy absences were not disturbing their families significantly. Hikers in transition between college and employment and between employment and retirement were likely modifying household arrangements. Hikers who had just left military service or residency at a university had already been away for months at a time. More-mature thru-hikers, who had been in the workforce, were often between jobs or had taken a leave of absence with their employer's and family's consent.

Families participated in the hikes by sharing e-mails or photos, sending packages, or even by joining the walk for a few days. Figure 8.3 shows a hiker wearing a kilt handmade for the trip by his mother. Just before this photo was taken, he had called her with instructions for a new kilt, for upcoming summer conditions. She was shipping it to a post office near the trail. One interviewee reported that after an automobile accident killed his wife and child, his father, also an AT hiker, put him on the trail to help him cope with grief and despondency. As trail journals verified, hikers slipped off-trail for short periods to attend weddings, spend a few days with their spouse, or visit a sick grandparent. The "vacationers" then returned to the corridor and tried to regain their pace. Well-planned ventures included meeting with other family members who hike. When he reached a stretch close to his home in Pennsylvania, Earl Shaffer met with his brother to hike together for a few days.[9] Jeff Alt's *Walk for Sunshine*, which was already dedicated to his handicapped brother, included some light-distance hik-

Fig. 8.3. A thru-hiker wearing a hiking kilt made by his mother, Weser, North Carolina.

ing with members of his immediate family, meeting up with an old friend and his dog (the dog got skunked), and a hiatus with both on- and off-trail time, to join his fiancé and his future brother-in-law.[10]

Although families did object to the AT trips as frivolous or dangerous, and could suffer from financial deficiencies stemming from a missing breadwinner, a common denominator among successful thru-hikers was that their families were either supportive or little bothered. The effect of the long absence on families deserves further study, and is also a major element in extended religious pilgrimage. The hiker or pilgrim can share the rewards of the journey with her or his family, including a sense of achievement, and in the religious case, the blessings conveyed by the saint or deity honored. Parents, siblings, and spouses of AT thru-hikers often formed a support network, shipping supplies, managing a blogging site, informing the local newspaper about a hiker's progress, and even driving to the trail with a change of clothes. Hikers frequently discussed the people at home in ways that revealed Mom and Dad had been bragging to the neighbors about their kid who was hiking THE ENTIRE Appalachian Trail.

Since the 1960s, wilderness advocacy organizations, backcountry resources managers, and park professionals have been concerned about overuse of trails and campsites. The surge in family automobile ownership after World War II brought even the wilds of the Rockies and the Cascades into accessible range for weekend jaunts. National and state park visitors began to complain about crowding on popular day-loop paths, at waterfalls, and on famous peaks (fig. 8.4). Interestingly, considering the recent flooding of many of the hostels with thru-hikers and the systematic planning to foster a wilderness ambiance on the AT, the survey respondents did not report feeling crowded. The respondents, on average, thought the statement "The large number of hikers on this route

Fig. 8.4. The crowded top of Mount Washington, New Hampshire. Appalachian Trail thru-hikers showed little negativity toward crowding on the Appalachian Trail, despite the fact that scenes like this are common where the trail intersects tourist roads or popular hiker stopovers.

interfered with my trail experience" was untrue (mean=1.9). Only 7 percent rated this statement as true or very true. The number and variety of thru- and section hikers was adding to the trail experience rather than detracting from it. In parallel, the respondents did not report feeling alone or separated. Only 8 percent thought the statement "I feel very isolated while I am on the trail" was true or very true (mean=2.1). A National Park Service study of a heavily impacted AT campsite at Annapolis Rocks, MD, found that hikers were "more satisfied with social and environmental indicators" after visitation was regulated and constructed campsites were added to mitigate damage.[11] Conditions were so variable along the trail, however, that end-to-enders and section hikers apparently invoked wide-ranging and undemanding standards for deciding what comprised a pleasant experience.

PERSONAL ISSUES AND PROBLEM SOLVING

The personal domain incorporated three major components: individual issues and problem solving, self-view and interior life, and physical and emotional health. The respondents reported the trip has given them "time to think about personal problems and concerns" (mean=4.4). Overall, 80 percent reported it was true or very true that an AT hike had given them time to consider personal issues. This outcome and the parallel mean score of 4.4 for the communal statement "This trip has given me time to think about my relationships with other people" demonstrated that the value of the long-distance walk for self-reflection was high and was not necessarily introverted and self-serving, in cases where sojourners formed a distinctive and very supportive, itinerant community.

While the hikers found that the AT "provided relief from daily stresses" (mean=4.1, mode=5), a result backed by other studies on backpacking and hiking, the ratings for breaking a bad habit were much lower (mean=2.1, mode=1). A smaller contingent (19 percent)[12] scored "This trip has helped me to break a bad habit" as true to very true. One hiker wrote in the survey margin: "Cocaine!!!"—verifying being out in the Appalachian wilds had assisted in battling drug dependence. An informant mentioned section hikers who had purposefully used a two-week walk to wrestle with destructive cravings, and I have chatted with thru-hikers escaping easy access to controlled substances. The AT had limitations for fighting some forms of addiction, such as alcohol abuse, because of the sporadic partying and the ease of finding hikers willing to join in for a night on the town. A recent college graduate with a dangerous binge drinking habit could find company and opportunity for pursuing his vice.

In responding to "This trip has helped me to manage a life transition (divorce, job change, illness, death of a loved one, etc.)" the hikers again produced three marked peaks (mean=2.8). More than one-third (34 percent) considered support for life transition to be true to very true, which was greater than the 23 percent reporting a life transition as a major motive for initiating a long-distance hike. Although this third consisted of fewer hikers than found building new friendships relevant, this was a still a remarkable percentage. The hiker perceptions were in concert with the observations of the trail angels, who believed many trekkers were transitioning between life phases or repositioning themselves professionally or relationally. Interestingly, hikers reporting a life transition as a major motive for their hike were not more likely to report success in this area than those who did not consider this a primary goal. Hikers believed the AT experience "will help me to cope with difficulties in my life" (mean=3.4)—45 percent rated this statement as true to very true. An even greater percentage verified that the experience "changed my life for the better" (mean=4.2); 75 percent rated this statement as true to very true (appendix II.1).

On average, hikers believed they had improved their physical fitness (mean=4.5). A resounding 85 percent rated this statement as true or very true, and the number of hikers affirming this statement increased with mileage accomplished. A small percentage of hikers (9 percent) reported help healing a physical injury or illness as a result of their trip, and about twice that (19 percent) report the "trip has helped me to heal an emotional or psychological illness or condition." Hikers reported a wide range of levels of physical fatigue (not necessarily a negative outcome), from high to low (mean=3.2), and relatively low levels of emotional distress (mean=1.9). Because hikers with serious injuries dropped out, the level of injury reported was presumably below that for AT thruhikers overall (fig. 8.5). Hikers who considered challenge or adventure primary goals for their hike were less likely to report healing from a physical illness or injury as true or very true (p=.067, trend), perhaps owing to a higher level of physical fitness at the start.

Fig. 8.5. Taping feet at Neel's Gap, near the beginning of a thru-hike, Georgia. This hiker is trying to prevent blisters, and is also limiting mileage in order to "break his body in."

SELF-ACTUALIZATION AND SELF-VALUATION

The SH4DI incorporated measures of self-perceived adequacy. The AT trip provided a strong sense of accomplishment (mean=4.5) and of enjoyment of life on the trail (mean=4.5). In fact, only two respondents gave enjoyment a rating below 3. Fewer hikers reported a strong "sense of harmony with my life" (mean=3.7) or "a sense of inner peace" (mean=3.6), although there was still a notable positive effect. Both these questions had peaks at 3 and 5, suggesting that some hikers were disinterested in these hidden emotions or self-perceptions or were not experiencing either turmoil or harmony, while others were feeling more internal balance. Conversely, the hikers reported low levels of self-doubt over their own abilities (mean 1.8, mode=1) and of fear or worry (mean=2.1, mode=1) (appendix II.1 & II.2).

In response to a statement summarizing the personal value of the trail, "This trip made me feel positive about who I am and the meaning of my life," the average score, 3.9, was lower than that for a sense of accomplishment. The third (34 percent) who were equivocal or believed the statement was untrue proved the AT was not a panacea for every case of low self-esteem or lapse in personal direction. For a solid majority, though, the AT long-distance hiking cultivated positive self-perspective and optimism about the future. The final statement in the personal experience portion of the questionnaire was "I am planning to take another trip like this in the future." The mean was 3.9, indicating many hikers were considering similar expeditions in the future—64 percent, or more than two-thirds, indicated this statement was true or very true. Hikers who find the experience exceptionally enriching sometimes hike the AT again the next year, or head west to take on the Continental Divide or the Pacific Crest Trails.

AGE, GENDER, AND EDUCATION AND THE AT EXPERIENCE

Gender was unrelated to differential outcomes in the environmental, communal, or personal domains on the AT, with two general exceptions: women were more likely to report an improvement in their relationship with their significant other (p=.018) and to find the trip caused emotional distress, worry, and doubt about their own abilities.[13] A greater percentage of women (50 percent) were traveling with a significant other, while only 19.4 percent of men were (p=.000). Considering only those hikers traveling with a significant other, there was no gender difference in perceived relational benefits (p=.223). A number of the published trail diaries were the reflections of women, yet these accounts differed little in substance from those of the men.[14] Other variables, such as goals for the trip, masked any obvious gender-related outcomes, as did the common elements in the trail experience, such as the exhilaration of scrambling up into the clouds, or the dejection of losing one's footing and tumbling into a creek. The women contemplating personal issues were well educated and professional and had much the same concerns as men, including compatibility with their jobs and finding fulfilling personal relationships. Leisure research has shown that outdoor experience can deconstruct gender stereotypes and that women can gain self-sufficiency, new worldviews, a strengthening of interpersonal relationships, and greater mental clarity for problem solving in the course of wilderness recreation.[15] The trail logs and personal accounts made it clear that woman and men mixed easily on the trail, and observation of hiking parties also pointed to easy acceptance. Individuals traveling with a significant other reported little difference in experience, except that they were more likely to find overnight accommodations were unpleasant or uncomfortable[16]—no surprise there.

Age significantly influenced multiple aspects of the AT experience.[17] Interestingly, many of the correlations between age and personal outcomes were negative—older hikers were less likely to experience relief from stress, to think about their relationships with other people, to believe the trip had changed their life for the better, and had added meaning to their life or had harmed relationships with their friends. Interestingly, the strongest correlations concerned fear and distress—younger hikers were much more likely to report they felt fearful or worried or experienced emotional distress during the trip. In terms of environment, older hikers were both more likely to experience discomfort resulting from weather and other factors and to simultaneously perceive the natural environment as pleasing. Younger hikers (nonparametric) were more likely to report the trip as a learning experience and/or useful for breaking a bad habit[18] (table 8.1). More mature hikers, on average, have more settled personal trajectories in terms of family and employment, and may have perceived the trip more as a capstone of a life well lived than as a guidepost to future opportunities. They were potentially better planners, and more likely to have financial resources adequate to complete their hike—characteristics that relieve stress. Senior backpackers may not have considered the AT a bridge from employment to retirement, because many of them had been dreaming about finishing the entire AT for years. Younger hikers struggling with finding a career or a life trajectory potentially found that the AT offered more meaningful social support or adequate time to structure a viable redirection.

Table 8.1

Correlations between age and personal outcomes

Statement	Corr. Coef.	Statement	Corr. Coef.
Negative correlations			
This trip caused emotional distress	-.316**	I felt fearful or worried on this trip	-.293**
This trip has given me time to think about my relationships with other people	-.241**	I have more time to think about personal problems	-.234**
This trip has changed my life for the better	-.226*	This trip caused me to doubt my own abilities	-.215**
This trip provided relief from daily stresses	-.205**	I felt isolated on this trip.	-.197**
I plan to take another trip like this in the future	-.197**	I feel bored on the trail	-.192**
Harmed relationships with my friends	-.144*	Made me feel positive about the meaning of my life	-.141*
Positive correlations			
The natural environment is pleasing	+.154*	Environmental or weather conditions have been uncomfortable	+.144*

NOTE: Negative correlations mean that older hikers give the question lower scores than younger hikers do. This table is organized from most negative to most positive. Correlation coefficients were computed via the Pearson method. (p=.05*, p=.01**).

GROUP SIZE, MILEAGE, AND BACKPACKING EXPERIENCE

Solo versus group hiking seems, a priori, to be very different enterprises. Among AT thru-hikers, larger group size appeared to have a minor positive impact on both making new friends and strengthening or improving old friendships. The pattern makes sense because people hiking together have extended opportunities to chat, assist each other, and share meals. Larger group size had a negative impact on the hiker's time to think about personal concerns and belief that the AT experience has changed their life for the better. The reason for these outcomes was not clear, although they may have arisen from reduced personal time and quiet time. Nonparametric analysis credited solo hikers with a greater sense of inner peace.[19] On the AT, group size effected personal experience related to self-reflection and building interpersonal relationships. These outcomes may not apply to other backcountry ventures, because the composition of individual hiking parties on the AT is smaller than for U.S.-designated wilderness areas overall.

Among motivations for undertaking an AT hike, only the social goals, including hiking with friends or family, or an interest in meeting new people or partying, were significantly correlated to personal experience. Hikers with communal goals were less likely to report physical discomfort in their accommodations (p=.009) and less likely to report boredom (p=.050). They were more likely to report relief from daily stresses (p=.000) and to provide high ratings to making new friends on the trip (p=.038). Hikers who had a strong desire to be in groups may have adapted better to hostels and shelters and been more willing to tap the benefits of trail society.

The amount of mileage already completed on this AT trip was significantly correlated to thirteen of thirty-four of the personal experience outcomes (table 8.2). Distance traveled, which served as a rough measure of the overall extent of the experience, was a better indicator of personal response than the length of time since the last major off-trail break. The significant correlations were predominantly to environmental factors and to shared communal or social experience. The highest correlation was to making new friends, suggesting that friendship building was not a phenomenon of the initiation of the trail but an ongoing process. The trail journals also confirmed that hikers tended to meet new people or to renew friendships from one terminus to the other. Hikers who have covered more AT distance reported greater levels of interest, learning, relief from daily stress, improved physical fitness, and enjoyment. Distance improved several forms of relationship, or at least the hikers' perceptions of them. Aside from forming new friendships, AT hikers with more miles under their cleat soles reported improved family relationships, more learning about care for the trail environment, and greater benefit in managing life transitions. Mileage was negatively correlated to self doubt. By inference, the more mileage completed, the more AT backpackers believe they were gaining ground in knowledge, strength, and interpersonal interactions.[20]

Table 8.2

The relationship of mileage completed to outcomes

Personal, community, or environmental outcome	Mileage	Time on trail	Prior hiking
Positive correlation with mileage			
I have made new friends on this trip	.361**	.294**	-.030
This trip produced many interesting events and experiences	.337**	.243**	-.004
This trip was a learning experience	.229**	.133	-.071
This trip has helped me to manage a life transition	.197**	.091	-.125
The more time I spent on this trip, the more I learned about caring for the trail environment	.184**	.130	-.169*
This trip has provided relief from daily stresses	.169*	.124	-.144*
This trip has improved my physical fitness	.167**	.117	.045
This trip has strengthened and improved my relationships with my family	.154*	.020	.003
I really enjoyed myself on this trip	.144*	.055	.011
Negative correlation with mileage			
This trip caused me to doubt my own abilities	-.150*	-.009	-.070

NOTE: The table displays correlation coefficients. The more mileage hikers have completed, the more they believe they are making new friends, learning, and relieved from stress. ($p=.05^*$, $p=.01^{**}$).

One might make the assumption that previous hiking experience had the same effect as mileage conquered during a single journey on the AT. The survey asked not about previous day-hiking experience but about overnight trips of one week, two weeks, or four weeks and more. The AT attracts many thru-hikers with minimal accumulated backpacking time. Even authors of published trail journals have bought their first set of quality backpacking gear while preparing for a single season, end-to-end attempt. This included Bill Bryson, who in his inexperience penned the national best seller *A Walk in the Woods*. The amount of prior backpacking was not significantly related to the mileage completed by the

Table 8.3

The correlations between levels of prayer and meditation and personal outcomes

Personal , community, and environmental outcomes	Pre-AT prayer	Prob.	On-AT prayer	Prob.
This trip has made me feel positive about the meaning of my life	.247	.001**	.219	.003**
This trip provided a sense of harmony with my life	.201	.005**	.147	.041*
This trip gave me a sense of inner peace	.194	.006**	.167	.020*
This trip has changed my life for the better	.193	.007**	.162	.024*
This trip will help me to cope with the difficulties in my life	.175	.014*	.134	.061
This trip has helped me to heal from a physical injury or illness	.167	.019*	.097	.181
This trip has given me time to think about my relationships with other people	.162	.023*	.153	.032*
This trip caused me to doubt my abilities	.151	.034*	.144	.043*
This trip has helped me to heal from an emotional injury or illness	.142	.047*	.122	.089
I felt worried or fearful while on this trip	.141	.049*	.158	.028*

Note: Prayer is especially effective for producing a sense of internal harmony and a positive outlook on one's life. The probabilities are displayed separately, so the differences in the degree of correlation are clear. (p=.05*, p=.01**)

survey respondents. Very seasoned hikers showed up both among the section hikers and the walkers who had completed 1,400 miles. Previous backpacking experience had no positive correlation to personal outcomes, but produced negative relationships to four outcomes, three of which concern self-reflection—time to think about personal problems, time to think about relationships with other people, and relief from daily stresses (appendix II.2). AT hikers who had already taken multiple overnight backpacking trips may be more challenge-oriented and less likely to be contemplating personal issues.

Religious Background and Personal Experience

Whether a hiker had a religious affiliation or not was largely unrelated to hiking outcomes in terms of personal experience.[21] A comparison of Christians and Jews with other faiths (primarily Buddhists, Taoists, and adherents of alternative religions) produced no statistically valid differences in personal experience, with one exception: Christians and Jews were less likely to consider the AT a learning experience than adherents of other faiths (p=.046). Christians, particularly, may find the AT support network is more similar to their home cultural experience. These scattered correlations, however, did not provide a clear picture of what religion meant on the AT.

A superior measure of religious engagement is the frequency of religious or spiritual practice. Hikers with at least moderate religious engagement (attending service monthly, or praying at least weekly) to higher levels of religious participation were more likely to believe that the trip was changing their life for the better, providing time to think about relationships with other people, making them feel positive about themselves and the meaning of life, providing a sense of harmony with their life, and helping cope with difficulties in life.[22] Participation in pre-trail prayer or meditation was significantly correlated to ten of thirty-four personal experience variables, while frequency of on-trail prayer or meditation was significantly correlated to seven of thirty-four with two positive trends (p=10) (table 8.3). In contrast, pre-AT service attendance levels and time committed to reading sacred and religious texts only had positive correlations with one personal outcome (statement) each. In this analysis it is useful to divide personal experience into four categories: communal (such as friendship), problem solving (such as coping with life transitions), self perception or interior (such as experiencing inner harmony), and environmental (such as comfort with the accommodation). Prayer and meditation were most strongly associated with positive perceptions in the interior personal domain and to building ties between the individual and the communal.

Hikers who participated in frequent prayer (the scale extended to several times a day) prior to the AT walk experienced as much enhancement in these spiritual domains as hikers who continued prayer or meditation on the trail. Engagement in prayer prior to beginning the long-distance hike potentially served as a form of preparation in the interior or self-perceptive, and to a lesser extent, the communal domains. Hikers who committed time to prayer or meditation felt positive about themselves and their ability to cope with difficulties. They were more likely to experience a sense of inner peace or harmony and to experience both physical and emotional healing. Notably, the frequency of prayer and meditation did not correlate to quality of experience with nature (table 8.3).

Mileage was more important than frequency of prayer or meditation to the experiences or outcomes with the highest overall ratings and those that were in the environmental domain. Of the fifteen experiential statements with the highest average ratings, only three were significantly tied to the frequency of prayer or meditation. In contrast, eleven were significantly correlated to the distance walked (appendix II.1). The correlation of prayer and meditation was proportionately higher than mileage in terms of outcomes reflecting personal problem solving and healing and interior state. This included experiencing feelings of peace or harmony with one's life, or conversely, fear and doubt. Interestingly, AT mileage was significantly correlated to hiker perceptions of accomplishing or resolving a life transition (a historic motive for undertaking walking pilgrimage), while frequency of prayer and meditation were not. Prayer and meditation appear to enhance the value of an AT sojourn for personal problem solving or healing, while adding less to environmental experience or personal enjoyment of the ambiance.

NOT GETTING ALONG

The logs at hostels and the interviews provided cases of hikers leaving the trail because of poor interpersonal interactions with other hikers. One irate comment in a hostel log declared that the other thru-hikers were self-centered "wankers" and the hiker who penned the remark was quitting, because the company was so incompatible. Some of the more astute angels described larger groups of backpackers who rejected others who did not fit in. One interviewee had observed several seasoned trekkers eating and chatting together while a new arrival was sitting off in a corner, with no one inviting him to join them. Angels also suggested that these misfits were inclined to give up and drop out. Logs and journals singled out hikers who rubbed others the wrong way because of bragging, commandeering limited resources, or being restless sleepers. Tight quarters at hostels and shelters led to strained relationships (fig. 8.6).

The published journals documented thru-hiker suspicion or avoidance of hikers who were too weird or who seem threatening. The trail does pose a risk of wanton physical violence from a stranger. Over the years, both murders and rapes have occurred at random points along the corridor.[23] Some of the angelic interviewees, in contrast, mentioned their attempts to assist AT travelers suffering from mental illness. One outfitter, for example, had given odd jobs to two perpetual thru-hikers who were mentally disabled. He had tried to assist them in maintaining healthy societal contacts. Both angels and hikers were at least moderately tolerant of difference, and willing to extend kindness to those with had little in common with themselves.

Fig. 8.6. Sleeping area in a hostel loft, Virginia. Tight quarters make for close and sometimes strained relationships.

CHAPTER 9
SPIRIT IN NATURE: RELIGIOUS MEANING AND THE TRANSCENDENT
INQUIRING ABOUT GOD AND THE TRANSCENDENT OTHER

The fourth element in the SH4DI was the transcendent domain: the relationship to God or "the relationship of self with something or someone beyond the human level a *Transcendent Other*."[1] The final section of the survey concerned explicitly religious or spiritual responses to the Appalachian Trail. To remain open to a variety of religious traditions, the questions in the survey referred to God (or gods or spirits). Finding appropriate interreligious vocabulary was difficult. Using a list of all the supernatural or philosophical alternatives would have made the questions too complex to read. The mix of monotheism, polytheism, and animism/pantheism drew no margin comments from practitioners of alternative religions objecting to the structure of the statements, though some Buddhists did note that the vocabulary was inaccurate from their perspective.[2] A few nonreligious respondents made margin comments to indicate they did not think God existed. The design incorporated an open-ended question allowing the respondents to describe spiritual experiences on trail in their own words. This question appeared prior to the section on transcendence, to reduce the impact of the language utilized in the survey on the hikers' personal articulation of their encounters with the sacred or completely other.[3]

Peter Ashley, who surveyed Tasmanians concerning their thoughts about wilderness spirituality, summarized some of the possible relationships as a "feeling on connection and interrelationship with other people and nature; a heightened sense of awareness and elevated consciousness beyond the everyday and corporeal world; cognitive and affective dimensions of human understandings embracing peace, tranquility, harmony, happiness, awe, wonder, and humbleness; and the possible presence of religious meaning." Ashley notably removed vocabulary concerning God or the creator from his summary, even though a number of his subjects made statements such as: "As I observe and experience the beauty of the wilderness creation, I stand in awe and wonder of God who designed and created it."[4] In the AT hiker survey, the section on transcendence did utilize terms for deity (God, spirit, gods), while the section on personal experience did not.

In response to the question in the first demographic section, 62 percent of the respondents indicated they were having spiritual or religious experiences on the trail, while 32 percent checked no, and an additional twelve (6 percent) did not answer this question. Of hikers with some form religious identity (all religions), 75.5 percent reported religious or spiritual experience on the AT, while 38 percent of those without a definite religious identity indicated religious or spiritual experience on trail (p=.01). Of the sixty-one respondents who reported current membership in a Christian church or organization (also about 30 percent of the hikers), fourteen indicated that they were not engaged in any spiritual or religious experience on the trail, or 23 percent of the active Christians.

In terms of demographic characteristics, the hikers' age, education level, or hiking partnerships made little difference in the level of on-trail religious practice, such as reading sacred texts, with two notable exceptions. The change in the amount of time spent in prayer or meditation was correlated to the size of the hiking group. Hikers who were traveling with companions were more likely to report a decrease in prayer and meditation over their usual practice (p=.001). The amount of time spent reading sacred or spiritual materials was negatively correlated to education level in pre-trail terms (p=.057), and this pattern was even more distinct on the trail (p=.006). Because the majority of hikers who had religious affiliations were Christian, this reverse relationship of education level to reading probably reflects differences between evangelicals and mainline or liberal Protestants. National surveys have found evangelicals purchased more religious-based reading materials while having lower incomes and educational levels on average than mainline Protestants.[5]

The hiker logs included quotes from Buddhist sacred texts and poetry, providing evidence that the more-committed Buddhists brought religious reading materials or had memorized texts and were thinking about them. Evangelical jottings in logs sometimes expressed theological concepts intended to influence other hikers, such as declaring Christ as the Only Son of God or as the exclusive way to salvation. They also included biblical passages, along with scribbled fragments of favorite hymns from childhood. The remarks let a Christian hostel staff know that a thru-hiker appreciated the dry carpet and access to a washing machine. Adherents of alternative religions also decorated the logs and were inclined toward drawings of mystical beings and lines from popular songs.

CONTACT WITH NATURE

The survey format allowed the respondents to officially skip the section rating individual statements concerning the transcendent (section V) if they considered it not relevant (this also allowed nonreligious hikers from feeling pressured and rejecting the survey completely). The maximum number of responses to this section was 149, a few more than the number initially affirming religious experience on trail.[6] The average scores reported here are for those hikers who responded to the section on transcendence. For selected variables below, however, I discuss the responses incorporating the hikers who did not think they were having a spiritual experience on the trail, as well as those who did.

A key question is: does contact with nature cause hikers to think about God, spirits, or the greater other? Three of the most positive religious responses had to do with access to God or seeing God in nature. In fact, the hiker scoring of "Contact with nature inspires me to think about God (or gods or spirits)" was the highest of any statement in the transcendent section of the survey, with a mean of 3.6 (appendix III.1). Of those who answered this section of the survey, 55 percent rated this as true to very true. Adjusting, however, for those hikers who did not answer this question, these eighty-two hikers who think about God when in the wilds are approximately 40 percent of the total respondents. Two related positive responses were: "This trip made me more aware of the beauty of God (spirit, gods)" with a mean of 3.3, and "I have felt close to God (or spirit or gods) while on this trip," with a mean of 3.4, and 36 percent believing this statement was true or very true. Natural aesthetics were an important source for contemplation of the divine, and for a significant number of respondents, tramping the ridges provided an opportunity to experience the presence of God or the transcendent other.

In terms of spiritual or religious practice, the hikers gave slightly lower ratings to questions concerning the potential of the AT journey for enhancing internal or personal spiritual practice. Respondents provided somewhat true ratings to "I think about religious or spiritual matters more when I am hiking," with a mean of 3.2, and "This trip facilitated prayer or meditation," a mean of 3.1. Interestingly, "Participating in religious ritual, prayer or meditation in nature or outdoors has exceptional spiritual, religious, or personal meaning" fell just below 3.00 at 2.98—moving toward the category of somewhat untrue on average. Among those replying to the directly religious statements, 38 percent verified the special nature of spiritual practice in the wilds as true or very true. Weighting for those who did not answer the question, just more than one-quarter (28 percent) of all respondents confirmed that they think of nature as having special value for spiritual practice. John Muir would shake his head. The thru- and section hikers were not, on average, pilgrims to the temple of the God among the venerable trees and ancient mountain ranges (fig. 9.1).

INTERPERSONAL RELATIONSHIPS AND SPIRITUAL COMMUNITY

For at least some hikers, the AT sojourn encouraged self-reflection over right attitudes and actions. In response to "This trip has made me aware of my personal deficiencies and failings," seventy-five hikers, or 51 percent of those rating the statement, indicated it was true or very true (mean=3.5). A smaller number, fifty-one (35 percent of those answering the question), indicated that it was true or very true that "This trip has helped me to correct my own wrong doing or negative attitudes" (mean=3.1). The results from the ethics and personal experience sections also found recognition of personal effects on other people and on the environment to be important outcomes of long-distance hiking. A fair conclusion, therefore, is that such extended walks or withdrawals from home environments support the historic religious belief that pilgrimage is inherently penitential or can promote repentance and self-understanding. Potential causative factors were relief from daily stresses, participation in a new and unfamiliar community, time to consider life, and frequent contact with harmonious nature. Or perhaps there was a "Canterbury Tales effect," where sharing the life story of others becomes a mirror of one's own spiritual and personal journey. Fewer hik-

Fig. 9.1. A hiker enjoys a reflective moment on a viewing stand above the Appalachian Trail near Highpoint, New Jersey. Even a very developed spot, such as this viewing stand, with heavy day hiker traffic, can provide opportunities for contact with the transcendent.

ers believed, however, that the trip provided "more time for spiritual or religious opportunities than I usually have" (mean=2.5). Thirty-nine hikers (19 percent overall) reported it was true or very true that they had more time for spiritual or religious engagement, suggesting that it is not greater opportunity for spiritual introspection alone that produced reflection on the adequacy of one's relationships to others.

The Appalachian Trail lacks spiritual guidance provided by master teachers or by the great saints (other than Thoreau). The trail does not have the sequences of prayers, confessions, or penitential rituals, such as walking barefoot up Croagh Patrick. Nor does it have the mythic identification with the deity itself of Mount Kalias. Pilgrims to the jagged, soaring Himalayan sacred residence visit landscape features, such as lakes and passes, that recall myths and religious teachings. Yet, many AT hikers reported a form of self-examination consistent with the goals of these ancient religious paths, and did so without continual availability of spiritual guides, confessors, or the company of coreligionists.

Selfexamination

A notable result was that the AT hikers, on average, *did not* feel a "sense of spiritual community" with the people they encountered on their trip (mean=2.7); and only about one-quarter of all respondents (fifty-seven hikers) perceived the AT trip as "a religious spiritual or learning experience" (mean=2.9). Yet a very high proportion of AT hikers responding to the survey engaged in spiritually formative friendship building or spent time thinking about their own ethical roles. A majority of hikers did not think of the AT as a source of practical spiritual strength (mean=2.7) or as assistance in thinking "about my religious or spiritual responsibilities to the environment" (mean=2.8). The questionnaires provided repeated evidence that the AT hikers did not consistently recognize self-examination, ethical formation, or generating positive relationships with fellow travelers as forms of spiritual wellness.

EPIPHANIES, CONVERSIONS, AND SPIRITUAL FORMATION

Religions that have spread widely from their regions of origin, or that appeared with the development of cities and major trade routes from the Iron Age onward, emphasize conversion or development of intellectual religious discipline. Christianity, Judaism, Buddhism, and Islam all value epiphanies or sudden insights into the meaning of life or the essence of God, and encourage life transitions from a nonreligious state to a religious commitment. The question then becomes, does the Appalachian Trail hike precipitate conversions, moments of enlightenment, or major religious change? In response to the surveys, hikers gave very low ratings, on average, to the statement "This trip precipitated a major change in my spiritual life" (mean=1.8). Only seven respondents gave this concept a top rating of 5. During the interviews with volunteers and businesspeople who offered assistance to hikers, we gathered only a few descriptions of religious conversions. Twelve Tribes had gained a fully committed member from the hikers they sheltered in their hostel, and one of the informants, who was a 2,000-miler, had returned to a town she had visited along the way, joined a local church, and became a church hostel volunteer. One informant described a hiker experiencing a sudden Christian conversion on a mountain in Georgia, where he returned to Neel's Gap and proclaimed he had literally met Jesus Christ on the AT. Trail Days in Damascus gleaned a half-dozen Christian commitments each year. Informants reported hikers who had teamed with another hiker to learn more about a religious belief system. Both hikers and the support network included individuals who openly proselytized, and evangelization was a component of church-sponsored services and events, particularly in the southern states.

Two of the 205 survey forms (1 percent) described a major change in religious orientation, one on a previous AT section hike and one on the concurrent section walk. A forty-eight-year-old male section hiker wrote: "1980—didn't believe in God much less Christ. Started 3 week hike in VA w[ith] a wish of death; came off w[ith] a wish of life. Hiked alone. Age 20. Romans I: Man is without excuse. He knows it instinctively & is evident in divine nature (paraphrase)." A nineteen-year-old section hiker reported that he had attended church for the first time in his life when on the trail, and he was planning to continue to attend when he finished his trip. His description of his spiritual experience emphasized joy: "Joy from nature. Joy from the church. Joy from interacting with nice people. Some feelings of the eternal. Guilt & penance (penitence?) from indulgences in town. Much, much peace & feelings of Love. Almost the whole trip has been some sort of spiritual experience." Against the total number of thru-hikers each year, however, conversions, self-reported radical change, or instances of committing fully to a religious denomination owing to an AT hike were uncommon.

Far more evident among hikers without a religious identity was a new or heightened appreciation of spirituality. One hiker wrote: "I am not a religious person, however this trip has given me a much deeper appreciation for spirituality. It has also made me think more critically about my beliefs." Another hiker without a religious identity commented: "Religion is a subject that gets constantly brought up in trail registers. It's almost impossible to not question your own beliefs." Three important themes were: the time the trip provided for reflection or for asking key questions about personal meaning, beauty and awe in nature, and the kindness and support of the trail community, which inspired thoughts about the transcendent (fig. 9.2). These effects of the AT sojourn were shared with other hikers and emerged as part of a gradual process of spiritual reassessment. Previously nonreligious hikers were far less likely than Christian respondents to attribute their experiences in nature to the presence of God. (See appendix IV.1 for additional nonreligious hiker statements.)

Also likely to experience a feeling of awakening on the trail were the "nominal" Christians who were brought up in a congregation or parish but now rarely attended, or who currently belonged to a church but infrequently participated in religious practices such as worship or prayer. Although they shared their wonder

Fig. 9.2. Sunset over Kent Pond adjoining the Appalachian Trail, Vermont. Numinous experience, or a feeling of the divine in nature, is often associated with very dramatic if mundane natural events or peculiarities of light or reflection.

with nature with nonreligious hikers, they were more likely to associate their experiences with God and to discuss a change in their engagement in prayer or contemplation. One fifty-year-old female hiker stated succinctly: "I began praying to God, now, I am conversing with him." A twenty-four-year-old woman commented: "Awe at the beauty of creation; including nature and the remarkable kindness of strangers (which I never noticed in my ordinary life.) Feeling with certainty that God exists, based on vast/beautiful creation." Some comments were "repentant," such the twenty-six-year-old who wrote that his experience provided "A better understanding of myself to others. A greater ability to try to empathize with others and see other points of view." (See appendix IV.2 for additional responses.)

There was little evidence that AT hikers suddenly plunged into religious alternatives, such as Wicca or Paganism, with a focus on ritual in or with nature. Though proportionately more common on the AT than in the greater U.S. population, the AT hikers who identified with alternative religions represented a wide

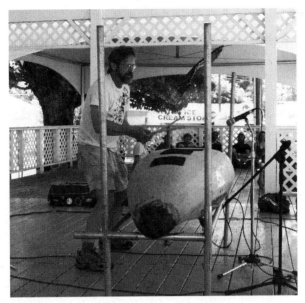

Fig. 9.3. Drumming at Trail Days 2009. The context here is not explicitly religious.

variety of religious preferences and did not tend to travel in like-minded groups, thus they often escaped notice. The raves of radical environmental organizations and New Age bookstores that sponsor educational events likely formed more effective recruitment settings for alternative religions than the AT, because they offer community and instruction in religious belief systems through ritual participation, contact with symbols and ritual objects, and exposure to religious literature.

Leaders of two integrative communities, with foundations in new religions, confirmed that hikers staying at their facilities participated in dances or musical performances conveying religious content or symbolism, including Native American–style drumming and circle dances originating in the Findhorn community in Scotland. Drumming has been a feature of Trail Days, while lacking a religious context at this country-fair–like event (fig. 9.3). Interviewees from the three integrative communities and two alternative or interreligious retreat centers, including Twelve Tribes with its Christian base, confirmed that several hikers had remained in these live-in options for longer stays and formed new religious interests, while only one reported gaining a fully committed member from the AT.

NUMINOUS AND MYSTICAL EXPERIENCE

More puzzling was the sparse reporting of intense numinous or mystical experience. Although a significant percentage of hikers felt close to God, gods, or spirit on the AT (36 percent overall), somewhat fewer "felt God (spirit, gods) was guiding me" (27 percent overall) (appendix III.1). One religious professional who ministered to hikers did describe hostel guests seeking her out to ask about very intense encounters with something outside themselves. The hikers often did not have cultural context for a feeling of divine presence or contact with the essence of the cosmos. Individual survey responses proved, in contrast, that a low-key, yet heightened perception of God in nature was relatively common on the AT. The very first respondent wrote: "Feeling more a part of God's creation constantly. At least once per day (often more) I reflect on this, then smile and offer a prayer of thanks." The overwhelming feelings of cosmic unity, visions of angels or God, or sense of irresistible immersion in God consistent with nature-based mysticism were, in contrast, rare. The hikers were not, on average, overwhelmed by God's spirit sweeping across the summits, nor were they seeing the splendid Blue Ridge sunset as a holy kaleidoscope.[7] The irresistible and overpowering encounter with God's reflection in nature, typical of Western mystics such as Julian of Norwich or Hildegard von Bingen, was not a prevalent feature of AT spirituality.

While often describing the thru-hike as a "pilgrimage," the published AT journals, by and large, did not provide vivid descriptions of spiritual experience with nature. These diaries were toned down and interpersonal, compared with John Muir's *My First Summer in the Sierra*.[8] Enjoyment of natural features and phenomena in the AT journals rarely extended past aesthetic appreciation. Pilgrimage meant self-actualization or self-discovery. The diarists who mentioned God, while describing awe in nature, were more likely to treat the Creator or Spirit in nature as a hiking buddy than as the foundation of all that is and all that will be. The natural settings along the AT provided repeated contact with dramatic sunsets, open peaks, and quiet glades—the types of locales American art and literature associate with contact with the divine (fig. 9.2).

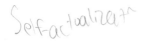

Among the notable minority of published diaries recording a sense of the divine in nature was the journal of Cindy Ross, a committed Roman Catholic. Ross's log was handwritten and homey, decorated with her own sketches of well-loved trail friends, cute animals, and sore feet. Cindy related her mainstream Catholicism to home and family, yet often touched the transcendent. As she passed through the Great Smokies, she penned: "As I hike north, my personal relationship with the mountains is becoming almost sacred. I am going up. Up to meet my Creator. Up to where the sweet wind can caress my tired body like a Father's loving hand."[9] Cindy also greeted God in the forests. More than halfway to Katahdin, strolling through one of the few old-growth forest tracts left in southern New England, she mused, "The 'Cathedral Pines' are awe-inspiring. I feel the presence of God here like nowhere before. Walking through them hushed, silent and reverent, it feels as though I'm in a huge glorious cathedral. I stop. There is no sound. The trees are so massive, I almost expect something extremely powerful to be heard. Just silence, which is itself powerful. And all this silence seems to thunder above everything else like a huge granite mountain."[10] Julian of Norwich, Lao Tze, and John Muir would all affirm what Ross heard and felt.

SPIRITUAL GROWTH AND RELIGIOUS COMMITMENT

When asked if "Trips like this interfere with my religious life," the respondents were resoundingly negative (mean=1.5). They did not perceive the AT as barrier or a temptation, despite decreased service attendance. Nor did they believe, on average, "Being away from home has separated me from people with religious or spiritual beliefs like my own" (mean=2.3). Though most hikers did not feel isolated from their faith base, hikers with a high level of participation in ritual did differentially report feeling separated from their home community. A twenty-four-year-old Lutheran remarked: "People out here are definitely less religious than I expected and I really miss my community from back home. I also really feel not being able to attend church at all. And I have not been able to meditate as much as I wanted." The surveys provided just slightly more evidence of interreligious dialogue or exposure. In response to "This trip has made me more aware of the religious or spiritual heritage of other cultures or people," the mean was still a relatively low 2.6. Considering that religious dialogue appeared in hostel logs, and discussions about personal meaning were relatively common in the casual evenings at shelters, the hikers were apparently treating these conversations as interpersonal rather than interreligious.

Among the hikers who described their spiritual or religious experience in their own words, Christians who regularly attended services or engaged in prayer at least daily were the most likely to attribute the beauty they observed and their rewarding interactions with other hikers to God. They also were less likely to report the journey as a time for questioning whether the spiritual was valid or beneficial. Their descriptions were primarily intensifications of their preexisting beliefs and practices or examination of their faith with the intent to improve themselves as Christians. A forty-four-year-old who described herself as Charismatic, wrote: "Too many [experiences] to list. God has provided for me every step of the way. My strength and comfort who answers my every need and knows my need before I even ask." A sixty-eight-year-old Congregationalist described his spiritual engagement on trail as: "Hav[ing] felt a closeness to God—increased loving thoughts towards my wife and family. More positive self awareness. Reflecting on my life's worth and mission to do a better job of doing God's will." A twenty-two-year-old nondenominational Christian confirmed, "I experience God through his creation and the beautiful natural world. God gives me the inspiration, guidance & strength to continue." The Christian hikers who attended services monthly or more frequently were more inclined to discuss "God" than "Jesus," "Christ," or the "Holy Spirit" as the source of their experience, suggesting that they were identifying the Creator with God the Father, in Trinitarian terms (see appendix IV.3. for more comments from Christians).

The AT hikers did not, on average, believe that the trail experience had "increased their religious or spiritual commitment" (mean=2.7). This outcome presents a notable contrast to their more positive response to the statement "I plan to Integrate more experiences such as this trip into my religious or spiritual life" with its significantly higher mean of 3.5 (p=.000). The hikers were not affirming the benefit of the sojourn in how religious they had become but in terms of the personal fulfillment and sense of spiritual presence they enjoyed on the Appalachian Trail. Further, hikers ranging from those with no religious ties to those heavily engaged in spiritual practice mentioned that being in nature enhanced their belief in a creator God or a unifying essence of the cosmos. A Baptist noted: "When you see the beauty of the trail you realize that there has to be a creator or God that made all this."

Christians or Jews engaged in regular religious practice were more likely than nonreligious hikers or nominal Christians to remark on their potential to pray for or minister to people they met along the way. A Jewish hiker who regularly attended synagogue also verified her engagement in reaching beyond the self in prayer: "I recite the morning prayers (those I know by heart) throughout the day. I feel I have some protection as I focus on prayer." A twenty-one-year-old United Methodist commented on his spiritual experience: "It's shown me that the AT is not human. In other words, I did not create the beauty. I see it's astonishing, but puts the human in perspective. It's also led me to believe I must minister to the world. Hikers are looking for something, like all are, and need an answer." A twenty-year-old nondenominational Christian described his efforts in "Learning how to pray & intercede for others—to feel their pain as well as their hope & joy. To know how & when to pray for them when you have no contact w[ith] them. It is glorious." A nineteen-year-old Episcopalian described her trail experience in light of other hikers' personal journeys: "Seeing people seeking w[ith]/o[ut] Christianity—thinking about God in new ways as it relates to peoples actions. God is who you ARE not your accomplishments. Questions of self-worth, punishment, judgment, grace, creation, beauty."

NATIONALISM, HISTORY, AND ENVIRONMENTALISM

A common feature of nineteenth-century literary and artistic depictions of the Appalachians is the association of the divine with nationalism. The Hudson River School artists painted the rugged crags of the White Mountains as a residence for the Creator God. Rain and rainbows are metaphors for divine blessing pouring over the Hudson and the Connecticut Rivers. Mountain travelers in the panoramic oils are on both a national and a Christian quest for righteousness.[11] Figure 9.4 shows a flag flying next to the historic First Baptist Church in Cheshire, MA. Baptists from Cheshire fought in the Continental Army during the Revolutionary War.

Despite such obvious visual associations, today's AT hikers do not, on average, interpret the great expanses of the Appalachians, and the thundering waters of the rivers that drain them, as a font of divine providence, nor do they associate the hike with their religious heritage (despite that for mainline and

Fig. 9.4. Historic First Baptist Church, Cheshire, Massachusetts, visible from the Appalachian Trail. Baptists from Rhode Island settled Cheshire and fought in the Continental Army in the Revolutionary War.

evangelical Protestants, the rolling chain of moist, forested slopes is very much a part of their historic religious roots). The postmodern trekkers did not realize that their great-grandparents would have seen the cascades, misty glens, and moss-covered boulders as religious metaphors or as mini-lessons in God's character. In response to "This trip has made me more aware of my religious heritage or roots," thirty-one hikers reported this was true or very true (mean=2.3). In response to "Participating in religious ritual, prayer or meditation at historic religious sites has exceptional spiritual, religious or personal meaning" (mean=2.2), only twenty-four hikers thought this was true or very true—16 percent of those filling out the spiritual portion of the survey, and about 12 percent overall. The response to "This trip has made me aware of how important religious/spiritual belief has been in the history of this country" was similar (mean=2.4). A few more hikers responded positively to "This trip has made me more aware of how God (spirit) has blessed this country" (mean=2.9). Approximately one-quarter of the respondents overall indentified this statement as true or very true (27 percent). Correcting for those did not answer the survey section on transcendence, only about 15 percent of today's hikers think the Appalachian landscape is important to the religious foundations of the United States, and 27 percent strongly believe the mountains and their natural bounty are an outpouring of divine care and love. For the majority, the national scenic trail is not an experience in religious nationalism. Ralph Waldo Emerson would be amused, William Cullen Bryant would write an editorial, and Fredrick Edwin Church would lecture them on God's beauty emanating from Katahdin.

A final question is: Does the AT experience increase religious or spiritual commitment to environmental care? The answer is yes—but again for a minority. In response to "This trip has helped me to think about my religious or spiritual responsibilities to nature or the environment" (mean=2.8), fifty-one hikers responded that this was true or very true, or about one-quarter of the total. This is a far lower number than responded positively to the statement "Experiencing natural beauty increases my motivation to care for the environment," where 82 percent of all the respondents overall confirmed this statement as true or very true. In addition, when answering the ethics section, 42 percent of hikers gave "Spiritual or religious experience with nature increases my motivation to care for the environment" a true or very true score. Again, the development of an activist stance was disconnected from the AT experience, even for those who believed religion might motivate environmental action.

AGE, GENDER, AND GROUP SIZE

Age was important to ethical and personal experience on the Appalachian Trail, and more-mature hikers were more likely to report a religious affiliation. Age, however, was only moderately correlated to transcendent outcomes—the amount of current religious engagement being a more robust indicator. Older hikers were *less likely* to read sacred texts and to believe the trip had helped to correct their own negative attitudes or wrongdoing. Conversely, they were more likely than younger hikers to find that the AT caused them to think about how God has blessed the United States, to feel they are close to God and God is guiding them, and to experience the beauty of God.[12] The more-mature hikers thus related to a personal and present deity, whose providence flows through the American countryside. Field observation confirmed that middle-aged and senior hikers were less given to partying and yellow blazing and were likely to set an even pace and savor the scenery. Hiking strategy, as well as more-traditional Christian beliefs, could thus have influenced age-related perceptions of the transcendent.

Women gave higher ratings than men to the trip facilitating prayer or meditation, to other hikers encouraging them in their spiritual lives, to increasing awareness of personal deficiencies, and to correction of personal wrongdoing. Group size significantly affected only one perception in the transcendent—the larger the group, the less the belief that the trip had facilitated prayer or meditation.[13] In addition, hikers traveling with a significant other were less likely to believe the AT sojourn provided additional time for spiritual or religious activities (p=.038) and to experience a sense of spiritual community with the people they met on the trip (p=.043).[14] AT hikers did not feel a strong sense of spiritual or religious community in any case, and traveling with a significant other, family, or large group could internalize the relationships to the hiking team, perhaps leaving God out on the margins. Educational level had little consistent relationship to perceptions of transcendent values.[15]

MILEAGE AND PREVIOUS HIKING EXPERIENCE

As was demonstrated in the previous chapter, AT hikers with more completed mileage had higher scores in thirteen outcomes reflecting the personal and communal domains. In the transcendent domain, three outcomes were significantly positively correlated to mileage completed: an increase in spiritual commitment, correction of wrongdoing or negative attitudes, and awareness of one's own religious heritage or roots.[16] Previous backpacking experience with longer trips was, in contrast, significantly negatively related to a number of outcomes in the transcendent domain, including: whether the trip facilitated prayer or meditation, increased religious commitment, helped one think about religious or spiritual responsibilities to other people, was a spiritual learning experience, or provided time to think about religious matters while hiking. There were, however, trends toward hikers with more backpacking experience feeling close to God, being more aware of the beauty of God, or experiencing guidance from God (or spirits or gods). An additional variable provided a negative trend: hikers with more backpacking experience were less likely to think about personal responsibilities to nature and the environment! Hiking experience was also negatively correlated to the belief that participating in religious activities outdoors has special meaning, and to the frequency of reading spiritual or religious writings while on trail.[17] Hikers with prior long-distance hiking experience were, again, less concerned about reflecting on their personal and ethical responsibilities. These experienced hikers may have been participating for athletic or challenge motives, and may have been less likely to begin the AT sojourn for personal or spiritual reasons.

Religious Affiliation and the AT

In environmental ethics and history circles, academics delight in contrasting Christianity and Judaism with "nature religions" to argue that mainstream American and European religion needs an eco-friendly overhaul. Because religious affiliation is neither a measure of religious effort nor of spiritual training, just dividing hikers into Christian versus world religions did not provide useful insight into the spiritual experience of the Appalachian Trail. In examining responses of hikers mentioning Buddhism, for example, three hikers who were affiliated with a specific sect reported much higher levels of engagement in meditation than other hikers who listed Buddhism among several religions, conforming more to a New Age or alternative religious approach.[18] Comparing the frequency of religious practices of Christians and Jews to those of a combination of all other religions, the surveys indicated that prior to the trip, the Abrahamic faiths had higher rates of attendance at services, with proportionately fewer not attending at all, and proportionately more attending services weekly than the world and alternative religions (p=.0001). This differential, though still significant, declined on the AT, because the Christians and Jews reduced attendance. There were not, however, pretrip differences in the levels of prayer and meditation among the two major faith categories, nor were there on the AT. On trail, however, the combination of world and alternative religions had a slightly greater proportion of adherents who believed they experienced an increase in prayer and meditation (p=.041). This subgroup of religious hikers is potentially more open to nature as a setting for internal spiritual practice. There were no differences in the level of reading sacred or spiritual texts in any setting.

Hikers who had a religious affiliation versus those without, not surprisingly, gave higher scores to transcendent experiences on the trail, with five exceptions. Nonaffiliated hikers were as likely as affiliated to report major change in one's spiritual life, increased time for religious or spiritual activities on trail, assistance thinking about spiritual responsibilities to the environment, correction of wrongdoing or negative attitudes, and a sense of spiritual community with people encountered on the hike.[19] For most of the transcendent statements, there was a no significant difference between Christians and Jews and the group consisting primarily of Buddhists, Taoists, and alternative religionists. Abrahamic versus other faiths was not a powerful predictor of the total impact of the AT on spiritual and religious experience. Because you must like forests and crags to hike any distance on the Appalachian Trail, AT hikers did have common values that rose above religious preference.[20] There was nearly a significant difference in "Contact with nature inspires me to think about God (or gods or spirits)," with higher than expected numbers of hikers from the Eastern and alternative religions giving both the highest and lowest ratings (p=.056). This question, though, does present a problem for Buddhists, who may not have validated the vocabulary of God, gods, and spirits. The non-Abrahamic respondents showed a greater split over the question of the value of historic sites for religious practice, with more being strongly positive or negative (p=.034). Christians and Jews were more likely to feel isolated from their home religious community than adherents of other religions (p=.038).

The survey question that solicited the hikers' own description of their religious and spiritual experience on the trail allowed a comparison between hikers who were members of Christian churches or organizations and those who were not, in terms of what they thought was most important or distinctive about the AT experience.[21] There was no significant difference concerning the percentage of churched versus non-churched hikers recording spiritual experience with nature or engagement in prayer or meditation. Members of Christian organizations were more likely to report experiencing God as caring or close, while non-churched respondents were far more likely to articulate their interior state in terms of feelings of inner peace, mystic presence, patience, or the flow of life (p=.01) (table 9.1). The survey was not detailed enough to determine if these experiences were similar, while being interpreted differently in terms of the ultimate transcendent source. In other words, church members might interpret feelings of inner harmony as closeness to God, which non-church members the same experience as peace or Zen.

The Buddhists and Taoists who provided a reflection on their spiritual experience, unlike the Christians who regularly attended church, did not emphasize God but, consistent with Buddhist belief, mentioned meditation, connectedness, or lack of worldly attachments. A Buddhist and Taoist who was chanting and meditating during his hike summarized: "Being able to leave the crazy consumer culture that we live in and be closer to the sky has been fantastic." The most extensive comment by a Buddhist, a student of Soto Zen, emphasized dissolution of ego: "The trail is. Sometimes hard, sometimes easy, but every day I

Table 9.1

Respondents' self-described spiritual experience in terms of vocabulary and descriptions of God's role

Type of religious or spiritual experience	Churched number	Churched %	Non-church number	Non-church %
God as creator, God in nature, nature as spiritual	14	29.8	23	32.4
God as close, caring, providential, or in conversation	12	25.5	5	7.0
Engagement in prayer, meditation, reflection, or more time for God	10	21.3	15	21.1
Peace, harmony, simplicity, non-ego, mystic , patience, life	2	4.2	17	23.9
Community, conversation, sharing, relationship with other people	6	12.8	7	9.8
Other	3	6.3	4	5.6
Total	47		71	

walk until I am exhausted, and it's never what I expect. Katahdin might as well be the moon for all the bearing it has on my daily work. The ego falls away—if you push as hard as you can you will only burn out. Material things cannot help you, they only weigh you down. A pretty morning with mild terrain and feel rich as a king, learning to love the as much is a challenge, but sometimes it is enough to keep walking." (Appendix III.4 provides additional comments of Buddhists and Taoists.)

A last cadre of hikers were those who identified with Buddhism along with another religion or religions and those who identified with contemporary alternative religions. Only one respondent who had a clear Christian denominational affiliation (Roman Catholic) appeared to be utilizing Buddhist and Daoist philosophy and practice as an enhancement to Christianity. The other respondents who were combining Buddhism with other religious traditions concentrated on their experience in nature. A comment from a hiker log compared: "This Trail has helped me to see many things about my life, relationships, our Great and Loving Creator & God's spirit, of the Living Breathe as Buddha would call [it]. I am ready to further develop and learn more." Although the sources of inspiration were similar to those of Christians, including beauty in nature and care provided by others, hikers with mixed religious or alternative religious interests were, like Buddhists, less likely to associate the source of their inspiration with God. A Pagan, for example, recognized the awe in nature and the goodness in other people when he attributed his spiritual experience to:

- Being in the wilderness & appreciating the beauty & power of nature & its simplicity.
- I am in touch with how little I need, its all on my back in my pack.
- I have seen the good side of human beings—generosity, kindness, sharing, trustworthiness.

Appendix III.5 records the comments of hikers who combined Christianity or Buddhism with other religions or identified themselves as shamans or New Age.

Peter Ashley took personal statements from experts and nonexperts (in Tasmania) about the spiritual values of wilderness. Nonexperts preferred terms like peace, harmony, connection, and awe. Experts were less likely to identify wilderness with peace or harmony and awe, while invoking vocabulary such as interconnectedness, transcendence, joy, and freedom. Ashley's findings are very similar to the AT results in terms of vocabulary, with the exception that his "down-under" respondents referred to God less frequently.[22]

RELIGIOUS PRACTICE AND EXPERIENCE WITH GOD

All three forms of religious practice—service attendance, prayer, and reading sacred or spiritual texts—were positively correlated to high ratings for explicitly religious experience while on the Appalachian Trail. As was the case with personal experience, prayer and meditation, both prior to the journey and while on the AT, had the greatest relationship. Those hikers who reported that the Appalachian Trail hike was providing an opportunity for prayer or meditation were hikers who frequently practiced prayer or meditation prior to their trip (p=.000). Prayer gave significant positive correlations to all religious or spiritual statements, except for two: hikers who engaged in prayer with high frequency were not more likely than other hikers to believe they had more time for religious or spiritual activities than they usually had while off-trail, and they were not more likely to believe the AT hike helped them to correct their own wrongdoing or negative attitudes (table 9.2).[23]

Overall, areas where prior prayer or meditation practice had a very high correlation with transcendent outcomes (cc =.5 or higher) included an increase in religious commitment, thinking about God in contact with nature, feeling close to God, being aware of the beauty of God, thinking of the trip as a spiritual learning experience, and planning to integrate similar future trips into one's spiritual life. In other words, AT hikers engaged in prayer and meditation had a predisposition to (or adequate preparation for) encountering the person of God or spiritual essence of the divine in nature (fig. 9.5).

Hikers also perceived the AT experience as a clear enhancement of their spiritual lives and practice. A Baptist who prayed more than once a day described his experience as:

Table 9.2

The relationship of the frequency of religious practice at home or prior to the AT trip, and the frequency during the long-distance hike to experience with the transcendent while hiking

Religious outcomes	Home prayer	AT prayer	Home ritual	AT ritual	Home reading	AT reading
I think more about spiritual matters when I am hiking	.411**	.457**	.327**	.349**	.372**	.359**
Participating in religious ritual, prayer, or meditation in nature or outdoors has exceptional religious meaning	.365**	.382**	.212**	.273**	.326**	.279**
I have felt close to God while on this trip	.584**	.562**	.372**	.298**	.437**	.398**
Contact with nature causes me to think about God	.509**	.470**	.386**	.310**	.356**	.309**
This trip precipitated a major change in my spiritual life	.318**	.391**	.202**	.318**	.257**	.291**
This trip has been a religious or spiritual learning experience	.549**	.503**	.356**	.355**	.441**	.422**
This trip made me more aware of the beauty of God	.557**	.520**	.519**	.355**	.490**	.402**
Participating in religious ritual, prayer, or meditation at historic sites has exceptional spiritual, religious, or personal meaning	.462**	.476**	.293**	.287**	.312**	.305**

NOTE: The numbers are Pearson correlation coefficients. (p=.05*, p=.01**)

- A great awareness of God's goodness by his design of creation to provide food and water (Immeasurable).
- A greater awareness of his power evidenced by his creation (Incomprehensible).
- More mindful of how glorious God must be and our inability to fully comprehend his glory (Unbeholdable).

A Presbyterian who accomplished a section hike each year, and prayed more than weekly, provided a thorough description of her time on the AT: "Being in the woods reaffirms my belief in God's presence. It is mentally calming and joyful for me. It gives me a deeper appreciation of my husband, those around me, and myself. It brings out the best in my thoughts and actions. It really aids in my comprehension of awe and timelessness. Problems become both puny and workable." Despite these correlations, religious motives for undertaking the AT hike were weak indicators of transcendent outcomes, perhaps owing to the small number of hikers who reported these goals among their top three reasons for the trip.[24]

Fig. 9.5. A team of volunteers, including both hikers and non-hikers, praying before serving a free breakfast to Appalachian Trail hikers, First Baptist Church, Franklin, North Carolina. Prayer has a significant impact on the hiking experience.

Pretrip and on-trail service attendance gave fewer significant correlations and generally weaker correlations to spiritual outcomes. Very strong relationships (cc=.5) between pre-AT ritual participation and religious outcomes included a feeling of being close to God and an awareness of the beauty of God. Respondents with high levels of ritual participation, however, also strongly held that being away from home had separated the hiker from people with similar religious beliefs (cc=.626, p=.000). Although hikers who continued service attendance during their hike also believed this, hikers with greater loss of ritual participation between home and the AT were more likely to feel cut off (cc=-.375, p=.000). High levels of negative correlations (cc=-.3) with service attendance concerned the belief that the trip separated the hiker from people with similar beliefs, and that the trip interfered with the hiker's religious life and even the experience of the beauty of God. A potential lesson from this outcome is that personal prayer may not compensate for loss of ritual, in cases where religious practitioners build social relationships through participation in organized worship, teaching, or celebrations.[25]

Cindy Ross's AT journal provided insight into the impact, on a Christian who visits church regularly at home, of attending a service that was also embedded in the AT and its volunteer network. Writing in the 1980s, Cindy praised Graymoor Christian Unity Center's food and hospitality (they no longer serve hikers), then lauded another form of refreshment: "But this morning, before breakfast, the most incredible thing happened . . . the real gift of Graymoor Monastery. It feels like years since my soul had the pleasure of attending Mass, so I'm seeking out the small room where the celebration will take place."[26] Ross was the only layperson among the friars. After a friar commented on the day's biblical reading, she spoke up: "I bring in my feelings of the trail and JoAnn [her hiking partner] and how hard it is for us sometimes. They all seem quite touched that I'm speaking out. At the 'Prayer of the Faithful' the balding Friar prays for all the hikers and their sister (myself), for me to find my way. My heart is melting."[27] Cindy was rejuvenated by the Mass, and experienced the service as a link between her background and her future on trail.

High levels of service attendance were not significantly related to hikers' beliefs about having more or less time for religious participation, being aware of personal deficiencies or failings, correcting wrongdoing or negative attitudes, being aware of the spiritual heritage of others, and having a sense of spiritual community with others on the AT trip. The disassociation of both religious affiliation and service attendance from repentance might superficially appear to be a form of self-righteousness. Actually, the result emerged from the equal impact of the AT experience, on both religious and nonreligious hikers, in terms of reflection on personal behavior. Hikers who do not attend church, temple, or synagogue were thinking about their impacts on other people as much as those who did. Unlike the difference in prayer practice between home and the AT, which was largely neutral, the difference in service and ritual attendance between the hikers' home communities and the AT provided a number of significant negative correlations with religious outcomes, implying that hikers with greater disruption of their religious routines may find their spiritual experience constrained by the trail environment.

Although the correlations were generally weaker than those for prayer, reading sacred or spiritual texts both prior to and while on the AT was significantly positively correlated to most spiritual outcomes, except the perception of having more time for religious participation, being aware of personal deficiencies or failings, correcting wrongdoing or negative attitudes, and having a sense of spiritual community with others on the AT trip.[28] The difference in reading frequency between home and the AT had little significant impact on religious outcomes, especially in comparison with differences in service attendance. Only one Baptist survey respondent mentioned provision of reading material along the way (no one else specifically commented about this). He was also the only respondent to remark specifically on the provision of pastoral ministry outside the hostel services context: "Some good Christian books were in some of the shelters that I really enjoyed. I also met several pastors on the trail & had great conversations."

SHADOW AND REALITY ON THE TRAIL

The public understanding of the Appalachian Trail has been that hikers are close to foundations of the universe in the bosom of the mountains. The published journals describing AT thru-hikes, however, rarely treated nature as a shadow or reflection of God. Even evangelicals, who still deployed typological interpretation when comparing the Hebrew Scriptures to the New Testament, stopped well short of Jonathan Edwards in seeing God's handwriting in every flower-covered forest floor, and each clear vista with fluffy white clouds cruising at an

perception v. reality

even pace across a perfect azure dome.[29] The microcosm of Ralph Waldo Emerson, Henry David Thoreau, or Asher Durand was equally absent.[30] Today's hike is filled with struggle and impatience. The length of the trail and the goal-driven nature of thru-hiking turn microcosms into step-overs. AT journals contained few accounts of hikers who stopped to appreciate a single nurse log, with a scattering of tree seedlings poking up through wet birch leaves and moss. Tarrying after dinner to enjoy the clear flow of an Appalachian river was, however, common practice for hikers of all religious backgrounds (fig. 9.6).

In all the world religions, prayer, contemplation, or meditation are prescribed training for solo wilderness residence and for extended pilgrimage. Early Christian monastics believed the unprepared would either emotionally unravel during long stints in the desert or receive little true insight into the nature of the divine. Eastern religions have advocated developing spiritual discipline with a religious master as a preliminary step to entering a wandering or ascetic venture into the forest or a hermitage. For AT hikers, prior spiritual practice enhanced experience, not just the transcendent but also the personal and environmental domains—heightening the perception of divine beauty in nature, the feeling God was close or available, and the perceived level of spiritual learning. Prayer and meditation, however, influenced different components of spiritual wellness than accumulated trail mileage did, a phenomenon that may extend to some forms of walking religious pilgrimage.

An unexpected conclusion of the AT survey was that a significant portion of a population predominantly nonreligious and under thirty engaged in reflection about right and wrong action relative to the needs of other people. Although the social source of this "repentance" deserves more study, the processes of constantly meeting new companions and having to compromise with their needs were likely formative factors. The removal of the usual competitive pressures of work and school may have eliminated rationales for taking actions that put other people at a disadvantage. The AT was clearly an environment where everyone could win. Holding common goals provided cohesion. These processes are also at work in religious pilgrimages, where participants walk long distances over a period of days or weeks and encounter other seekers along the way.[31]

Fig. 9.6. A recreationist contemplating the Nantahala River, in the Appalachian Trail corridor just below the Founder's Foot Bridge at Weser, North Carolina.

CONCLUSION
GAINS IN FOUR SPIRITUAL DOMAINS
GAINS AND INTERACTIONS

Other studies have confirmed that wilderness recreation has positive correlations to self-actualization, self-esteem, emotional or psychological healing, building teamwork, and reducing antisocial behaviors.[1] The AT surveys verified that the trail filled a remarkable range of individual needs for change and life reorientation and provided benefits in all four spiritual domains, particularly in cases where time to gain perspective was likely to be effective. Probable contributing factors were physical exercise, simple lifestyle, peer feedback, and support offered by other hikers.[2] The most widely shared outcomes of the AT hike were those that concerned the physical and social environment of the AT itself, including making new friends, experiencing natural beauty, and acclimating to physical stresses of the trail. Statements with 70 percent and greater "true" or "very true" ratings had low dependence on individual issues, personal circumstances, or religious background. The transcendent domain was the least evident and most particular to a subgroup of hikers, with 62 percent reporting some level of spiritual or religious experience, and maximum "weighted percentages" of 40 percent of hikers rating statements concerning the transcendent as true or very true. A significant minority of respondents, however, believed they were greatly increasing the depth of their relationship with God or the transcendent.

A pivotal question is: do all the spiritual domains equally influence each other? In table 10.1 the personal domain is divided into three subcategories: personal concerns and problem solving (such as managing a life transition), personal health, and self-perception, including feelings of achievement and inner peace. The responses to the questions reflecting the communal domain actually had the weakest relationship to the other two domains, with the exception of its high correlation with personal interior or self-perception. In other words, how well one was building relationships with others was strongly related to one's feelings of inner peace or of achievement. The weaker communal correlations with personal problem solving may originate in the universal importance of building friendships, while other communal variables were more particular to individual circumstances. Environmental perceptions were moderately correlated to all other domains and subdomains, with the exception of personal "interior," where the degree of correlation was elevated. Environmental satisfaction and coping were therefore closely related to self-image and self-perception. The personal domains displayed high correlations to each other, with the exception of personal health, which again was more likely to be linked to individual circumstances.

So what, in practical terms, do these results mean? First, the way hikers related to other people (communal) was, with the exception of making new friends, particular—individual hikers were experiencing their relationships with old friends, their significant other, and their family differentially. Some thru-hikers were finding the trip had a much greater impact on their family relationships than others, owing to their personal circumstances. How hikers felt about themselves was related to a combination of the other domains: environmental, communal, and personal. Although it was difficult to distinguish cause and effect, a marked interior experience and a very intense environmental experience

Table 10.1

The percentage of variables showing significant correlations among the domains

	Communal	Environment	Personal health	Personal concerns	Personal interior
Communal	Very Low 18%	Moderate 42%	Low 29%	Low 23%	High 50%
Environment	Moderate 42%	Moderate 43%	Moderate 39%	Moderate 33%	High 62%
Personal health	Low 29%	Moderate 39%	High 60%	High 60%	Moderate 35%
Personal concerns	Low 23%	Moderate 33%	High 60%	Very high 70%	Very high 73%
Personal interior	High 50%	High 62%	Moderate 35%	Very high 73%	Very high 80%

tended to co-occur. Hikers who were having a strongly positive experience in terms of feeling inner peace or self-worth were also likely to feel they were working out their personal problems and improving their lives for the better. Though the frequency of prayer was not significantly correlated to the perception of nature, both enjoyment of nature and prayer were correlated to feelings of inner peace, suggesting a synergistic effect between the two.

The surveys provided some surprises. Gender was less important than age to perceived benefits from the journey. The AT thru- and section hikers were tolerant of the high traffic on the trail, probably because of their enjoyment of the interpersonal and communal aspects. Perhaps the most unexpected result was that higher frequencies of prayer and meditation prior to the initiation of the trip improved personal interior and communal outcomes, while prior backpacking experience was largely neutral. Mere religious membership or ritual participation (service attendance) was not as robust an indicator of AT personal experience as frequency of prayer or meditation. These outcomes supported the belief, widespread among the world's religions, that contemplative practice is an important preparation for pilgrimage, wilderness residence, or vision quest.

The survey verified the "Canterbury Tales effect."[3] People sharing long-distance journeys with strangers form beneficial new relationships and contemplate the quality of their interactions with others. The "secular" long-distance journey on foot can provide some of the benefits traditionally associated with religious pilgrimage, particularly assistance with life transitions, time for reflection, improved self-control, and the ability to live in simple or austere environmental conditions. A small, while notable, subset of AT hikers self-reported physical and emotional healing. Marni Goldberg and her coauthors, in a qualitative study (nonnumerical), identified "self-fulfillment, self-reliance, fun and enjoyment of and warm relationships" as AT hiker values, without determining their relative importance.[4] As other studies of wilderness experience have predicted,[5] the mega-hike and the community of travelers generated spiritual benefits, without any formal or denominational religious context.

In investigating the relationship of the transcendent to the other three domains, I deployed multivariate statistical techniques for clustering similar responses to questions concerning communal, personal, and environmental experience and those concerning the transcendent.[6] The transcendent statements consistently separated from the others, suggesting that level of individual religious commitment and engagement was a dominant factor in determining hiker perception of the transcendent domain, while other variables such as friendly atmosphere of the AT environment were more influential in the other three domains. A second method for comparing the relationships among the domains was to search for statements hikers answered in a parallel way. The individual statements concerning transcendence produced no significant correlations at all with hiker experience of gaining physical fitness, fatigue, injury, comfort in

Fig. 10.1. Appalachian Trail thru-hiker on another uphill pitch, North Carolina. Though the concept of sustained effort suggests spiritual formation, physical experience was weakly correlated to the experience of transcendence.

overnight accommodations, feelings of boredom, or feelings of isolation (table 10.2). Hiker experience with transcendence had few correlations to making new friends, perceptions of the trail environment, or the experience of the trail as a learning experience. For the AT thru-hikers, experience of transcendence over-all had a weak relationship to perceptions of the trail environment, including its demanding physical conditions. Although Christianity has historically used uphill struggle as a metaphor for reaching God, the surveys did not confirm this as literally true for twenty-first-century hikers (fig. 10.1).

The transcendent domain produced a moderate number of correlations with managing a life transition and managing self-doubt and personal stresses, and a higher number of correlations with understanding one's impacts on other people, healing past physical and emotional injuries or illnesses, conquering bad habits and personal problems, and improving family relations. The tran-scendent statements were very frequently correlated (70 percent to 90 percent of the statements) to the feeling of peace or balance in one's life and to beliefs the trip was changing life for the better, leading to positive feelings about one's self, and believing the hiker could cope with difficulties in life. The single transcen-dent concept most frequently correlated to other domains was: "This trip has helped me to correct my own wrongdoing or negative attitudes."[7] Statements from the transcendent domain with few positive correlations to outcomes in the other domains included feeling separated from the home religious community (none!), and feeling God's guidance (three of twenty-nine)! Feeling interference in one's religious life, spending time reading sacred texts, and visiting religious buildings or monuments also had few significant correlations, indicating these factors were perhaps not negative but were, at best, neutral.

A third method for comparing the domains, and perhaps the most easily un-derstood, was to consolidate an index of the level of spiritual response by hiker. A simple way to accomplish this is to take an average of all the positive state-ments. Table 10.3 displays the correlations of this index of spiritual experience to the other three domains. Nine of the ten greatest correlations concerned the personal domain, which is also the sphere where frequency of prayer had the most correlations. The highest correlations concerned positive feelings about life and feelings of inner peace and harmony. The level of religious and spiritual engagement with the AT was notably correlated to a perceived increase in posi-tive feelings about the meaning of life. Gwyther Rees, Leslie Francis, and Many

Table 10.2

The number of correlations between statements in the section of the survey using explicitly religious language and expressing transcendence, and statements concerning personal experience in the environmental, communal, and personal domains.

Significant correlations w/ transcendence	Statements concerning the environmental, communal, and personal domains—from lowest number of correlations to the highest
None	Feelings of isolation, feelings of boredom, discomfort with accommodations, gaining physical fitness, experiencing fatigue, trip caused physical injury or illness
Low 1 to 4	Harmed relationships with friends and family, strengthening relationship with significant other, cope with life's difficulties, gain sense of accomplishment, discomfort with environmental conditions, experiencing enjoyment, the natural environment is pleasing
Moderate 5–10	Strengthening old friendships, planning to take another trip like this, managing a life transition, relief from daily stress, making new friends, encountering many interesting events and experiences
High 11–16	Time to think about personal concerns, heal from a physical illness, feeling fearful or worried on trip, strengthened family relations, heal from emotional or psychological illness, provided relief from daily stresses, time to think about relationships with other people, helped to break a bad habit
17–20 no cases	Gap to very high number of correlations
Correlated to most statements 21–26 (of 29 total)	Changed my life for the better, provided a sense of harmony with life, helps to cope with difficulties in life, feeling positive about life, provided a sense of inner peace

NOTE: The results reflect Pearson correlations among all possible combinations of statements from the two sections.

Table 10.3

The correlations of an average of the positive responses in the transcendent domain to statements concerning the environmental, communal, and personal domains

Statement	Domain	Corr.	Prob.
This trip made me feel me positive about the meaning of my life	Personal	.475**	.000
This trip will help me cope with the difficulties in my life	Personal	.445**	.000
This trip gave me a sense of inner peace	Personal	.421**	.000
This trip a sense of harmony with my life	Personal	.365**	.000
This trip has changed my life for the better	Personal	.313**	.000
This trip helped me to manage a life transition …	Personal	.293**	.000
This trip has given me time to think about my relationships with other people	Communal	.290**	.000
This trip has helped me to heal from an emotional or psychological … condition …	Personal	.285**	.001
This trip has helped me to break a bad habit	Personal	.248**	.002
This trip helped to heal from a physical … condition …	Personal	.228**	.002
I felt fearful or worried on this trip	Personal	.225**	.002
This trip has produced many interesting events and experiences	Environmental	.206*	.012
This trip was a learning experience	Environmental	.206*	.005
I have strengthened old friendships on this trip	Communal	.200*	.014
I have made new friends on this trip	Communal	.192*	.019
This trip has caused me to doubt my own abilities	Personal	.187*	.022
This trip has given me time to think about personal problems or concerns	Personal	.173*	.035
The large number of hikers on this route interfered with my trail experience	Communal	.166*	.044
The natural environment on this trip is pleasing	Environmental	.158*	.027

Robbins, using the SH4DI, found that religious affiliation and personal prayer were predictive in terms of Welsh young peoples' sense of purpose in life.[8]

THE TRAIL AS LIVED-IN EXPERIENCE

The concepts of peak experience and of temporary exposure to nature were too constrained to capture the comprehensive effect of the lived-in AT. Different aspects of mega-hiking[9] functioned on variable temporal and spatial scales. Though the AT presents physical stresses similar to other "wilderness," the personal outcomes were probably atypical of shorter-term wilderness experience and were influenced by the time spent off-corridor. AT thru-hikers rarely stayed in the backcountry or away from developed zones for more than five nights at a time, and, with the exception of the Great Smoky Mountains and northern New England, thru-hikers were likely to visit stores, munch deli sandwiches, and use accommodations with Web access and washing machines on average every third day, if not more frequently. Further, a very high level of interaction among hiking parties and an elevated percentage of seniors characterized the AT. Age is likely an important factor in contemporary religious walking pilgrimage[10] and individual experience in other natural settings.[11]

William Borrie and Joseph Roggenbuck have defined short-term wilderness visits in phases, including entry, immersion, and exit.[12] This system does not properly characterize the Appalachian Trail end-to-enders, because of the repeated exit and entry from the corridor. For the AT, the first, brief phase—*entry*—is abrupt and requires an immediate reorientation of the most basic tasks of daily living. The trail is not what novices expect. Some would-be end-to-enders quit and get off at the first road crossing, or call home for a ride from Neel's Gap. The second phase is *accommodation,* where the walker adjusts to the physical and social environment and makes initial contacts with other hikers. The journals indicated that this phase requires two to three weeks, or about one hundred to three hundred miles, depending on individual levels of physical fitness, expectations for the journey, the difficulty of the start (such as encountering a snowstorm on the third day), and the level of preparedness. Most relationships with other hiking groups are tentative, and mom is still mailing the supplies on the wrong schedule. Some gear needs to be dropped or replaced. Lasting friendships begin, while the great number of would-be thru-hikers and the high drop-out rate provide considerable interference and social clutter. Many would-be thru-hikers fail to complete this phase, due to everything from disappointment over the trail lifestyle to an early injury. Nationally, the majority of short-term wilderness trips never emerge from this necessary *accommodation.* The one- or two-week backpacking adventure is in perpetual start-up, and the sore muscles never completely subside.

The third phase is establishment or *community formation,* where trail "families" begin to consolidate, and loose confederations of hikers walking at a similar pace begin to meet repeatedly at shelters. While there is still high attrition, the thru- and section hikers begin to monitor each other's welfare. They inquire regularly about others who have fallen behind, and make arrangements to meet members of other hiking parties at a specific shelter or in town. News of a hiker in trouble or of a hiker making exceptional progress begins to circulate up and down the AT. The volunteer-sponsored events such as Trail Days, the various festivals, and free meals at churches contribute to the development of social networks by providing venues where hikers beginning at different times or preferring different forms of accommodation can mix, chat, and share activities such as tossing a Frisbee. This phase is also marked by improved fitness, acclimation to the milieu, and more astute management of camping gear.

Unlike the open campsites of most U.S. wilderness areas, where backpackers space their tents and do not share meals among parties, the shelters and hostels prevalent on the AT accommodate various soloists and partnerships in close proximity. The AT encourages inter-group communication and trust because of the strong identity with the Appalachian Trail itself. Thru-hikers test strangers (such as researchers conducting interviews) by opening conversations about who the unfamiliar individuals know or by asking how many trail miles they have walked themselves. A new acquaintance who recognizes other trail figures, such as well-known hostel managers, the staff of the ATC in Harpers Ferry, or thru-hikers currently on the trail, is accepted, at least tentatively, as part of the community, as is someone who has knowledge of Appalachian Trail geography.

A similar phase of community formation is possible for large, organized wilderness expeditions and outdoor schools, particularly if they remain together for more than one or two weeks. The AT travelers differ from these team adventurers, however, in their potential for forming new friendships throughout their sojourn. This phenomenon is more similar to historic walking pilgrimage, as is the opportunity for converging at festivals and social gatherings in town. The need to continually adjust to unfamiliar hikers, while retaining ties with established trail "families" or hiking partnerships, potentially contributes to the "Canterbury Tales effect." Organized or guided wilderness group travel also has low contact with farmers, café owners, and Baptists who cook pancakes. While the AT hiker develops the self-actualization, self-reliance, and confidence offered by a well-managed wilderness skills course, the growing belief in the goodness of other people is potentially enhanced by the host of trail angels, who serve the role of caring strangers in the midst of a difficult personal challenge.

The fourth phase of the journey is the *functional network*, where hikers have gained familiarity both with the skills necessary to success and with their fellow hikers. For northbounders this develops after the additional attrition caused by the physical rigors of the Great Smoky Mountains and the financial shortages that remove many poorly prepared thru-hikers prior to southern Virginia. Trail Days is both a temporal and a psychological milestone. Timed to attract the maximum number of northbounders, it is a rite of passage for those most likely to survive the unending striding toward sacred Katahdin. Even fast-paced end-to-enders who have already reached Shenandoah and do not return for the parades and parties know it marks the boundary between those able to become 2,000-milers and those who are not. Hikers are feeling increasingly comfortable, both with their own abilities and with the availability of community support as they reach Damascus. Unfortunately, in ethical terms, the sense of entitlement often creeps into interactions with volunteers and near-trail businesses at this point.

The fifth phase is deciding to finish, or determining how much trail is enough. This might be termed the *commitment* phase. Many AT hikers initiate the trail foray intending to just find out how far they can go. Some began their hike to escape a problem, and either found they cannot escape it or have resolved their issue well before the end of the trail. A handful suffer from boredom or miss their spouse or family. College is starting again, or an employer calls and says if you want your job back you need to come home now. Others feel they have proven themselves. Each summer, would-be end-to-enders who are physically able to finish, but are disorganized or inclined to dally, fall behind schedule. They eventually recognize they are running out of time to reach Maine before snow closes Baxter State Park. Particularly in the stretch from Pennsylvania through Massachusetts, the angels remarked on the potential for a crisis of meaning in

Fig. 10.2. Photos on the Appalachian Trail wall, Inn at the Long Trail, Vermont. Friendships last long after the two thousand miles is finished. Hikers mail Christmas cards with a Katahdin photo, as verification of the accomplishment. The cards are sent to fellow hikers and to the angels (hostels, inns, cafes, and outfitters) who helped along the way.

midjourney. This did not affect all thru-hikers, but a significant number begin to consciously ask themselves: "Do I need to walk the whole trail?"[13] The volunteers assist in resolving these doubts, as do supportive relationships with other hikers. Hikers experience both encouragement and common sense offered by strangers. Some thru-hikers with chronic injuries, Lyme disease, or financial woes do need to stop. Others require a hug and some cold ice cream, or Lynn Setzer hiking nude in front of them to cheer them on through the boggy, isolated reaches of Maine. Although this type of process also occurs on short-term wilderness expeditions, the individual thru-hiker's personal and time investment in the AT is much greater. Dropouts often leave because they were experiencing severe physical discomfort or because they were not compatible with other hikers.[14]

The sixth and final on-trail phase of the hike is the *celebration phase,* or the completion of the journey (fig. 10.2). The trail journals described the sense of euphoria and achievement this brings. Other people often inquired: "Have you walked the whole AT?" Thus the onlookers, including family and friends, distinguished between the job half done and the job completed. This sense of finality and of reaching a new level of personal success is absent from shorter wilderness rambles on loop trails. Completing the AT is a dramatic form of self-actualization and self-affirmation, as is walking the Camino or the Pacific Crest Trail. The trim and athletic college student joins the ranks of American folk heroes. She sends Christmas cards with a photo of herself embracing the sign on top of Katahdin to all her relatives and college friends and everyone who helped her along the route. She becomes the pioneer who explored the Appalachian frontier with Davy Crockett, or the student of Thoreau, who strolled the woods around Concord. The survey found, however, that AT hikers felt a sense of accomplishment almost from the initiation of their journey, and it was not necessary to complete the entire trail to experience deep affirmation of one's ability to rise to the challenge.

The AT and other mega-hikes offer a seventh phase, and that is *reintegration* with off-trail life. From a spiritual perspective this is a critical phase because it determines what a hiker will take away with him after half a year on the trail. For 2,000-milers, the AT has become "home," and for some, the most welcoming and comfortable habitat they had ever known. A handful of 2,000-milers never leave the trail. They take on the Pacific Crest Trail the next year, or spend their time planning a second hike on the AT. A few move close to the trail, find a job, and buy a cabin. The majority become "alumni," returning periodically for Trail Days or a weekend hike with their children. Becoming a 2,000-miler is a fondly remembered honor and a lifelong element in self-identity. Though this project incorporated interviews with former thru-hikers, all were individuals living close to the trail and continuing to serve the hikers. They testified that the AT had assisted them in taking their bearings on life, and in three cases, informants had joined a religious organization or undertaken a ministry as the result of an end-to-end walk. The highly committed cadre was not typical of the reintegration process, however, and an accurate overview of what happens to hikers after they leave the trail would require additional study. My informal contacts included multiyear hikers and those returning for festivals and short-term service. Those attending Trail Days marked their T-shirts with white blazes, indicating the number of all-AT hikes completed or in progress. The "alums" wore hiking clothes and shoes (whether hiking or not during the event). The easy assumption of hiker garb and merger back into the activities of the AT implied that the trail had made a lasting impact on the end-to-enders, and they never lost the constellation of friendships spinning through the 2,000-mile walk.

Spiritual Outcomes and the Length of the Journey

A second pivotal question is: do hikers reach a point of maximum spiritual effect early in the journey? The length and route of the AT are based on the topography of the Appalachians and the positions of the higher ranges, rather than on the psychological dynamics of backcountry rambling. This investigation was not structured to fully address the process of individual adaptation, which would be better analyzed by sampling hikers at different points along the entire national trail, or by interviewing the same hikers multiple times. A preliminary analysis,[15] intended to determine whether there were "caps" on the impacts of a long-distance walk correlated to mileage, found that perceived effects such improved physical fitness, enjoyment, interest, and a pleasing natural environment began early, within the first hundred to three hundred miles, and gradually increased. These are all outcomes that are largely contingent on environmental immersion.

Rather than displaying caps (asymptotes), the communal variables appeared to have thresholds. In other words, hikers traveling short distances and underway for very short periods gave proportionately fewer high ratings to the statement "This trip has given me time to think about my relationships with other people." Hikers' belief that they were making new friends and were experiencing relief from stress was also delayed. Higher scores for these three outcomes were prevalent after the first three hundred miles (plus or minus). Hiker reports that the trip had changed their life for the better initiated early, while showing increasing gain in scores after three hundred miles. These results paralleled the accounts in the published trail journals of 2,000-milers, which verified that the excitement and aesthetics of the trail start at Springer or Katahdin, while new relationships require time to stabilize. The struggle to harden one's feet and tighten one's muscles, as well as the need to rearrange gear, which characterize the first few days on trail, affect enjoyment and constrain focus on the range of personalities sharing the sound of rain pounding on a shelter roof. Although the transition varied by walker, the more enriching elements of the communal domain initiated two or three weeks after entering the woods.[16]

An interesting property of the AT environmental domain was the lack of correlation between mileage completed and the belief "the natural environment is pleasing." In my own experience, Appalachian backpackers enjoy the views from the very beginning of their trips. On a trip north from Springer, a friend and I stayed at the shelter on Tray Mountain, GA—not very far up the AT. After dinner, we relaxed on the open bald of the peak. She was stunned by the sunset and remarked that she always had thought the stark silhouettes of line-on-line of ridges were created by photographers using filters and doctoring their images. The hazy blue outlines shimmering in the crepuscular light were real and fully appreciated on first encounter. Field observation suggested that long-distance backpackers became accustomed to the vistas, and began to skip opportunities to take a short detour off-trail and gain a break from the curtain of leaves by stepping out on a ledge or reaching a clearing in the trees.[17] End-to-enders were still thrilled as they struggled above tree-line on reaching the Presidential Range. They no longer stopped, however, at every rivulet or uniquely shaped boulder. Repeated exposure to sweeping vistas and to quiet, sun-specked glades may, however, have raised the positive scores for the learning experience offered by the trail and outcomes resulting from a combination of variables, such as enjoyment of the hike. Though hikers may acclimate to the overlooks, pinnacles, and cascades, their perception of the AT as interesting continued to increase for more than a thousand miles.

Research on wilderness recreation has focused on the concept of "peak experience" and documented the emotional responses of rafters as they plunge down canyons and glide between boulders and towering red-rock walls, even on single-day forays. Psychological studies have demonstrated that wilderness or hiking trips of a few hours to a month can result in a range of outcomes from changes in mood in response to contact with nature, such as the immediate calming effect of viewing outdoor scenes, to establishment of new and lasting interpersonal relationships.[18] The results of the AT survey suggested that the range of nature-initiated mood change or emotional stimulation changed relatively little from the beginning of the AT hike to the end. D. L. Ben Zequeira-Russell, in a study of fifteen Christians on a wilderness leadership course in the Sierras, concluded "no relationship was found between items used to measure peak experience and changes in spirituality scores." Zequeira-Russell also found that wilderness participants who reported "the beauty and majesty of the wilderness were important to their spiritual experience" also showed an increasing disappointment with the sacred.[19] Among AT hikers, perceiving the natural environment as pleasing had a very low number of significant correlations with statements describing specific outcomes concerning the transcendent, while it was significantly correlated to an overall index of perceptions of the transcendent (table 10.3). For hikers who were religious, an appreciation of natural aesthetics may have led to more positive feelings about their journey, including the belief that the mega-hike was spiritually beneficial. The popular notion that viewing beauty in nature, on average, leads to a better understanding of God or a sense of closeness to the divine is, however, too simple a model.

THE ETHICS OF FOREST TO TOWN

The communal domain has undergone substantial modification since Earl Shaffer completed the first end-to-end hike in 1948. The center of hiker-human interaction has shifted from contact with upland farmers, fire tower monitors, and country store proprietors, to the streams of thru-hikers heading north or south, and to businesses and organizations that specifically support recreationists. The AT has evolved terminology specific to AT thru-hiking, in recognition of an alternative peripatetic trail subculture. Hikers are reborn and assume trail names. They form trail "families" and identify with the "class" or the year they begin an end-to-end hike. Hikers build reputations, not based on their environmental or geographic knowledge, but on their walking prowess or the individual roles they play in trail culture. As a diverse, democratic, and fluid social entity, the AT allows experimentation with new relationships. Successful AT hikers develop highly positive perceptions of this process of restructuring one's life and merging with trail culture.

Recent research has found that exposure to nature can stimulate ethical thinking, such as feeling a sense of humility in the midst of high peaks and valleys spreading to the far horizon.[20] Controlled experiments have proven that images of natural landscapes evoke value orientation toward intrinsic or prosocial aspirations—in other words, immersion in photographs of natural settings elicited thoughts of caretaking.[21] Some AT hikers developed a sense of entitlement with accumulated mileage, however, which was a form of arrogance and self-oriented acquisitiveness. The challenge and achievement aspects of mega-hiking, and the social status they convey, were apparently countering some of the humility generated by hikers' encounters with the magnificence of the Appalachians and the powerful natural forces that still rule the ridges. All sources of information utilized in the AT project verified that thru-hikers demonstrated caretaking behaviors toward their fellow hikers, the service providers, and the AT corridor. The hikers had their lapses in virtue, though, and the sources of the caretaking ethic extended beyond the natural environment to the examples set by Franciscan friars, managers of sugar maple bush, café cooks, fire chiefs, and even Irish bartenders. The mountain landscape and its residents, as well as the hikers themselves, all acted as teachers in the weave of independence and interdependence forming the fabric of the AT journey.

Recent research has found that immersion in landscapes dominated by human constructions thwarts valuing of intrinsic aspirations, such as caretaking, community, and personal growth, and instead prompts extrinsic aspirations, such as fame, money, and image.[22] A reasonable hypothesis is, therefore, that frequent hiker trips to town may mute some of the spiritual effects of the daily ramble through the protected natural corridor. The tendency of hikers to utilize the trail towns as environments of excess or release, including drinking and heavy food consumption, could accentuate extrinsic values such as personal acquisition of culinary resources. The importance of the volunteers and their modeling of giving to others is a counterbalance to a strong dichotomy between city and wilds in terms of value formation.

Ethically, the AT experience encouraged simultaneous positive valuation of human beings and nature—the hikers, on average, did not have a conflicted philosophy, which excluded people from the Appalachians, and did not view humankind as an unrelenting threat to the wild. The long-distance hike may actually foster the belief that compromise between human interests and development and the health and integrity of natural ecosystems is possible. The hikers displayed a concern for conserving rural and agricultural landscapes, as well as for wilderness. The constant shift from forest to town, however, generated many of the tensions concerning right and wrong behavior along the AT. The increasing intrusion of information technology into the AT lifestyle has emerged as a key ethical issue that deserves further conversation, especially as the millennial generation begin to graduate from college and buy their first lightweight backpack with a pocket for inserting a smart phone.

Despite all the services offered to hikers by trail clubs, churches, and municipalities, the AT hikes were not universally generating a desire to join service organizations. This pattern may have been influenced by the age of the hikers and the fact that many are between jobs or even permanent residences. The hikers, on average, did not believe they had made major gains in environmental knowledge, at least resulting from access to educational materials. Further, only one-quarter of the respondents reported applying what they learned environmentally to their home region. At Trail Days 2009, a booth was selling T-shirts with the message, "Give back to the Trail" printed on the front to raise funds for trail maintenance. The thru-hikers remain very willing to give back. The question is of the scale of response and whether the recipients are their immediate friends or the trail community as a whole—the difference between offering small favors among buddies or within a trail "family" and pitching in on larger chores, such as building a footbridge, conducting a wildlife survey, or packing in lumber to renovate a shelter. Increased contact with service opportunities during the course of a hike and greater access to environmentally astute interpretive information, particularly at overnight accommodations, could improve hiker engagement with the most critical environmental concerns for the trail and for their home communities. The evidence credited the AT with building individual character and stamina. The hikers learned to trust humanity while developing a new level of self-reliance. On average, the process of ethical formation was greatest at the proximate and interpersonal scale and declined at broader scales, ascending to all-trail, to the regional, and to the national-level environmental and social ethical concerns.

MEGA-HIKING AND RELIGIOUS PILGRIMAGE

Bron Taylor has proposed: "Outdoor adventure and other recreational practices can express, evoke, and reinforce religious perceptions and orientations to natural and social worlds. Some participants in them understand nature itself to be sacred in some way and believe that facilitating human connections to nature is the most important aspect of their chosen practice."[23] This is potentially true for a small subgroup of AT hikers, while the majority either believe spirituality and sacred terrain have nothing to do with their hike or are more traditional theists who are pursuing contact with God's creation as a secondary or tertiary motive for their expedition. Even practitioners of alternative religions prioritize self-actualization, contact with other hikers, and fulfilling personal needs at levels parallel to their relationship with the Earth.

Historically, world religions have pursued longer pilgrimages for accommodating life transitions, increasing religious commitment, and fostering major "attitude adjustments."[24] Recent diaries and journals from El Camino de Compostela confirm that today's Western religious pilgrims engage in self-reflection, develop new friendships, and consider the next phase of their lives. Roman Catholic priest Kevin Codd took a break from his position as seminary director to limp along the Camino. His journal records his slow grappling with both his transition from middle age to senior status, and the evolution of his relationships with God and his fellow walkers through the course of the trip.[25] Shirley MacLaine, a New Ager, took a more mystical excursion on the Camino, while also enjoying the encouragement of her fellow travelers.[26] The medieval rituals and centuries-old churches were only half the spiritual fuel—the casual companions who offered treatment for inflamed blisters and the Spanish landscape were the other half.[27]

Today, the roles of historic saints' roads and modern national trails and footpaths appear to be merging in terms of user goals. Even at Lourdes, the younger generation are primarily interested in recreation, while the older generation is still focused on receiving help from God and saintly intercession.[28] In 1995, only 9 percent of walkers on the Camino started with explicitly religious interests.[29] On El Camino, many of the hikers and bicyclists are nominal Roman Catholics or not Catholic at all. As one can discern from the published accounts, pilgrims open café conversations about religion tentatively, even on the way to the shrine of St. James the Greater. Today's hikers are fitting the available trails to their spiritual needs, particularly in terms of private and introspective spiritual practice. The documented shift in emphasis from religion to spirituality, particularly among younger Americans and Europeans, is likely to further advance the strategy of adapting the hiking opportunity to the backpacker's spiritual needs, rather than the adapting of the walker to the ritual structures of the pilgrim's road. In terms of feeling part of a spiritual community, AT hikers provided much lower ratings than they did concerning friendship overall. As the recreational mixes with the religious, a similar individuation and diversification of "pilgrims" on historic saints' roads will potentially emphasize democratization and exploring personal spiritual options, while reducing the sense of shared religious experience.

The temporal demands of the AT end-to-end adventure reduced attendance at religious services, and were break-even in terms of time for prayer. The necessity of beating the snow to Katahdin, the rough surfaces, and steep rock outcrops give precedence to tromping away available daylight. The programmed stops at shrines characterizing religious pilgrimage may enhance outcomes in the personal as well as in the transcendent domain, through slowing the pace and increasing the frequency of prayer. Shorter as opposed to longer routes with clear foundations in Western religious heritage, such as Cuthbert's Way (a new countryside path crossing the border from Scotland to England) versus El Camino (France to Spain), should produce different spiritual outcomes.[30] While further research is definitely required, preliminary hypotheses project the longer Camino, with its refugios for pilgrims, as providing the better platform for wrestling with life transitions and for benefiting from insights generated by the Canterbury Tales effect. Cuthbert's Way, with its charming ramble along the Tweed River and ruined monasteries, is likely to be an equally effective environment for introspective prayer and for appreciating nature, at least per unit time invested, while reducing the communal interactions.

Hikers tolerated low-key outreach and the religious motivations of the trail angels, as long as they had the option to participate without being forced to absorb the views of others. The perception of the volunteers that thru-hikers are closer to God on the AT might be more accurately stated as, thru-hikers are open to new life phases and potentials, including spiritual formation, while on the long journey. Today's theologians of pilgrimage are still struggling with the question of mission.[31] Martin Robinson portrayed Christian pilgrimage of all sorts as progressing through stages: the call of God, the encounter with God, the beckoning of God, and finally, traveling for Christ.[32] The AT hikers of all religious backgrounds, indeed, were at different stages, although they might be better titled: exploration (examining the spiritual self), relation (recognizing and accepting the transcendent), maturation (growing in understanding), and incorporation (thinking about ministry to or care for others). "Hike your own hike" remained the basis of thru-hiker values. Despite the variation in "spiritual experience"— from not at all to fully life changing—the Appalachian Trail thru-hike remains a valid and powerful platform for ethical and spiritual formation, and for nurturing a love for wild landscapes and for nature as planetary partner and friend.

APPENDIX I

TABLES OF ETHICAL VALUES

Table I.1

Ethical values of Appalachian Trail hikers

Topic	Question	Mean	Median	Mode
	Equal to or greater than 4.0, very true			
Pollution				
	Proper waste management is a responsibility of all good citizens.	4.64	5	5
	Water and air pollution are threats to human health.	4.35	5	5
Biodiversity				
	Humans should do more to protect wildlife.	4.49	5	5
	We should preserve as many of the earth's wild plants and animals as possible.	4.47	5	5
Care & Service				
	Care for nature should be an integral part of my life.	4.31	5	5
	Service to other people should be an integral part of my life.	4.11	4	5
	Between 3.50 and 3.99—True			
Rural scene				
	Humans should do more to prevent loss of agricultural lands and the rural scene.	3.96	4	5
Threats				
	Industrialized human culture is a threat to the earth's environments.	3.93	4	5
	Environmental degradation could result in the disappearance of humanity from the earth.	3.89	4	5

Table I.1 (cont.)

Topic	Question	Mean	Median	Mode
Ecojustice 1				
	Caring for the environment is important to caring for the world's needy people.	3.88	4	5
Population				
	Increasing human population is a threat to the earth's environments.	3.82	4	5
Trail				
	Human developments, such as roads and buildings, are damaging our parks and hiking trails.	3.50	3	3
Between 3.0 and 3.49—Somewhat true				
None				
Between 2.50 and 2.99—Equivocal to somewhat untrue				
Ecojustice 2				
	People who are poor do not have enough access to outdoor recreation.	2.61	3	1
Anti-Environmental				
	Environmentalists often exaggerate or make issues seem worse then they are.	2.59	2	2
Between 2.00 and 2.49–Untrue				
Environment vs. People				
	Caring for the environment can harm human welfare or interests.	2.46	2	1
	Money spent on the environment should be used to directly assist needy people	2.13	2	2

NOTE: These values are based on all completed responses in the hiker surveys, between 191 and 202 responses per statement. The scale is from 1 to 5, from "Not at all true" to "Very true."

Table I.2

Impact of the AT hike on personal values or ethical action

Topic	Question	Mean	Median	Mode
	Equal to or greater than 4.0, very true to true			
Aesthetics				
	Experiencing natural beauty increases my motivation to care for the environment.	4.25	5	5
	Between 3.5 and 3.9—True to somewhat true			
Wilderness				
	This trip has made me more aware of the value of wild or undeveloped lands.	3.68	4	5
Personal responsibility				
	This trip has made me more aware of how my behavior or ethics can effect the natural environment.	3.69	4	5
	This trip has made me more aware of how my behavior or personal ethics can affect other people.	3.56	4	5
Trail				
	The more time I spend on this trip, the more I learn about caring for the environment.	3.51	3	3
	Between 3.0 and 3.4—Equivocal to somewhat true			
Active				
	This trip has increased my motivation to join environmental organizations or to volunteer to care for the environment.	3.25	3	3
	This trip has made me more likely to take political action or to vote concerning environmental issues.	3.04	3	3
Spiritual experience				
	Spiritual or religious experience with nature increases my motivation to care for the environment.	3.25	3	5

Table I.2 (cont.)				
Topic	Question	Mean	Median	Mode
Between 2.5 and 2.99—Equivocal to somewhat untrue				
Learning				
	I would like to have more access to printed or educational materials concerning environmental issues along the trail	2.99	3	3
	Exposure to educational materials or programs about this trail has increased my interest in environmental care.	2.72	3	3
Active ethics 2				
	This trip has increased my motivation to join humanitarian or human service organizations or volunteer time to people in need.	2.85	3	3
Bioregion				
	This trip has made me more aware of environmental concerns in my hometown or region.	2.75	3	3
Between 1.5 and 2.0—Untrue to very untrue				
Anti-learning				
	I have not learned anything new about environmental care on this trip.	1.67	1	1

NOTE: These values are based on all completed responses in the hiker surveys, generally between 195 and 198 responses. The scale is from 1 to 5, from "Very untrue" to "Very true."

APPENDIX II

TABLES OF PERSONAL VALUES

Table II.1
The fifteen statements with the highest overall ratings from the personal experience section of the hiker survey.

Statement	% very true or true (or untrue or very untrue for negative statements)	Mean rating	Domain	Enhanced by mileage	Enhanced by prayer/ meditation
This trip produced many interesting events and experiences.	93	4.65	Envir	Yes**	No
The natural environment on this trip is pleasing.	89	4.53	Envir	No	No
I really enjoyed myself on this trip.	89	4.51	Pers	Yes*	No
This trip was a learning experience	88	4.50	Envir	Yes**	No
This trip has given me a sense of accomplishment.	87	4.50	Pers	No	No
This trip has improved my physical fitness.	85	4.48	Pers	Yes*	No
I have made new friends on this trip.	84	4.45	Comm	Yes**	No
Being away from home has harmed my relationships with my family. (negative)	85	1.60	Comm	No	No

Table II.1 (cont.)

Statement	% very true or true (or untrue or very untrue for negative statements)	Mean rating	Domain	Enhanced by mileage	Enhanced by prayer/meditation
This trip has given me time to think about my relationships with other people.	82	4.39	Comm	No	Pre* On*
This trip has given me time to think about personal problems or concerns.	80	4.37	Perso	No	No
The large number of hikers on this route interfered with my trail experience. (negative)	82	1.69	Comm	No	No
This trip has changed my life for the better.	77	4.22	Pers	Yes**	Pre** On*
This trip caused me to doubt my own abilities. (negative)	79	1.80	Pers	Yes* Neg.	Pre* Neg.
Overnight accommodations have been unpleasant or uncomfortable. (negative)	77	1.90	Envir	Yes* Neg.	No
This trip has provided relief from daily stresses.	71	4.05	Pers	Yes*	No
I often feel bored on the trail. (negative)	9	2.00	Pers	No	No

NOTE: Included are the environmental, communal and personal domain. A high proportion of these variables are positively correlated to the mileage walked during the current trip. "Neg." the greater the mileage or prayer the lower the rating of the statement.

Table II.2

The relationship of prior backpacking experience to outcomes.

Personal, community or environmental outcome *Negative correlations with prior long distance hiking experience*	Prior back-packing	Continuous time on Trail	Total Trail mileage
This trip has given me time to think about personal problems or concerns	-.185**	.062	.117
The more time I spent on this trip, the more I learned about caring for the trail environment	-.169**	.130	.184*
This trip has given me time to think about my relationship to other people	-.153*	.049	.114
This trip has provided relief from daily stresses	-.144*	.124	.169*

NOTE: The table displays correlation coefficients. The more backpacking experience AT hiker have, the less likely they are to report they are contemplating personal problems or experiencing relief from stress. (p=.05*, p=.01**).

TABLES OF SPIRITUAL AND PERSONAL VALUES

Table III.1

The transcendent outcomes with the highest average ratings, and those correlated to mileage completed.

Statement	% very true or true (or untrue or very untrue for negative statements)	Adjusted % very true or true	Average rating	Adjusted average rating	Enhanced by mileage	Enhanced by prayer/ meditation
Contact with nature inspires me to think about God	57	40	3.57	2.86	No	Pre** On**
This trip made me aware of my personal deficiencies and failings	51	37	3.46	2.79	No	Pre* On**
I have felt close to God (gods, spirit) while on this trip	50	36	3.36	2.71	No	Pre** On**
This trip made me more aware of the beauty of God (spirit, gods)	49	36	3.29	2.66	No	Pre** On**
I think about religious or spiritual matters more when I am hiking	45	33	3.24	2.63	No	Pre** On**
This trip has facilitated prayer or meditation	42	31	3.14	2.56	No	Pre** On**
This trip has helped me to correct my own negative attitudes or wrong doing	35	25	3.05	2.49	Yes*	No

Participating in religious ritual prayer or mediation in nature or outdoors has exceptional spiritual, religious or personal meaning	38	28	2.98	2.17	No	Pre** On**
This trip has been spiritual or religious learning experience	39	28	2.95	2.42	No	Pre** On**
This trip has helped me to think about my religious or spiritual responsibilities to other people	35	25	2.94	2.41	No	Pre** On**
While on this trip I felt God (spirit, gods) was guiding me	37	27	2.75	2.27	No	Pre** On**
Mileage correlated statements						
This trip has increased my religious or spiritual commitment	29	21	2.66	2.21	Yes	Pre** On**
This trip has made me more aware of my religious heritage or roots	20	15	2.30	1.94	Yes*	Pre** On**
Statement concerning on-trail community						
I had a sense of spiritual community with the people I encountered on this trip	29	21	2.67	2.21	No	Pre** On**

NOTE: (p=.05*, p=.01**) The adjusted values assign a "1" to the blank responses of those hikers not answering Section 6 of the survey, thus provide *an estimate* of the scores if all hikers, including the very unreligious.

Table III.2

Hiker response to statements that concern personal needs or circumstances or that reflect self-perception.

Statement	% very true or true	Average rating	Domain	Enhanced by mileage	Enhanced by prayer
This trip made me feel positive about the meaning of my life.	66	3.89	Personal	No	Pre** On**
This trip provided a sense of harmony with my life	57	3.73	Personal	No	Pre** On*
This trip gave me a sense of inner peace	58	3.65	Personal	No	Pre** On*
This trip will help me to cope with difficulties in my life	48	3.41	Personal	No	Pre*
I have strengthened old friendships on this trip	38	3.01	Communal	No	No
This trip has helped me to manage a life transition	36	2.87	Personal	Yes**	No
This trip has helped me to break a bad habit	19	2.07	Personal	No	No
This trip has helped me to heal from an emotional or psychological illness, condition or injury	19	2.03	Personal	No	Pre*
This trip has helped me to heal from a physical illness, condition or injury	9	1.56	Personal	No	Pre* On*
This trip has strengthened or improved relationships with my significant other	30	2.58	Communal	No	No

APPENDIX IV

WRITTEN COMMENTS BY RELIGIOUS BACKGROUND

Table IV.1

Selected descriptions of spiritual or religious experiences on the AT from hikers *without a religious identity or affiliation*

Gender and age	Description of spiritual or religious and spiritual experience on trail
Male 24	Spending extensive time in nature provides much time to question the meaning of existence. It has made me think about spirituality and religion and what they mean to me.
Female 30	You have a lot of time for reflection. Also any 'issue' you have in real life will present itself while on the trail, but without the distractions of modern life to interfere with your need to just "deal" with them. You're more likely to consider these things from a deeper spiritual level than just a self-help pop psy[chology] sort of way. Also spending more time in the woods you begin to feel the "imprint" that everyone & everything has left behind. You begin to contemplate the mark you leave behind—both on nature and the people you encounter. You begin to value both a lot more as well.
Male 25	Spiritually, this trail has provided me with time to perfect on my own philosophies and beliefs.
Male 23	Just extend time alone really allows me to do a lot of me-time thinking, which has extended into just allowing myself to calm myself in a way I haven't before.
Male 46	I've had time to contemplate some questions and work out some answers for me regarding spiritual questions.
Male 49	Spiritually more at ease.
Female 25	Being in the wilderness is a religious/spiritual experience, being in God's creation, no?
Male 47	Thankful for the spirit that made the beautiful earth and giving me the ability to experience it.
Female 26	Seeing so many beautiful things in the natural world & experiencing very kind people—all adds to the feeling that there is some kind of spiritual force that touches all of us.
Female 30	It's difficult to define a spiritual experience but I have had moments of peace, awe, and wonder not associated with the everyday and inspired by the vastness of the mountains and the kindness of others.

Male 47	I feel being alone & out in close contact with nature is a chance to become more "in tune" with one's self as well as getting a much broader view of society. In a sense being close to nature is being close to God.
Female 26	"Spiritual" to me is a vague term. Being on the trail has made me feel connected to nature that I feel a part of something larger than humanity. I now see nature from a human perspective like a child learning the people around him are his family. Nature has brought me a certain peace that is its own fulfillment.
Female 23	I've had a chance to read a bit about Zen Buddhism, and I make a point of praying for other people.

Table IV.2

Selected descriptions of spiritual or religious experiences on the AT from hikers who self-identify as Christians but attend services only a few times a year or less.

Gender and age	Description of spiritual or religious and spiritual experience on trail
Male 26	I see God every day in the mountains and the forests and the rivers and the sunsets and the people I've met and I marvel at the fact that God let me live long enough to see all this.
Male 24	Not really sure about specific experiences but hiking has made me think much more about my beliefs or lack thereof.
Male 25	I have learned a lot about my role in a group of people, how people interact with each other & with nature.
Male 41	Not to worry. God takes care of the sparrow, why should I worry.
Female 26	This trip has made me more reflective on my spiritual beliefs—I would like to find a church to join when I return home.
Female 32	God is so evident in the outdoors. People are praying for me and it works. So much Christian ministry along the trail is inspiring.
Male 54	Contemplation on Creation. God vs. science, etc. The evils that men do in the name of God.
Male 59	Mystical experiences are impossible to put into words.
Male 63	The act of meditation is a spiritual experience in and of itself. I am able to center myself and contemplate issues while hiking. It is refreshing to tune out for minutes or hours of activity and not to remember what was happening while in that state.
Male 24	This is God's country. Every sunrise, sunset, or view reflects his gifts to us.
Male 35	Walking through God's creation everyday is an experience but the surprise is that I also find God in the people on the trail and off the trail. We are all children of God. [We are all] creations of God. One day I climbed up a steep rocky vista to take pictures of the views, a storm rolled in one and forced me off the mountain, in haste, I went down the wrong way and was lost in the rain without my pack or rain gear. In a panic I was looking for the trail, the terrain was steep and bushy, and after an hour I threw my hands up. "I'm lost, I can't find my way, lord can you help me." I took a deep breath and started walking within 5 minutes back to the trail. "Amen."
Male 24	By going away from distraction I'm able to focus my life and how to live a more effective Christian life, also the beauty in nature helps me to appreciate God's creation.
Male 26	This hike has provided a spiritual experience through my connection with nature. I wouldn't label it a "religious experience." I've recognized therapeutic benefits by being in the woods all day, every day. It restores balance and relieves stress. It brings forth connection to the earth and other people.
Male 24	Spiritual uplifting—becoming patience & people-helper. Understanding the significance of a mile.

Table IV.3

Selected descriptions of spiritual or religious experiences on the AT from hikers who self-identify as Christians and attend services more than monthly and pray more than weekly

Gender and age	Description of spiritual or religious and spiritual experience on trail
Male 50	I have lots of "free time" on the trail to spend thinking about my life, my purpose, or to talk to God about these things. I also have time to talk to God about others.
Male 51	Thoughts about God and his creation, thoughts about my father who passed away in Jan., and my family.
Male 20	Chance to get away from bustle of "regular" life and contemplate my faith. Also gives me time to read the Bible and experience God's creation.
Male 29	Greater appreciation for the natural world around me. Continually in awe over the "handiwork" of God's creation.
Male 57	I have been able to experience God through the relationships on the trail. The beauty of the landscape has made me experience the face of God.
Male 57	Asceticism—thirst, hunger, extreme physical exhaustion, inner strength summoned when none apparently. Thunderstorms, Sunrise, Sunset, Beautiful Vistas, Animals Fauna/Flora.
Male 54	I am always attempting to stay in the moment and to see how God fills that moment. I turn my will and my life over to God over and over again, only to find worldly thoughts creeping back in—So then I start all over turning my will and my life over for the care of God—I'm attempting to be more faithful—so that when God directs me—I will follow his path without hesitation instead of being tempted to worldly ways.

Table IV.4

Descriptions of spiritual or religious experiences on the AT from hikers who self-identify as Buddhists or Taoists, with identification with other religions, or identify with New Age or earth-centered religion

Gender, age, religion	Description of spiritual or religious and spiritual experience on trail
Male 25, Roman Catholic, Buddhism, Taoism	An understanding of the Catholic Mass as a celebration designed to work through caste boundaries. Everyone is equal and sharing is the point of transubstantiation. Therefore it can be a faith of works, not confined in politics or ritual. That and everybody needs reconciliation.
Male 25, Pagan, Buddhist, Unitarian, Agnostic	Nature is amazing. You see and experience it every day. You have a short finite time on this planet. Too many of us DO NOT take advantage of what we have, or can experience. Spirituality can be viewed as what we take away from an experience.
Male 25, Pagan, Buddhism, Hinduism, Native American, New Age	Occasional moment of mind-body "Zen" unity.
Male 50, Buddhism, Christianity, Native American	Uplifting—To be away from civilization and in tune with nature.
Male 22, New Age, Buddhism, Presbyterian, Grand Unified Theory	A general/specific connectedness to the world around me. Feeling part of a larger whole.
Male 28, all religions checked	I have come to realize the flow of the universe. That if you let go of the ego/self and submit/surrender to this flow, you may enter into a period of growth not known—in fact unknown by our small ego. Our ideas of what is best for us and what is TRULY best for us are different things. When we empty ourselves some divinity rushes in to fill the void. Love is all you need.
Female 39, Christianity, Islam, Buddhism, New Age	Connection to God via natural world, introspection.
Male 33, Earth-centered	I am in church every day as I walk in the woods.
Male 47, New Age	I ask him about things I should do. He tells me my answers. Most of the time they don't come when I ask but sometimes days after.

Appendix IV.5

Descriptions of spiritual or religious experiences on the AT from hikers who self-identify as Buddhists or Taoists, without identification with other religions.

Gender, age, religion	Description of spiritual or religious and spiritual experience on trail
Male 24, Taoism	Spiritual connection w[ith] the earth, feel my presence in the circle of existence. *Comment on God:* Either the universal intelligence puts itself in motion for every separate effect, and if this is so, be content with that which is the result of its activity; or it has put itself in motion once, and everything comes by way of sequence in a manner: or indivisible elements are the origin of all things. In a word, if there is a god, all is well, and if chance rules, do not thou also be governed by it? (Marcus Aurelius)
Male 22, Taoism & Buddhism	Lots of time to meditate. Lots of valuable life lessons learned from nature. *Comment on God:* Whatever he/she/it is I have no reason to put it into words. It would be impossible to describe accurately, and right to describe inaccurately.
Female 27 Buddhism	On the trail, you tend to realize that many situations go beyond "mere coincidence." There is definitely a higher power overseeing things in life.
Male 22 Theravada Buddhism	The trip has given me lots of time to think and gain insights from some wise and interesting figures. Most of all it has given me the opportunity to try and stay calm and at peace during hardship.
Male 39 Mahayana Buddhism	Daily meditation. *Comment on God:* God is not a separate being. God is a force that is present in all.

NOTES

PREFACE

1. Susan Bratton, *Christianity, Wilderness and Wildlife: The Original Desert Solitaire* (Scranton, PA: University of Scranton Press, 2009); Belden Lane, *The Solace of Fierce Landscapes: Exploring Desert and Mountain Spirituality* (New York: Oxford University Press, 1998).

2. Jamie Korngold, *God in the Wilderness: Rediscovering the Spirituality of the Great Outdoors with the Adventure Rabbi* (New York: Doubleday, 2007)

3. Mike Comins, *A Wild Faith: Jewish Ways into Wilderness, Wilderness Ways into Judaism* (Woodstock, VT: Jewish Lights Press, 2007).

4. John Lionberger, *Renewal in the Wilderness: A Spiritual Guide to Connecting with God in the Natural World* (Woodstock, VT: Skylight Press, 2007).

5. Laura Waterman and Guy Waterman, *Forest and Crag: A History of Hiking, Trail Blazing, and Adventure in the Northeast Mountains* (Boston: Appalachian Mountain Club Books, 2003).

6. Rebecca Solnit, *Wanderlust: A History of Walking* (New York: Penguin Books, 2000).

7. Stephen Altschuler, *The Mindful Hiker: On the Trail to Find the Path* (Camarillo, CA: DeVorss Publications, 2004).

8. Jill Dubisch, "Healing 'the wounds that are not visible': A Vietnam veterans' motorcycle pilgrimage," in Jill Dubisch and Michael Winkelman, *Pilgrimage and Healing* (Tucson: University of Arizona Press, 2005), 135–54.

9. Lee Gilmore, "Embers, dust, and ashes: Pilgrimage and healing at the Burning Man Festival," in Dubish and Winkelman, *Pilgrimage and Healing,* 155–78.

10. Roderick Nash, *Wilderness and the American Mind,* 4th ed. (New Haven, CT: Yale University Press, 2001).

11. Because I am often asked, I have, as of this writing, walked somewhere between seven hundred and eight hundred miles of the AT one-way, and because I have strolled some sections multiple times, and most of the sections I have covered were walked in both directions, my total mileage is more than 1,600. I am most familiar with the southern end of the AT, specifically the Great Smokies, and am least familiar with the far north.

CHAPTER 1

1. Russell Johnson and Kerry Moran, *Tibet's Sacred Mountain: The Extraordinary Pilgrimage to Mount Kailas* (Rochester, VT: Park Street Press, 1989).

2. James Harpur, *Sacred Tracks: 2000 Years of Christian Pilgrimage* (Cambridge, MA: Harvard University Press, 2002).

3. Marc P. Keane, *Japanese Garden Design* (Rutland, VT: Charles E. Tuttle, 1996); David A. Slawson, *Secret Teachings in the Art of Japanese Gardens: Design Principles, Aesthetic Values* (Tokyo: Kodansha Int., 1987).

4. Information on the history of the Trail may be found on the official Web site of the Appalachian Trail Conservancy, www.appalachiantrail.org.

5. S. Steven Hawks, 1994, "Spiritual health: definition and theory," *Wellness Perspectives* 10, no. 1: 3–13. Paul Heintzman's leisure studies articles utilize this definition.

6. Gordon Mursell, ed., *Christian Spirituality: Two Thousands Years from East to West* (Minneapolis: Fortress Press, 2001), 9.

7. Benton MacKaye, "An Appalachian Trail: A project in regional planning," *Journal of the American Institute of Architects* 9 (October 1921): 325–30. Larry Anderson, *Benton MacKaye: Conservationist, Planner and Creator of the Appalachian Trail* (Baltimore, MD: Johns Hopkins University Press, 2002) contains a copy of the original proposal on pages 372–79. See also Waterman and Waterman, *Forest and Crag*; Georgia Appalachian Trail Club History Committee, *Friendships of the Trail: The History of the Georgia Appalachian Trail Club, 1930–1980* (Atlanta: Georgia Appalachian Trail Club, 1995).

8. Barbara Novak, *Nature and Culture: American Landscape Painting, 1825–1875* (New York: Oxford University Press, 1980); Robert L. McGrath, *Gods in Granite: The Art of the White Mountains of New Hampshire* (Syracuse, NY: Syracuse University Press, 2001).

9. John Gatta, *Making Nature Sacred: Literature, Religion, and Environment in American from the Puritans to the Present* (New York: Oxford University Press, 2004).

10. I wrote this section after hearing William Cronan speak at the Amon Carter Museum in Fort Worth, TX, on November 10, 2007. Cronan was interpreting an exhibit of the photographs of Frank Goehlke, many of which unite human development with natural features, rather than separating them.

11. The Appalachian Trail Conservancy Web site provides statistics on 2,000-milers.

12. Victor Turner and Edith Turner, *Image and Pilgrimage in Christian Culture: Anthropological Perspectives* (New York: Columbia University Press, 1978); Peter Brown, *The Cult of the Saints: Its Rise and Function in Latin Christianity* (Chicago: University of Chicago Press, 1981).

13. Joseph L. Price, "Naturalistic Recreations," in Peter van Ness, ed., *Spirituality and the Sacred Quest* (New York: Crossroads Press, 1996), 414–44.

14. A. Whitney Sanford, "Pinned on karma rock: Whitewater kayaking as religious experience," *Journal of the American Academy of Religion* 75, no. 4 (2007): 875–95. See also Bron Taylor, "Focus introduction: Aquatic nature religion," *Journal of the American Academy of Religion* 75, no. 4 (2007): 863–74.

15. Samuel Snyder, "New streams of religion: Fly fishing as a lived, religion of nature," *Journal of the American Academy of Religion* 75, no. 4 (2007): 896–922. See also Bron Taylor, "Surfing into spirituality and a new, aquatic nature religion," *Journal of the American Academy of Religion* 75, no. 4 (2007): 923–51.

16. Paul Heintzman and Roger C. Mannell, "Spiritual functions of leisure and spiritual well-being: Coping with time pressure," *Leisure Sciences* 25 (2003): 207–30.

17. Paul Heintzman, "A conceptual model of leisure and spiritual well-being," *Journal of Park and Recreation Administration* 20, no. 4 (2002): 147–69.

18. John Fisher, Leslie Francis, and Peter Johnson, "Assessing spiritual health via four domains of spiritual well-being: The SH4DI," *Pastoral Psychology* 49, no. 2 (2000): 133–45; Gwyther Rees, Leslie Francis, and Many Robbins, *Spiritual Health and the Well-Being of Urban Young People* (Bangor, Wales: Commission on Urban Life and Faith, University of Wales, 2005).

19. Gwen K. Neville, *Kinship and Pilgrimage: Rituals of Reunion in American Protestant Culture* (New York: Oxford University Press, 1987); Harpur, *Sacred Tracks;* Sarah Hopper, *To Be A Pilgrim: The Medieval Pilgrimage Experience* (Phoenix Mill, UK: Sutton Publishing, 2002).

20. Numerous guides to pilgrimage in Europe and elsewhere in the world are available and they offer insights into pilgrimage landscapes. Examples are: Jennifer Westwood, *On Pilgrimage: Sacred Journeys around the World* (Mahwah, NJ: Hidden Spring of Paulist Press, 2003); Kevin J. Wright, *Catholic Shrines of Western Europe* (Liguori, MO: Liguori Press, 1997); and Bernard Jackson, *Places of Pilgrimage* (London: Geoffrey Chapman, 1989).

21. Juan Eduardo Campo, "American pilgrimage landscapes," *Annuals of the American Academy of Political and Social Science* 588, Americans and Religions in the Twenty-First Century (1998): 40–56.

22. Matthew Davis and Michael Farrell Scott, *Opening the Mountain: Circumambulating Mount Tamalpais, A Ritual Walk* (Emeryville, CA: Shoemaker & Hoard, 2006).

23. Sarah M. Pike, *New Age and Neo-Pagan Religions in America* (New York: Columbia University Press, 2004), 33–34.

24. Bratton, *Christianity, Wilderness and Wildlife;* Lane, *Solace of Fierce Landscapes.*

25. Simon Coleman and John Elsner, *Pilgrimage: Past and Present in the World Religions* (Cambridge, MA: Harvard University Press, 1995); Richard Barber, *Pilgrimages* (Suffolk, UK: Woodbridge Press, 1991).

26. Peter Harbison, *Pilgrimage in Ireland: The Monuments and the People* (Syracuse, NY: Syracuse University Press, 1991).

27. Paul Post, Jos Pieper, and Marinus van Uden, *The Modern Pilgrim: Multidisciplinary Explorations of Christian Pilgrimage* (Lueven, Netherlands: Peeters, 1998).

28. Ralph Waldo Emerson, Henry David Thoreau, and J. Elder, ed., *Nature/Walking* (Boston: Beacon Press, 1994).

29. Donald McKinney, *Walking the Mist: Celtic Spirituality for the 21st Century* (London: Hodder and Stoughton, 2004).

30. Altschuler, *The Mindful Hiker.*

31. Geoffrey Chaucer and Nevill Coghill (trans.), *Canterbury Tales* (New York: Penguin Group, 2003).

32. I have hiked Cuthbert's Way from Melrose to Lindisfarne, and day hiked some short sections of Declan's Way.

33. David Adam, *Fire of the North: The Illustrated Life of Cuthbert* (London: SPCK Press, 1993). Walkers headed for Lindisfarne or Holy Island can also enjoy Adam's volumes of religious poetry.

34. John W. Neff, *Katahdin: An Historic Journey* (Boston: Appalachian Mountain Club Books, 2006); Henry David Thoreau, "A week on the Concord and Merrimac Rivers," in Catherine Albanese, *The Spirituality of the American Transcendentalists* (Atlanta: Mercer University Press, 1988), 241–65; Eric Pinder, *North to Katahdin* (Minneapolis: Milkweed Editions, 2005).

35. Campo, "American pilgrimage landscapes," 50–51. Graceland was the home of rock and roll icon Elvis Presley.

36. Kip Redick, "Wilderness as *axis mundi:* Spiritual journeys on the Appalachian Trail," in Gary Backhuas and John Muungi, eds., *Symbolic Landscapes* (New York: Springer Verlag, 2009), 65–90.

37. John C. Hendee and Chad P. Dawson, *Wilderness Management: Stewardship and Protection Resources and Values,* 3rd ed. (Golden, CO: Fulcrum Press, 2002).

38. L. Graber, *Wilderness as Sacred Space,* Monograph Series, No. 8 (Washington, DC: American Society of Geographers, 1976).

39. Thomas Vale, *The American Wilderness: Reflections on Nature Protection in the United States* (Charlottesville: University of Virginia Press, 2005), 13–17.

CHAPTER 2

1. William Birchard and Robert Proudman, *Appalachian Trail Design, Construction and Maintenance*, 2nd ed. (Harpers Ferry, WV: Appalachian Trail Conference, 2000), 3.

2. Appalachian Trail Conservancy Web site, September 20, 2009.

3. Regional descriptions rely on my field experience and the Trail guides for the sections. These are listed in the references at the end of this volume.

4. Appalachian Trail Conservancy Web site.

5. To get an overview of just how treacherous the weather can be, see Nicholas Howe, *Not Without Peril: 150 Years of Misadventure on the Presidential Range of New Hampshire* (Boston: Appalachian Mountain Club Books, 2000).

6. MacKaye, "An Appalachian Trail."

7. Neff, *Katahdin.*

8. The Web site of the Appalachian Trail Conservancy will offer current data.

CHAPTER 3

1. Rick Sawatzky, Pamela Ratner, and Lyren Chiu, "A meta-analysis of the relationship between spirituality and quality of life," *Social Indicators Research* 72 (2005): 153–88; Lawrence Beck, "The Phenomenology of Optimal Experiences Attained by Whitewater River Recreationists in Canyonlands National Park," Ph.D. diss., University of Minnesota, 1987; Roland Mueser, *Long Distance Hiking: Lessons from the Appalachian Trail* (Camden, ME: Ragged Mountain Press, 1998); Todd Ogryzlo, *The Outcomes of a Wilderness Experience: Perception and Trip Intensity of Stress Reduction,* master's thesis, Laurentian University of Sudbury (Ontario), 1998.

2. Appalachian Trail Conservancy Web site, September 20, 2009.

3. While notifying the ATC about the survey, I made no attempt to obtain permission to sample on the AT itself, owing to the religious content of the questionnaire. I did obtain permission to contact hikers from private property adjoining the trail, at church-run facilities, and at a municipal park. The original design called for two hundred hiker surveys and anticipated that about 20 to 30 percent would be individuals attempting the entire trail, while the remainder of the respondents would be section hikers and backpackers on short trips.

4. Those needing supplies may decide to reach a hostel in midafternoon so they have time to shop, while others may straggle in just after dark, having maximized their mileage for the day. When we tried midday sampling near two road intersections where AT hikers frequently stop for ice cream or sandwiches, two problems emerged immediately. We could wait for two or three hours and not see anyone. Second, the hikers did

not wish to delay their walk during prime daylight hiking time. We thus offered them surveys to take and fill out later, but very few of these were returned via mail. Distribution and mail back is simply too logistically complex along the trail, and the hikers resist carrying any additional clutter.

5. Saint Thomas Episcopal Church in Vernon, NJ. We tried offering both hiking food and necessary items such as boot laces as an incentive, while not requiring the hikers to fill out the survey, if they took a free dinner. We also offered to make a $5 donation to a church-run hostel for each completed survey.

6. We checked the hiker logs or the number of hikers encountered against the number of surveys received to obtain a rough estimate of percentage returns. Meeting in midday near the trail returned less than 15 percent. Hostel returns were generally between 40 and 50 percent per week of survey time. We inspected the drop box surveys to make certain the handwriting varied, and no respondents were filling out more than one. Initially we intended to collect only one survey from each group traveling together. This strategy proved impractical. If one member of a hiking partnership fills out the survey, other members are likely to want to participate. Further, because hiking partnerships often form informally among hikers keeping a common pace, the types of relationships vary from married couples to hikers who not only did not know each other prior to the trip, but they were resident on different continents. Considering that more men than women hike on the AT, having more than one member of a group respond probably did not prejudice the survey significantly and helped to prevent undersampling women and individuals traveling with family members.

7. The practice of off-trail and hostel collection also makes replies by high-mileage backpackers and those who prefer to stay at shelters or camp by themselves on trail less likely. Hikers with greater financial means often reserve better accommodations, such as hotel rooms, and are potentially undersampled. Because we began the survey in late June, we missed the first northbound through hikers crossing the New Jersey–New York line, although the hiker box continued through next spring and picked up surveys from early season northbound end-to-enders. Analysis of the first surveys did indicate minor increases in the proportion of female hikers and average age of the hikers as the summer wore on. We found no evidence that non-Christians avoid church-based hostels; however, it is possible that a few practitioners of alternative religions may not have been willing to stop where we operated the hiker drop box.

8. All the statistical analyses and summaries were conducted using SPSS version 16.0 or 17.0, SPSS, Inc., Chicago. The programs utilized were primarily Frequency, Crosstabs, and Correlation. The data were inserted in an Excel matrix and then converted to SPSS. Two respondents under the age of eighteen were eliminated from the data set.

9. Gerald Kyle, Alan Graefe, Robert Manning, and James Bacon, "An examination of the relationship between leisure activity involvement and place attachment among hikers along the Appalachian Trail," *Journal of Leisure Research* 35, no. 3 (2003): 249–73.

10. Mueser, *Long Distance Hiking,* 14–20.

11. Edward B. Garvey, *The New Appalachian Trail* (Birmingham, AL: Menasha Ridge Press, 1997), 9.

12. Posting from the Earl Schaffer Foundation, in the Place Hostel, Damascus, VA.

13. In 2007, a Japanese crew was filming a documentary on the trail, for release in Japan. Informants who manage tourist facilities mentioned that Japanese outdoor enthusiasts have shown an increasing interest in the AT in recent years.

14. Of the section hikers, 71 percent were traveling interstate, while 29 percent of the section hikers, or roughly 5 percent of the survey respondents, were traveling within New Jersey or New York, or were on a jaunt over the NY/NJ state line.

15. This figure had to be approximate, as some AT thru-hikers usually hitchhiked into town, while others were inclined to walk. Some "thru" hikers still skipped trail sections, and others backtracked or diverted—to visit nearby peaks, to find friends, or even to retrieve lost gear. The survey included questions about vehicle support and alternative transportation, but only one hiker reported using a bicycle, and no thru-hikers reported vehicle support, while several section hikers did. This may not be accurate, however, because friends and relatives do bring vehicles when they join thru-hikers for short sections, and some thru-hikers do park vehicles and return to them. The interpretation of the question probably varied among respondents.

16. Only three respondents, all section hikers, reported traveling in a hiking party with a guide or leader.

17. Mueser, *Long Distance Hiking,* 17.

18. Actual figures are 11.2, 4.9, and 3.4 percent.

19. Using the Pearson method of Chi-square.

20. I originally used Hendee and Dawson, *Wilderness Management,* 399.

21. Ibid., 399. After I completed the data collection for this study, Chad Dawson and John Hendee published a fourth edition reversing the senior authorship: *Wilderness Management: Stewardship and Protection of Resources and Values* (Golden, CO: Fulcrum Press, 2009). The trends in wilderness use remain the same into the twenty-first century. Their new demographic section is pages 375–85.

22. David Cole, Alan E. Watson, and Joseph Roggenbuck, "Trends in wilderness visitors and visits: Boundary Waters Canoe Area, Shining Rock, and Desolation Wilderness," *Wilderness Research Paper* INT-RP-483 (Ogden, UT: USDA Forest Service Intermountain Research Station, 1995).

23. Hendee and Dawson, *Wilderness Management,* 302–93.

24. The survey was not open to hikers under eighteen years old. Field observation at the hostels indicated a few parents going long distances were traveling with children,

particularly teenagers. This is relatively rare, however. Because parent-child combinations made up 3 percent of respondents, and the majority of these were parents walking with recent college graduates, parents with younger children are potentially less than 1 percent of the total thru-hiking parties.

25. Hendee and Dawson, *Wilderness Management*, 400.

26. Ibid., 276–79.

27. Ibid., 390–91.

28. Ibid., 390–92.

29. M. E. "Postcard" Hughes, *We're Off to See the Wilderness, The Wonderful Wilderness of Awes* (Bloomington, IN: Xlibris Corporation, 2005), 11.

30. Robert Alden Rubin, *On the Beaten Path: An Appalachian Pilgrimage* (Guilford, CT: Lyons Press, 2001), 3.

31. David Miller, *AWOL on the Appalachian Trail* (Livermore, CA: Wingspan Press, 2006), 1.

32. J. R. "Model T" Tate, *Walkin' on the Happy Side of Misery* (Bloomington, IN: Xlibris, 2001), 13.

33. Adrienne Hall, *A Journey North* (Boston: Appalachian Mountain Club Books, 2000), ix.

34. Solitude was, more precisely, a major goal for 7.6 percent.

35. Jay Platt, *A Time to Walk: Life Lessons Learned on the Appalachian Trail* (Carterville, GA: Eagle Eye Publishing, 2000), 4–8.

36. Bill Irwin with David McCasland, *Blind Courage* (Waco, TX: WRS Publishing, 1996), 22–31.

37. Ibid., 51.

38. Harold Howell and Amy Adams, *Encountering God on the Appalachian Trail* (Colorado Springs, CO: Peak Press, 2003).

39. Madeline Cornelius, *Katahdin with Love: An Inspirational Journey* (Lookout Mountain, TN: Milton Publishing, 1991); Jean Deeds, *There are Mountains to Climb: An Inspirational Journey* (Indianapolis, IN: Silverwood Press, 2003).

40. Marni Goldenberg, Eddie Hill, and Barbara Freidt, "Why individuals hike the Appalachian Trail: A qualitative approach to benefits," *Journal of Experiential Education* 30, no. 3 (2008): 277–81.

41. Mueser, *Long Distance Hiking*, 7–8.

42. Michael Murray and Brian Graham, "Exploring the dialectics of route-based tourism: the Camino de Santiago," *Tourism Management* 18, no. 8 (1997): 513–24.

43. Because the Baylor team had just released their first findings, I initially utilized their Internet report for the original survey design: Christopher Bader, Kevin Dougherty, Paul Froese, Byron Johnson, F. Carson Mencken, Jerry Z. Park, and Rodney Stark, *American Piety in the 21st Century: New Insights into the Depth and Complexity of Religion in the US, Selected Findings from The Baylor Study of American Religion* (Waco, TX: Baylor University, 2006). Rodney Stark then published a very readable paperback, *What Americans Really Believe* (Waco, TX: Baylor University Press, 2008). The Baylor survey, which was originally conducted in 2006, followed by additional surveys in 2007 and 2008, drew a large, randomly selected sample of U.S. residents and determined their degree of religious affiliations and engagement in religious activities. In 2006, useful papers on alternative religions and nature included: Bron Taylor, "Earth and nature based spirituality (Part II): From Earth First! and Bioregionalism to Scientific Paganism and the New Age," *Religion* 31 (2001): 225–45; and Phillip C. Almond, "Druids, patriarchs and the primordial religion," *Journal of Contemporary Religion* 15, no. 3 (2000): 379–94.

44. Adding to 101 percent because of rounding up—21.6 percent had no religious or spiritual engagement on or off trail, 21.6 percent had a nominal tie, and 56.9 percent were regularly engaged.

45. Stark, *What Americans Really Believe*, 1–16.

46. Ibid., 61–68.

47. One response of a hiker who wrote "Methodist, Episcopal" could mean either two denominations or Methodist-Episcopal which is a largely African American denomination. From a survey of about two hundred, the expected memberships in African American denominations would have been about ten responses, instead of one or zero.

48. Such as United Methodists as opposed to Free Methodists. The survey included both Southern and American Baptists, for example.

49. Goldenberg, Hill, and Freidt, "Why individuals hike the Appalachian Trail."

50. M. T. Allison and J. E. Schneider, eds., *Diversity and the Recreation Profession: Organizational Prospective* (State College, PA: Venture Publishing, 2000); Paul H. Gobster, "Managing urban parks for a racially diverse and ethnically diverse clientele," *Leisure Sciences* (2002): 143–59; Staron Faucher, *Ethnic Preferences in Outdoor Recreation, Cameron Park, TX*, master's thesis, Baylor University, 2009.

51. Stark, *What Americans Really Believe*, 95–100.

52. Patterns differed by region, however. High-income individuals were more likely to be involved if living on the West Coast, but in the South, lower-income women outscored women with higher family incomes on the New Age index. Stark, *What Americans Really Believe*, 125–31.

53. A recent study in the United Kingdom found that individual construction of a religious belief system was becoming more common, and paralleled a reduction in

membership in the Church of England. Pauk Heelas and Linda Woodhead, *The Spiritual Revolution: Why Religion is Giving Way to Spirituality* (Oxford, UK: Blackwell Publishing, 2005).

54. Stark, *What Americans Really Believe,* 8–14.

55. Note that many of the respondents would not be on the trail for the two major Christian holidays, Christmas and Easter.

56. Stark, *What Americans Really Believe,* 1–16, 61–68.

57. Ibid., 61–68.

CHAPTER 4

1. The methods were reviewed and approved by the Baylor University Institutional Review Board. Additionally, in terms of protocol, we preferred a casual location, such as a kitchen, office, or front porch. If the interviewee became skeptical or wished to terminate the conversation, we stopped the interview immediately. We answered all queries from the interviewees, providing any requested background, such as graduate degrees, trail experience, and even denominational background. Where polite, we utilized the commercial facility in question, such as the food service or camping area, and if invited, had a cup of tea, lunch, or a snack. The student assistant, Robert Kent, was trained via practice interviews and was instructed in the use of release forms and in appropriate responses to individuals refusing an interview. The interviewees were given a chance to recover the release and the interview notes at the end of the conversation, and thereby not to have the conversation recorded. Interviewees who were clergy or spiritual advisors were assured they did not have to violate anyone's confidence. The release would indicate if the individual was willing to be quoted. The notes would remain confidential and the release of information about illegal activities or conflicts between hikers and service establishments has been edited to remove identifiers. Data collection was in handwritten notes stored in notebooks. Additional comments from the interviewer were assembled after each interview. The initial goal was forty interviews, but to obtain a north-south balance, a second sequence was added in 2008.

2. The interviews form three geographic sequences: in New England from Gorham, NH, through Connecticut; from Pawling, NY, to Palmerton, PA; and from Waynesboro, VA, south to the first road crossing north of Springer Mountain in Georgia. We located potential interviewees by two methods: 1) calling or e-mailing in advance and requesting an interview; or 2) preferably, going to the establishment and making arrangements for an interview. The minimum length for an interview was about fifteen minutes, while typical interviews lasted about forty minutes. Because the interviews were open-ended, however, a number of conversations with very well-informed individuals lasted as long

as three hours. We requested written permission to use the information, and interviewees provided a second, separate signature if they were willing to have their name or the name of their business attached to their statements. We allowed interviewees to delete material if they wished and to skip questions they did not want to answer, as well stop the conversation when they wished. Some of the comments reported in this chapter are anonymous, to honor the wishes of informants or to avoid identifying sources of commentaries on specific hiker or helper behaviors.

3. These questions were used as prompts. The vocabulary was varied to suit the context, and questions were dropped if inappropriate or already answered in the general course of the interview:

1. What services or assistance do you offer?
2. Why did you or your congregation, organization, family, etc. decide to open a hostel, campground, etc.? Why did you decide to get involved with AT hikers?
3. What is your background or training?
4. Do you see the hostel as a service to others (or ministry)?
5. Does interaction with hikers benefit your organization in any way?
6. Do you think your organization provides any social or personal (spiritual) benefits to hikers?
7. Are any of the founders of this operation or yourself AT hikers?
8. Have any hikers told you anything of their spiritual or personal motivations? Do any stories or individuals stand out?
9. What do you think motivates the thru-hikers?
10. What kind of positive interactions does your organization have with hikers?
11. Do hikers do anything that is a problem for the church or hostel? (no names, please)
12. What do you think is most important about your (hostel, campground, service)?
13. Anything else?

4. Cynthia Taylor-Miller, ed., *Appalachian Trail Thru-Hikers' Companion 2007* (Harpers Ferry, WV: Appalachian Trail Conservancy, 2007).

5. Cynthia Taylor-Miller and Carol Barnes, eds., *Appalachian Trail Thru-Hikers' Companion 2006* (Harpers Ferry, WV: Appalachian Trail Conservancy, 2006); Taylor-Miller,

ed., *Thru-Hikers' Companion 2007;* Leslie Mass, ed., *Appalachian Trail Thru-Hiker's Companion* (Harpers Ferry, WV: Appalachian Trail Conference, 2008).

6. The source is not Miss Janet, but other interviewees in Erwin, TN.

7. Luke 6:31. This version is from Bruce Metzger and Roland Murphy, *The New Oxford Annotated Bible* (New York: Oxford University Press, 1994).

8. The context is the parable of the talents. Matthew 25:34–40, which describes those individuals who join Christ in heaven, reads: "Then the king will say to those at his right hand, 'Come, you that are blessed by my Father, inherit the kingdom prepared for you from the foundation of the world; for I was hungry and you gave me food, and I was thirsty and you gave me something to drink. I was a stranger and you welcomed me, I was naked and you gave me clothing, I was sick and you took care of me, I was in prison and you visited me.' Then the righteous will answer him: 'Lord, when was it that we saw you hungry and gave you food, or thirsty and gave you something to drink? And when was it that we saw you a stranger and welcomed you, or naked and gave you clothing? And when was it that we saw you sick or in prison and visited you?' And the king will answer them, 'Truly I tell you, just as you did it to one of the least of these, you are members of my family, you did it to me.'"

9. The New Revised Standard reads: "Do not neglect to show hospitality to strangers for by doing that some have entertained angels without knowing it." (Hebrews 13:2) 1 Peter 4:9 advises: "Be hospitable to one another without complaining."

10. Bill Bryson, *A Walk in the Woods: Rediscovering America on the Appalachian Trail* (New York: Broadway Books, 1999).

11. Garvey, *New Appalachian Trail,* 289.

CHAPTER 5

1. Information was taken from logs at the retreat center.

2. Numinous experience is an intense feeling of the presence of the divine or of something beyond the individual self, or of the unity of the cosmos.

3. The passenger railroad for the United States.

4. Psalm 121. Other relevant passages include Psalm 46:1, 1 Corinthians 1:25, and Ephesians 6:10.

5. The team includes MDs and RNs rather than mere first-aiders.

CHAPTER 6

1. Field observation of pizza delivery in the mid-Atlantic region.

2. Rubin, *On the Beaten Path*, 167.

3. Hikers have been arrested for indecent exposure when they have gone "slow-streaking" over township lines.

4. This research was conducted in Great Smoky Mountains National Park and along the AT outside the park. The heavily used Smokies had much more evidence of problems with human waste disposal than the adjoining region. The information gleaned was used specifically to address privy management.

5. Color as of 2007.

6. Appalachian Trail Conservancy, no date, Suggestions for Trail Magic, pdf handout, accessed May 8, 2009, on http://www.appalachiantrail.org/what-we-do/trail-management-support/volunteer_toolkit/trail-management-policies.

7. Some of the project work I completed in the Great Smokies in the 1970s investigated the question of whether shelters caused excessive impact on natural resources.

CHAPTER 7

1. This is a standard method for preventing "cheating" when collecting surveys.

2. Historic accounts of tensions between human beings and nature in Western culture include Clarence Glacken, *Traces on the Rhodian Shore* (Berkeley: University of California Press, 1967); H. Paul Santmire, *The Travail of Nature: The Ambiguous Ecological Promise of Christian Theology* (Philadelphia: Fortress Press, 1985); Max Oelschalger, *The Idea of Wilderness: From Prehistory to the Age of Ecology* (New Haven, CT: Yale University Press, 1991); and Roderick Nash's very well-circulated review of Euro-American attitudes grading from antagonism to love for wilderness: *Wilderness and the American Mind*.

3. Vale, *American Wilderness*, 24–25.

4. Ibid., 34–36.

5. Overviews of the field of environmental ethics cover the first two questions and further define anthropocentric, biocentric, and ecocentric. Some useful volumes are Robin Attfield, *The Ethics of Environmental Concern* (New York: Columbia University Press, 1983); Susan Armstrong and Richard Boltzer, *Environmental Ethics: Divergence and Convergence* (New York: McGraw Hill, 2003); Baird Callicott, *Beyond the Land Ethic* (Albany: State University of New York Press, 1999); Eugene Hargrove, *Foundations of*

Environmental Ethics (Albany: State University of New York Press, 1992); Ralston Holmes III, *Environmental Ethics: Duties to and Values in the Natural World* (Philadelphia: Temple University Press, 2003); and Lisa Newton, Catherine Dillingham, and Joanne Choly, *Watershed 4: Ten Cases in Environmental Ethics* (Belmont, CA: Thomas Wadsworth, 2006).

6. The questionnaire utilizes a Likert scale. This allows for a gradation of answers. The method has been widely utilized in opinion surveys.

7. The nonparametric tests were Mann-Whitney U, Kruskal-Wallis, and Chi-squares. These are included here when they provide additional information.

8. Buddy Newell, *You Won't Get to Maine Unless You Walk in the Rain* (Littleton, NH: Bondcliff Books, 2002).

9. Jeff Alt, *A Walk for Sunshine: A 2,160 Mile Expedition for Charity on the Appalachian Trail* (Cincinnati: Dreams Shared Publications, 2000).

10. I have done this a number of times myself, including taking a trip to Lourdes when my mother and my aunt were both ill. And I immersed myself in the freezing water more than once, standing in for them. I have also brought water back from holy wells for my older Irish relatives. My own experience is that the emotional impact of these exchanges is high. The aspect of shared belief accentuates the meaning of going out of one's way to fetch the water, and such pilgrimage is an active attempt to seek healing in cases where the doctors have already run out of options.

11. The correlation coefficients in this section are determined by the Pearson method. Probability for the 3.6 and 3.7 being different was .117.

12. Alt, *Walk for Sunshine*, 105.

13. Ibid., 106.

14. Scott Weidensaul, *Mountains of the Heart: A Natural History of the Appalachians* (Golden, CO: Fulcrum Publishing, 1994).

15. Nancy Slack and Allison Bell, *The AMC Field Guide to the New England Alpine Summits*, 2nd ed. (Boston: Appalachian Mountain Club Books, 2006).

16. Steve Nash, *Blue Ridge 2020: An Owner's Manual* (Chapel Hill: University of North Carolina Press, 1999).

17. See, for example, Conrad L. Kanagy and Hart M. Nelson, "Religion and environmental concern: Challenging the dominant assumptions," *Review of Religious Research* 37, no. 1 (1995): 33–45; Andrew Greeley, "Religion and attitudes toward the environment," *Journal for the Scientific Study of Religion* 32, no. 1 (1993): 19–28; Douglas Lee Eckberg and T. Jean Blocker, "Christianity, environmentalism and the theoretical problem of fundamentalism," *Journal for the Scientific Study of Religion* 35, no. 4 (1996): 343–55.

18. Douglas Lee Eckberg and T. Jean Blocker, "Varieties of religious involvement and environmental concerns: Testing the Lynn White thesis," *Journal for the Scientific Study of Religion* 28, no. 4 (1989): 509–17.

19. Justin G. Longnecker, Joseph A. McKinney, and Carlos W. Moore, "Religious intensity, Evangelical Christianity, and business ethics: An empirical study," *Journal of Business Ethics* 55 (2004): 373–86.

20. The following are a selection of volumes on the topic. The most recent have extensive bibliographies referencing the available Christian literature. Catherine Albanese, *Nature Religion in America: From the Algonkian Indians to the New Age* (Chicago: University of Chicago Press, 1990) reviews nature religion during the historic period, from colonial contact through the twentieth century, for the United States. Sources on Christianity include: Robert Booth Fowler, *The Greening of Protestant Thought* (Chapel Hill: University of North Carolina Press, 1995); Loren Wilkinson, ed., *Earthkeeping in the '90s: Stewardship of Creation* (Grand Rapids, MI: William B. Eerdmans, 1991); Steven Bouma-Prediger, *For the Beauty of the Earth: A Christian Vision of Creation Care* (Grand Rapids, MI: Baker Academic Books, 2001); Robert J. Berry, ed., *Environmental Stewardship: Critical Perspectives, Past and Present* (London: Continuum Publishing, 2006); Willis Jenkins, *Ecologies of Grace: Environmental Ethics and Christian Theology* (New York: Oxford University Press, 2008); Roger S. Gottlieb, *A Greener Faith: Religious Environmentalism and Our Planet's Future* (New York: Oxford University Press, 2006); and Norman Wirzba, *The Paradise of God: Renewing Religion in an Ecological Age* (New York: Oxford University Press, 2003).

21. See Susan Power Bratton, "Ecology and Religion," in Philip Clayton and Zachary Simpson, *The Oxford Handbook of Religion and Science* (Oxford: Oxford University Press, 2008), 207–25; David Landis Barnhill and Roger S. Gottlieb, eds., *Deep Ecology and World Religions* (Albany: State University of New York Press, 2001); Laurel Kearns and Catherine Keller, eds., *Ecospirit: Religions and Philosophies for the Earth* (New York: Fordham University Press, 2007); David E. Cooper and Simon P. James, *Buddhism, Virtue and Environment* (Aldershot, UK: Ashgate Publishing, 2005).

22. Judaism and Christianity are dominant for this survey, while Islam is also considered an Abrahamic faith.

23. The sample size is small here, so additional completed surveys might have modified this outcome.

24. I did try separating the Christians and Jews from other belief systems, but this did not make a difference, probably owing to the dominance of Christians among the survey respondents.

25. Nonparametric tests gave different results, finding no relationship between service attendance and environmental values, and finding that higher levels of prayer

and meditation were negatively related to the belief that human population growth is damaging the Earth.

26. (cc=-.232, p=.001).

27. Lynn Huntsinger and Maria Fernandez-Gimenez, "Spiritual pilgrims at Mount Shasta, California," *Geographical Review* 90, no. 4 (2000): 536–58.

28. Gender difference significances are: threats to human health (p=.19 NP), people who are poor do not have enough access to outdoor recreation (p=.029 NP), industrialized culture is a threat to the Earth's environment (p=.04 NP), and care for the environment should be an integral part of their lives (p=.013 NP), environmentalists exaggerate issues (p=.003 or p=.016 NP), motivation to join environmental organizations (p=.05 NP), join humanitarian organizations (p=.03 NP), or to vote concerning environmental issues. (p=.037 NP).

29. Probabilities for age differences: increasing human population was a major threat (p=.047), air and water pollution are threats to human health (p=.001), money for the environment should be directed to needy people (p=.042), caring for the environment is important to the world's needy people (p=.031), human developments are damaging parks and hiking trails (p=.011), caring for nature should be an integral part of their lives (p=.016), awareness of environmental concerns in their hometown (p=.000), desire greater access to educational materials concerning environmental issues along the trail (p=.051).

30. There was a trend toward hikers with higher levels of education linking the environment to the circumstances of the world's needy people (p=.101) and believing care for nature should be an integral part of their lives (p=.107). Trends included individuals with higher levels of education being more likely to believe beauty inspired them to environmental care (p=.099) and less likely to believe they were learning more about the environment throughout the length of their trip (p=.071). An interesting result is that respondents traveling in larger groups were less likely to perceive human population growth as an environmental threat (p=.032) and human beings as damaging parks and trails (p=.012), while they were more likely to perceive caring for the environment as helpful to the world's needy people (p=.031). Hikers who were walking with companions were less likely to report that exposure to educational materials while on trail had increased their interest in environmental care (p=.000), and as a trend, to be less interested in access to further educational materials (trend, p=.092).

31. (cc=-.148, p=.036; cc=-.176, p=.014).

32. Nongovernmental organizations.

33. See Nash, *Wilderness and the American Mind,* or Vale, *American Wilderness,* 185. These volumes provide general overviews of the development of thought about wilder-

ness in the United States. Waterman and Waterman, *Forest and Crag: A History of Hiking, Trail Blazing, and Adventure in the Northeast Mountains* provides an excellent overview of the historic organization of trail clubs in New England.

34. Probabilities are: the concept that service to other people should be an integral part of their lives (p=.047, p=.022 NP); service to nature should be an integral part of their lives (p=.016, p=.004 NP); caring for the environment is important to caring for the world's needy people (p=.028, p=.028 NP). The concept that human developments were damaging parks and trails was split, with p=.039 for parametric analysis and p=.87 for Mann-Whitney U nonparametric. Nonparametric analysis also indicated a trend toward a greater belief that humanity could disappear because of environmental degradation, p=.087. There were also trends toward members of environmental organizations believing human developments were damaging parks and trails and that humanity might be at risk owing to environmental degradation of the Earth (a more radical environmental perspective).

35. Probability=.244 NP.

36. Probabilities for human population (p=.045, p=.025 NP) and air and water pollution as threats (p=.048 NP), and human beings should preserve as many of the Earth's wild plants and animals as possible (p=.054, trend, p=.109 NP). NP is Mann-Whitney U.

37. Probabilities for environmental organization members: desiring more access to environmental education (p=.022 NP), being more likely to vote on environmental issues (p=.007 NP), being motivated to join environmental organizations (p=.089 NP, trend), not having learned anything new (p=.088 NP, trend) and finding that exposure to environmental materials had increased learning (p=.063, trend).

38. Teresa Martinez and Steve McMullin, "Factors affecting decisions to volunteer in nongovernmental organizations," *Environment & Behavior* 36, no. 1 (2004): 112–26.

39. A full list of the published memoirs and journals is incorporated in the reference list at the end of the book.

40. Susan A, Korrick, Lucas M. Neas, Douglas W. Dockery, Diane R. Gold, George A. Allen, L. Bruce Hill, Kenneth D. Kimball, Bernard A. Rosner, and Frank E. Speizer, "Effects of ozone and other pollutants on the pulmonary functions of adult hikers," *Environmental Health Perspectives* 106, no. 2 (1998): 93–99; Steven P. Giardot, P. Barry Ryan, Susan M. Smith, Wayne T. Davis, Charles B. Hamilton, Richard A. Obenour, James B. Renfro, Kimberly A. Tromatore, and Gregory D. Reed, "Ozone and $PM_{2.5}$ exposure and acute pulmonary health effects: A study of hikers in the Great Smoky Mountains National Park," *Environmental Health Perspectives* 114, no. 7 (2006): 1044–52.

41. Reviews of transcendentalist attitudes towards nature or of their writings include: Albanese, *Spirituality of the American Transcendentalist;* Conrad Cherry, *Nature and Religious Imagination: From Edwards to Bushnell* (Philadelphia: Fortress Press,

1980); Emerson, Thoreau, and Elder, *Nature/Walking;* Henry David Thoreau, and Bill McKibben, ed., *Walden, or Life in the Woods* (Boston: Beacon Press, 2004).

CHAPTER 8

1. Fisher, Francis, and Johnson, "Assessing spiritual health"; Rees, Francis, and Robbins, *Spiritual Health.*

2. World Health Organization, *WHOQOL-SRPB: Field Test Instrument: Spirituality, Religiousness and Personal Beliefs* (Geneva: WHO, 2002). I also looked over studies of the trail itself, such as Gerard Kyle, Alan Graefe, Robert Manning, and James Bacon, "Predictors of behavioral loyalty among hikers along the Appalachian Trail," *Leisure Sciences* 26 (2004): 98–118.

3. I have visited a number of pilgrimage locales over the years, so I have had numerous opportunities to observe behaviors of modern religious walkers. Some of the locales I am personally familiar with include Cuthbert's Way, Lourdes, Chimayo, Lady's Island, the Columban routes in Ireland, Iona, Altotting, Knock, Croagh Patrick, and a variety of cathedrals and shrines in Europe, such as Durham, Walsingham, and Chartres.

4. Incidentally, not all of them finished on time, and when one of the team fell behind, he dropped out and let the others attempt to complete New Jersey in two days.

5. Bill Maroni, *When Straight Jacket Met Golden Sun: A Journey on the Appalachian Trail* (Bloomington, IN: Xlibris 2003); Lynn Setzer, *A Season on the Appalachian Trail,* (Harpers Ferry, WV: Appalachian Trail Conference, 1997).

6. Lynn Setzer, *A Season on the Appalachian Trail,* 167–68.

7. Ibid., 177.

8. 2.97 without rounding the number.

9. Earl V. Shaffer, *Walking with Spring* (Harpers Ferry, WV: Appalachian Trail Conference, 1983).

10. Alt, *Walk for Sunshine.*

11. Melissa Daniels and Jeffry Marion, "Visitor evaluations of management actions at a highly impacted Appalachian Trail camping area," *Environmental Management* 38, no. 6 (2006): 1006–19.

12. 18.500 percent.

13. Probabilities: the trip caused emotional distress (p=.029 NP), felt fearful or worried (p=.002 NP), and trip caused me to doubt my own abilities (p=.045 NP).

14. For example, Adrienne Hall, *A Journey North: One Woman's Story of Hiking the Appalachian Trail* (Boston: Appalachian Mountain Club Books, 2000); Leslie Maas, *In Beauty May She Walk: Hiking the Appalachian Trail at 60* (Jacksonville, FL: Rock Spring Press, 2005); Madeline Cornelius, *Katahdin with Love: An Inspirational Journey* (Lookout Mountain, TN: Milton Publishing, 1991); Danie Martin, *Always Another Mountain: A Woman Hiking the Appalachian Trail from Springer to Katahdin* (College Station, TX: Virtual Bookworm, 2005).

15. Academic studies of spirituality and long-distance hiking have specifically considered female experience. An example is Susan Glassman's interviews with seven female coresearchers, where she did not compare their responses to a comparable sample of men. It is not clear if her results apply primarily to women. Susan Glassman, "The Experience of Women Discovering Wilderness as Psychologically Healing," Ph.D. diss., Union Institute and University, 1995. Sarah Pohl, William Borrie, and Michael Patterson, "Women, wilderness and everyday life: A documentation of the connection between wilderness recreation and women's everyday lives," *Journal of Leisure Research* 12, no. 4 (2000): 415–34.

16. Probability=.031 NP.

17. Because of the high number of younger hikers in their twenties, many of whom had recently finished college, age and education level are correlated. The more mature hikers on average had high levels of education (p=.001). Both age and education influenced perceptions of personal experience on the trail.

18. I also ran the data by age classes through Kruskall-Wallis NP. All the following data give higher ranks to younger hikers. The trip has: given me time to think about personal problems or concerns (p=.011), helped me to manage a life transition (p=.108 trend), provided relief from daily stress (p=.073 trend), helped me to break a bad habit (p=.015), changed my life for the better (p=.094, trend), given me time to think about my relationships with other people (p=.024), felt fearful or worried (p=.010), caused me to doubt my own abilities (p=.094 trend), become a learning experience (p=.008), and I am planning to take another trip like this in the future (p=.014).

19. In terms of correlations and probabilities, larger group size correlated with making new friends (cc=.148, p=.037) and strengthening or improving old friendships (cc=.171, p=.016). Group size had a negative impact on the hiker's time to think about personal concerns (cc=-.137, p=.054) and belief that the AT experience has changed their life for the better (cc=-.157, p=.028). Nonparametric analysis credited solo hikers with a greater sense of inner peace (p=.043 NP) and with the least improvement in family relationships (p=.032). Couples felt less isolated (p=.000), and larger groups had a trend toward experiencing more emotional distress (p.=057). All Kruskall-Wallis.

20. I also divided mileage completed into categories and checked for relationships via nonparametric methods. Significant probabilities, using Kruskal-Wallis (all of them increased with greater mileage, unless otherwise noted) included: managing a life transition (p=.049), changing my life for the better (p=.014), time to think about relationships with other people (p=.021), being away from home has harmed my relationships with my family or friends (p=.055), made new friends on the trip (p=.000), improved family relations (p=.085, trend), caused emotional distress (p=.036), improved my physical fitness (p=.082), made me feel positive about who I am (p=.016), enjoyed myself (p=.090, trend), produced many interesting events and experiences (p=.000), provided a sense of harmony with my life (p=.069, trend, greater with less mileage), gave me a sense of inner peace (p=.077, trend), caused me to doubt my own abilities (p=.003, greatest rank in middle categories), given me a sense of accomplishment (p=.002), was a learning experience (p=.007).

21. Results were very inconsistent and depended on the methods used. In parametric Chi-square analysis, hikers who had religious affiliations were more likely to report strengthening old friendships (p=.03) and improving their relationships with a significant other (p=.04). Both of these interpersonal interactions are based at home, or in the off-trail life. These results only applied to parametric tests; nonparametric found no significant variables.

22. Nonparametric probabilities (Kruskal-Wallis) were: changing life for the better (p=.036), having time to think about relationships (p=.049), feeling positive about the meaning of life (p=.002), providing a sense of harmony with life (p=.011), having a sense of inner peace (p=.040), and help with coping with difficulties in life (p=.030).

23. Robert Manning, James Bacon, Alan Graefe, Gerard Kyle, Robert Lee, and Robert Burns, "'I never hike alone': Security on the Appalachian Trail," *Park and Recreation* (July 2001): 50–56.

CHAPTER 9

1. Fisher, Francis, and Johnson, "The SH4DI."

2. If I were redoing this survey in an environment such as the Sierras or Cascades, where the percentage of Buddhists would potentially be even higher, I would design a version especially for them. One of the difficulties in developing the survey is finding a cross-cutting vocabulary that works equally well for all religions. Much of the challenge lies in differences over what or who God is, and between monotheism and polytheism. I found the polytheistic perspective easier to incorporate, with a survey written primarily for adherents to the Abrahamic faiths rather than the concept of nothingness.

3. Brad Daniel, "The life significance of a spiritually oriented, Outward Bound–type wilderness expedition," *Journal of Experiential Education* 29, no. 3 (2007): 386-89.

4. Peter Ashley, "Toward an understanding and definition of wilderness spirituality," *Australian Geographer* 38, no. 1 (2007): 53–69.

5. Stark, *What Americans Really Believe*, 17–20.

6. A few hikers were tired of completing the survey at this point or were interrupted and just stopped. In interpreting the responses, it is important to recognize the absence of these hikers from the explicitly religious section of the surveys.

7. Mysticism is an elusive subject. Jordan Paper, *The Mystic Experience: A Descriptive and Comparative Analysis* (Albany: State University of New York Press, 2004) provides a recent overview. The classic work by Evelyn Underhill, *Mysticism: A Study in the Nature of Man's Spiritual Consciousness* (New York: Dutton, 1910) remains one of the most readable summaries of Western experience. The women mentioned, such as Hildegard von Bingen, are medieval Christian mystics.

8. John Muir, *My First Summer in the Sierra* (Boston: Houghton Mifflin, 1911).

9. Cindy Ross, *A Woman's Journey* (Harpers Ferry, WV: Appalachian Trail Conference, 1990), 14.

10. Ibid., 76.

11. Angela Miller, *The Empire of the Eye: Landscape Representation and American Cultural Politics, 1825–1875* (Ithaca, NY: Cornell University Press, 1993); Gene Edward Veith, *Painters of Faith: The Spiritual Landscape in Nineteenth-Century America* (Washington, DC: Regnery Publishing, 2001); Kelly Gould Ryan, *Frederic Edwin Church* (Washington, DC: National Gallery of Art, 1989).

12. Correlation coefficients and probabilities: reading sacred texts ($cc=-.164$, $p=.047$), belief the trip has helped to correct their own negative attitudes or wrongdoing ($cc=-.198$, $p=.017$), think about how God has blessed the United States ($cc=.296$, $p=.0001$), to feel they are close to God ($cc=.286$, $p=.0001$), feel God is guiding them ($cc=.234$, $p=.004$), and to experience the beauty of God ($cc=.185$, $p=.026$).

13. Probabilities relative to gender (NP Kruskal-Wallis) of the trip: facilitating prayer or meditation ($p=.046$), to finding contact with other hikers encouraged them in their spiritual lives ($p=.059$), to increasing awareness of personal deficiencies ($p=.043$), to encouraging correction of personal wrongdoing ($p=.019$). The concept that participating in spiritual activities outdoors had exceptional meaning presented a trend ($p=.078$), as did the perception God or spirits were providing guidance ($p=.078$). Solo hikers were more likely to find that the trip facilitated prayer or meditation ($p=.031$ NP).

14. There was also an interesting trend toward couples being less likely to feel God was guiding the long-distance walk (p=.093).

15. The results on education were mixed. Parametric methods produced no significant results. Nonparametric produced one significant result: visiting religious buildings or monuments inspires me to think about God (p=.022 NP, with a peak at the college level beneath graduate level) and a couple of trends—reports of increased spiritual commitment were lower for higher levels of education (p=.062 NP) and awareness of the importance of religious belief to the history of the country (p=.062 NP) was higher for college level.

16. Correlations and probabilities of increase with mileage were: an increase in spiritual commitment (cc=.221, p=.007), correction of wrongdoing or negative attitudes cc=.212, p=.010, and awareness of one's own religious heritage or roots (cc=.176, p=.032). Utilizing nonparametric methods by mileage category, only the trip as spiritual or religious learning experience gave a positive result (p=.027 NP), and this had the highest rank in the middle categories.

17. Probabilities using Kruskal-Wallis include the trip facilitated prayer or meditation (p=.019), increased religious commitment (p=.005), helped one think about religious or spiritual responsibilities to other people (p=.010), was a spiritual learning experience, provided time to think about religious matters while hiking (p=.014), feeling close to God (p=.055, trend), being more aware of the beauty of God (p=.071 trend), experiencing guidance from God (p=.066, trend), and provided time to think about personal responsibilities to nature and the environment (p=.062 NP, or cc=-.179, p=.040). Previous hiking experience was also related to the belief that participating in religious activities outdoors has special meaning (p=.043 NP, with a peak in the middle categories) and to the frequency of reading spiritual or religious writings while on trail (p=.079, trend NP; or cc=-.215, p=.009). The concept that the trip provided experience not available at home was significant, with a peak in the middle experience categories (p=.011).

18. The sample size concerning Buddhists is obviously too small to draw a major conclusion from this trend. It would take two to three years of similar sampling to accumulate enough responses to evaluate Buddhists properly.

19. Probabilities from Kruskal-Wallis: major change in one's spiritual life (p=.291), increased time for religious or spiritual activities on trail (p=.628), assistance thinking about spiritual responsibilities to the environment (p=.141), correction of wrongdoing or negative attitudes (p=.423), and a sense of spiritual community with people encountered on the hike (p=.241).

20. For example, there was no significant differences in response, between Abrahamic and other faiths, to "I think about religious or spiritual matters more when I am hiking," or in becoming "more aware of the beauty of God," or feeling "close to God" (p=.547,

.333, and .208). The survey may have been too general to detect some forms of differ-ence, however, and the sample size for non-Christian religions was very small.

21. In this case, the one synagogue member and two Buddhists who belonged to religious organizations were not categorized with the Christian church and fellowship members. The reader should therefore note the non-churched category includes Chris-tians and non-Christians. I read the qualitative descriptions and identified the most important element in each.

22. Ashley, "Wilderness spirituality."

23. These two statements almost gave statistically significant results, however, so it is best to treat them as the weakest areas of response, rather than outcomes of no significance. However, hikers who reported an increase in prayer during the AT hike were more likely to report that they did have more time for spiritual activities (cc=.165, p=.047), and even more important, and in conflict with the overall outcomes, hikers who increased prayer or meditation during the trip were more likely confirm that the AT trip had precipitated a major change in their spiritual lives (cc=.203, p=.014).

24. There was a trend toward hikers with the goal of self-reflection feeling a greater sense of inner peace and harmony and providing higher ratings to the AT as a spiritual learning experience (p=.065; p=.07).

25. Pilgrimages and other forms of spiritual trekking among the world's religions range from solo endeavors, such as vision quests, to venues, such as group tours to Lourdes, where the pilgrim travels with the home community. A group from an Irish parish visiting Lourdes will both attend Mass in the basilica with pilgrims from other nations and then hold their own Mass in front of the grotto where St. Bernadette saw the Virgin Mary. This venue is the opposite of the AT experience, because it increases rit-ual (there may be two or three services a day) and it continues participation in the Mass and group prayers with friends, relatives, and familiar religious guides, while integrating the parish into international Roman Catholicism.

26. Ross, *A Woman's Journey*, 71.

27. Ibid., 71.

28. There were again significant negative correlations with an experience of separa-tion from coreligionists and of interference in one's religious life.

29. Mark Stoll, *Protestantism, Capitalism and Nature in America* (Albuquerque: Uni-versity of New Mexico Press, 1997).

30. Albanese, *Spirituality of the American Transcendentalists*.

31. This is in contrast to an all-village or all-church pilgrimage, where a group of people who usually worship together take a day and walk to a shrine or a sacred spring, which builds depth with the transcendent domain through participation in the familiar.

Conclusion

1. Keith Russell, "What is wilderness therapy," *Journal of Experiential Education* 24, no. 2 (2001): 70-79; William Borrie and Joseph Roggenbuck, "The dynamic, emergent, and multi-phasic nature of on-site wilderness experiences," *Journal of Leisure Research* 33, no. 2 (2001): 208–28.

2. These partially parallel the findings of research on wilderness therapy. Unfortunately, most of these studies concern teens or late adolescents. Keith Russell and Dianne Miller have tracked interactions of clients in wilderness therapy with their peers and with their counselors. They confirm the importance of exercise, group counseling, wilderness living, and expert guides. The AT is less formal and social contacts change more frequently, while some of the same elements apply. See Keith Russell and Dianne Miller, "Perspectives on the wilderness therapy process and its relation to outcome," *Child and Youth Care Forum* 31, no. 6 (2002): 415–37.

3. Chaucer, and Coghill (trans.), *Canterbury Tales*.

4. Goldenberg, Hill, and Freidt, "Why individuals hike the Appalachian Trail."

5. The references used to design this study and Scott Fry and Bernd Heubeck, "The effects of personality and situational variables on mood states during Outward Bound wilderness courses: An exploration," *Personality and Individual Differences* 24, no. 5 (1998): 649–59; Denise Marie Hutter, "Weaving the Fabric of Culture: The Emergence of Personal and Collective Wisdom in Young Adults Participating in a Wilderness Rite of Passage," Ph.D. diss., Palo Alto, CA, Institute of Transpersonal Psychology, 1999; Paul Heintzman, "Leisure and Spiritual Well-Being: A Social Scientific Exploration," Ph.D. diss., University of Waterloo, Canada, 1999.

6. I utilized the Pieces Inc. version of Principal Components Analysis and their clustering procedures, both for the entire data set and with only the respondents who answered section VI on religion and spirituality. Classifying by question, the questions concerning transcendence consistently separated completely and clustered with other questions in the section. The most closely related questions among the domains were those about reflecting on one's own wrongdoing and impact on other people, which were replicated, using different language, between the two sections of the survey. This outcome is probably a result of the sharing of communal and environmental experience among the majority of the respondents and the very particular nature of the religious engagement on the trail.

7. Other concepts that were positively correlated to at least half the outcomes in the personal experience section of the questionnaire were: the trip serving as a religious or spiritual learning experience, the trip precipitating a major change in one's spiritual life, the trip creating more awareness of personal deficiencies or failings, contact with

other hikers was spiritually encouraging, and the trip enhanced awareness of the religious or spiritual heritage of other cultures.

8. Rees, Francis, and Robbins, *Spiritual Health,* 23–24.

9. Waterman and Waterman, *Forest and Crag.* The term applies to trips of more than two weeks, or with very high mileage, or crossing an entire state or region.

10. Studies of Lourdes have shown that younger pilgrims are more oriented than older ones toward recreation, for example, while more mature pilgrims are seeking help and assistance. See Paul Post, Jos Pieper, and Marinus van Uden, *The Modern Pilgrim: Multidisciplinary Explorations of Christian Pilgrimage* (Lueven, Netherlands: Peeters, 1998), 173–88.

11. Professional outfitters and tour guides may organize one- or two-week wilderness excursions as "women only" or "over fifty," particularly if they offer a variety of packages requiring different degrees of conditioning or effort. Some outfitters specialize in trips for women, and there are national organizations, such as Elder Hostel, that offer outdoor experiences for seniors. Retired seniors can have more time for travel off-peak season, and the tourist industry as a whole offers packages and discounts for seniors. The AMC has recently offered some packages for seniors, including overnight accommodation at their facilities, while specialized tours for women or for more-mature hikers remain rare on the AT. This AT study provides little insight into the dynamics of these limited cohort tours, because the average group size is smaller and the women and seniors on the AT are so well-integrated with the men under thirty. The AT thru-hiker is inherently more independent than a guided expedition or workshop participant. These data do suggest, however, different spiritual outcomes for groups with different composition, particularly those of different ages. Considering that the median age of hikers participating in the AT survey was around thirty, and very few respondents were in their late teens, should warn leaders of youth groups that the spiritual outcomes reported in the AT survey may not apply to teens and children. The AT thru-hikers are adults, with adult personal issues, and they have reached the point of independent decision making about their religious preferences and beliefs. See Lawrence S. Cunningham, *A Brief History of Saints* (Oxford, UK: Blackwell Publishers, 2005) for a history of some early female and senior pilgrims.

12. William Borrie and Joseph Roggenbuck, "The dynamic, emergent, and multiphasic nature of on-site wilderness experiences," *Journal of Leisure Research* 33, no. 2 (2001): 208–28.

13. I have personally been present for a number of conversations on this subject, and have chatted with hikers who were in good physical and financial shape but were contemplating quitting.

14. Not being adequately prepared, encountering difficult weather or wildlife, such as heavy rain or marauding bears, and injuries are the most frequent reasons for quitting, at least in the eastern wilderness where I have more experience. Hikers do discover that they cannot communicate with their friends in a stressful environment or in the close quarters of a backpacking tent.

15. Because the hikers belonged to cohorts, such as those coming from Springer, those coming from Katahdin, those coming from Harpers Ferry, and those coming from Wind Gap or starting locally, I divided the hikers into 100 miles or less, 101 to 300, 301 to 700, 701 to 1,000, and 1,001 to 1,400 miles. I then constructed probability tables and checked for cases where there were high numbers of lower ratings at the beginning of the trips. I also conducted regressions, but the presence of strong cohorts according to mileage walked may have distorted the fit of the curves.

16. I should note that the short-distance travelers in the survey were primarily hiking locally and did not fully integrate with the end-to-enders who dominate the sample. They have less in common. Also, by NY-NJ, the majority of end-to-enders had gotten to know other thru-hikers, while short-termers were still focusing on their own party.

17. This phenomenon deserves further study.

18. Additional studies aside from those already cited include: Prem Chhetri, Colin Arrowsmith, and Mervyn Jackson, "Determining hiking experiences in nature based tourist destinations," *Tourism Management* 25 (2004): 31–43; Henk Staats, Birgitta Gatersleben, and Terry Hartig, "Change in mood as a function of environmental design: Arousal and pleasure on a simulated forest hike," *Environmental Psychology* 17 (1998): 283–300.

19. D. L. Ben Zequeira-Russell, "Wilderness and Spirituality: Hikers' Experience of God in the Backcountry," Ph.D. diss., Fuller Theological Seminary, 2002, 26–27.

20. Wade Rowett and his students at Baylor University, including Salif Mahamme, have conducted studies that demonstrate university students feel humility on viewing grand natural settings. As of this writing, they have not published these results.

21. Netta Weinstein, Andrew K. Przybylski, and Richard M. Ryan, "Can nature make us more caring? Effects of immersion in nature on intrinsic aspirations and generosity," *Personality and Social Psychology Bulletin* 35 (2009): 1315–29.

22. Ibid.

23. Taylor, "Focus introduction."

24. See Mary Lee Nolan and Sidney Nolan, *Christian Pilgrimage in Modern Western Europe* (Chapel Hill: University of North Carolina Press, 1992) for a broad overview of European practice.

25. Kevin A. Codd, *To the Field of Stars: A Pilgrim's Journey to Santiago de Compostela* (Grand Rapids, MI: William B. Eerdmans, 2008). Joyce Rupp also has penned a very readable Christian account, *Walk in a Relaxed Manner: Life Lessons from the Camino* (Mary Knoll, NY: Orbis Books, 2005).

26. Shirley MacLaine, *The Camino: A Journey of the Spirit* (New York: Simon and Schuster, 2001). Paul Coelho, in *The Pilgrimage* (San Francisco: Harper San Francisco, 1998), weaves cosmic exploration with humanism and spiritual disciplines such as breathing exercises. He has also influenced alternative religious thought.

27. A less religious account may be found in Rob Neilands, *The Road to Compostela* (Bradford-on-Avon, UK: Dotesis, 1985). Among the many studies of pilgrimage that incorporate El Camino or today's long-distance pilgrim's roads are: Post, Pieper, and Uden, *The Modern Pilgrim;* Ellen Badone and Sharon R. Roseman, eds., *Intersecting Journeys: The Anthropology of Pilgrimage and Tourism* (Urbana: University of Illinois Press, 2004).

28. Post, Pieper, and Uden, *Modern Pilgrim,* 173–88.

29. Michael Murray and Brian Graham, "Exploring the dialectics of route-based tourism: the Camino de Santiago," *Tourism Management* 18, no. 8 (1997): 513–24.

30. I have walked all of Cuthbert's Way, though I have not, as of this writing, traveled El Camino.

31. Graham Tomlin, "Protestants and pilgrimage," in Craig Bartholomew and Fred Hughes, *Explorations in a Christian Theology of Pilgrimage* (Aldershot, UK: Ashgate Publishing, 2004), 110–25. See also Bratton, *Christianity, Wilderness and Wildlife.*

32. Martin Robinson, "Pilgrimage and mission," in Bartholomew and Hughes, *Christian Theology of Pilgrimage,* 170–83.

REFERENCES

Adam, David. *Fire of the North: The Illustrated Life of Cuthbert*. London: SPCK Press, 1993.

Albanese, Catherine. *Nature Religion in America: From the Algonkian Indians to the New Age*. Chicago: University of Chicago Press, 1990.

Albanese, Catherine. *The Spirituality of the American Transcendentalists*. Atlanta: Mercer University Press, 1988.

Allison, M. T, and J. E. Schneider, eds. *Diversity and the Recreation Profession: Organizational Perspectives*. State College, PA: Venture Publishing, 2000.

Almond, Phillip C. "Druids, patriarchs and the primordial religion." *Journal of Contemporary Religion* 15, no. 3 (2000): 379–94.

Alt, Jeff. *A Walk for Sunshine: A 2,160 Mile Expedition for Charity on the Appalachian Trail*. Cincinnati: Dreams Shared Publications, 2000.

Altschuler, Stephen. *The Mindful Hiker: On the Trail to Find the Path*. Camarillo, CA: DeVorss Publications, 2004.

Anderson, Larry. *Benton MacKaye: Conservationist, Planner and Creator of the Appalachian Trail*. Baltimore: Johns Hopkins University Press, 2002.

Armstrong, Susan, and Richard Boltzer. *Environmental Ethics: Divergence and Convergence*. New York: McGraw Hill, 2003.

Ashley, Peter. "Toward an understanding and definition of wilderness spirituality." *Australian Geographer* 38, no. 1 (2007): 53–69.

Attfield, Robin. *The Ethics of Environmental Concern*. New York: Columbia University Press, 1983.

Bader, Christopher, Kevin Dougherty, Paul Froese, Byron Johnson, F. Carson Mencken, Jerry Z. Park, and Rodney Stark. *American Piety in the 21st Century: New Insights into the Depth and Complexity of Religion in the U.S., Selected Findings from The Baylor Study of American Religion*. Waco, TX: Baylor University, 2006.

Badone, Ellen, and Sharon R. Roseman, eds. *Intersecting Journeys: The Anthropology of Pilgrimage and Tourism*. Urbana: University of Illinois Press, 2004.

Barber, Richard, *Pilgrimages*. Suffolk, UK: Woodbridge Press, 1991.

References

Barnhill, David Landis, and Roger S. Gottlieb, eds. *Deep Ecology and World Religions.* Albany: State University of New York Press, 2001.

Beck, Lawrence. "The Phenomenology of Optimal Experiences Attained by Whitewater River Recreationists in Canyonlands National Park." Ph.D. diss. University of Minnesota, Twin Cities, 1987.

Berry, Sam, ed. *Environmental Stewardship: Critical Perspectives, Past and Present.* London: Continuum Publishing, 2006.

Birchard, William, and Robert Proudman. *Appalachian Trail Design, Construction and Maintenance.* 2nd ed. Harpers Ferry, WV: Appalachian Trail Conference, 2000.

Blaney, Melody A., and L. K. Ullyart. *A Journey of Friendship: A Thru-hike on the Appalachian Trail.* Marietta, OH: River Press, 1998.

Borrie, William, and Joseph Roggenbuck. "The dynamic, emergent, and multi-phasic nature of on-site wilderness experiences." *Journal of Leisure Research* 33, no. 2 (2001): 202–28.

Bouma-Prediger, Steven. *For the Beauty of the Earth: A Christian Vision of Creation Care.* Grand Rapids, MI: Baker Academic Books, 2001.

Bratton, Susan. *Christianity, Wilderness and Wildlife: The Original Desert Solitaire.* Scranton, PA: University of Scranton Press, 2009.

———. "Power, Ecology and religion." In *The Oxford Handbook of Religion and Science,* edited by Philip Clayton and Zachary Simpson, 207–25. Oxford: Oxford University Press, 2008.

Brill, David. *As Far as the Eye Can See: Reflections of an Appalachian Trail Hiker.* Harpers Ferry, WV: Appalachian Trail Conference, 2004.

Brown, Peter. *The Cult of the Saints: Its Rise and Function in Latin Christianity.* Chicago: University of Chicago Press, 1981.

Bryson, Bill. *A Walk in the Woods: Rediscovering America on the Appalachian Trail.* New York: Broadway Books, 1999.

Callicott, Baird. *Beyond the Land Ethic.* Albany: State University of New York Press, 1999.

Campo, Juan Eduardo. "American pilgrimage landscapes." *Annuals of the American Academy of Political and Social Science* 588, Americans and Religions in the Twenty-First Century (1998): 40–56.

Chaucer, Geoffrey, and Nevill Coghill, trans. *Canterbury Tales.* New York: Penguin Group, 2003.

Cherry, Conrad. *Nature and Religious Imagination: From Edwards to Bushnell.* Philadelphia: Fortress Press, 1980.

Chhetri, Prem, Colin Arrowsmith, and Mervyn Jackson. "Determining hiking experiences in nature based tourist destinations." *Tourism Management* 25 (2004): 31–43.

Codd, Kevin A. *To the Field of Stars: A Pilgrim's Journey to Santiago de Compostela*. Grand Rapids, MI: William B. Eerdmans, 2008.

Coelho, Paul. *The Pilgrimage*. San Francisco: Harper San Francisco, 1998.

Cole, David, Alan E. Watson, and Joseph Roggenbuck. "Trends in wilderness visitors and visits: Boundary Waters Canoe Area, Shining Rock, and Desolation Wilderness." *Wilderness Research Paper* INT-RP-483. Ogden, UT: USDA Forest Service Intermountain Research Station, 1995.

Coleman, Simon, and John Elsner. *Pilgrimage: Past and Present in the World Religions*. Cambridge: Harvard University Press, 1995.

Comins, Mike. *A Wild Faith: Jewish Ways into Wilderness, Wilderness Ways into Judaism*. Woodstock, VT: Jewish Lights Press, 2007.

Cooper, David E., and Simon P. James. *Buddhism, Virtue and Environment*. Aldershot, UK: Ashgate Publishing, 2005.

Cornelius, Madeline. *Katahdin with Love: An Inspirational Journey*. Lookout Mountain, TN: Milton Publishing, 1991.

Cunningham, Lawrence, S. *A Brief History of Saints*. Oxford: Blackwell Publishers, 2005.

Daniel, Brad. "The life significance of a spiritually oriented, Outward Bound–type wilderness expedition." *Journal of Experiential Education* 29, no. 3 (2007): 386–89.

Daniels, Melissa, and Jeffry Marion. "Visitor evaluations of management actions at a highly impacted Appalachian Trail camping area." *Environmental Management* 38, no. 6 (2006): 1006–19.

Davis, Matthew, and Michael Farrell Scott. *Opening the Mountain: Circumambulating Mount Tamalpais, A Ritual Walk*. Emeryville, CA: Shoemaker & Hoard, 2006.

Dawson, Chad, and John Hendee have published a 4th edition reversing the senior authorship: *Wilderness Management: Stewardship and Protection of Resources and Values*. Golden, CO: Fulcrum Press, 2009.

Deeds, Jean. *There are Mountains to Climb: An Inspirational Journey*. Indianapolis: Silverwood Press, 2003.

Dubisch, Jill. "Healing 'the wounds that are not visible': A Vietnam veterans' motorcycle pilgrimage." In Jill Dubisch and Michael Winkelman, *Pilgrimage and Healing*. Tucson: University of Arizona Press, 2005, 135–54.

Eberhart, M. J. (Nimblewill Nomad). *Where the Path is Less Worn*. Bloomingdale, OH: Thirsty Turtle Press, 2004.

Eckberg, Douglas Lee, and T. Jean Blocker. "Christianity, environmentalism and the theoretical problem of fundamentalism." *Journal for the Scientific Study of Religion* 35, no. 4 (1996): 343–55.

———. "Varieties of religious involvement and environmental concerns: Testing the Lynn White thesis." *Journal for the Scientific Study of Religion* 28, no. 4 (1989): 509–17.

References

Emerson, Ralph Waldo, and Henry David Thoreau. *Nature/Walking,* edited by J. Elder. Boston: Beacon Press, 1994.

Faucher, Staron. "Ethnic Preferences in Outdoor Recreation, Cameron Park, TX." Master's thesis, Baylor University, 2009.

Fisher, John, Leslie Francis, and Peter Johnson. "Assessing spiritual health via four domains of spiritual wellbeing: The SH4DI." *Pastoral Psychology* 49, no. 2 (2000): 133–45.

Fowler, Robert Booth. *The Greening of Protestant Thought.* Chapel Hill: University of North Carolina Press, 1995.

Fry, Scott, and Bernd Heubeck. "The effects of personality and situational variables on mood states during Outward Bound wilderness courses: An exploration." *Personality and Individual Differences* 24, no. 5 (1998): 649–59.

Garvey, Edward, B. *The New Appalachian Trail.* Birmingham, AL: Menasha Ridge Press, 1997.

Gatta, John. *Making Nature Sacred: Literature, Religion, and Environment in American from the Puritans to the Present.* New York: Oxford University Press, 2004.

Georgia Appalachian Trail Club History Committee. *Friendships of the Trail: The History of the Georgia Appalachian Trail Club, 1930–1980.* Atlanta: Georgia Appalachian Trail Club, 1995.

Giardot, Steven P., P. Barry Ryan, Susan M. Smith, Wayne T. Davis, Charles B. Hamilton, Richard A. Obenour, James B. Renfro, Kimberly A. Tromatore, and Gregory D. Reed. "Ozone and $PM_{2.5}$ exposure and acute pulmonary health effects: A study of hikers in the Great Smoky Mountains National Park." *Environmental Health Perspectives* 114, no. 7 (2006): 1044–52.

Gilmore, Lee. "Embers, dust, and ashes: Pilgrimage and healing at the Burning Man Festival." In Dubisch and Winkelman, *Pilgrimage and Healing.* Tucson: University of Arizona Press, 2005, 155–78.

Glacken, Clarence. *Traces on the Rhodian Shore.* Berkeley: University of California Press, 1967.

Glassman, Susan. "The Experience of Women Discovering Wilderness as Psychologically Healing." Ph.D. diss. Union Institute and University, 1995.

Gobster, Paul H. "Managing urban parks for a racially diverse and ethnically diverse clientele." *Leisure Sciences* (2002): 143–59.

Goldenberg, Marni, Eddie Hill, and Barbara Freidt. "Why individuals hike the Appalachian Trial: A qualitative approach to benefits." *Journal of Experiential Education* 30, no. 3 (2008): 277–81.

Gottlieb, Roger S. *A Greener Faith: Religious Environmentalism and Our Planet's Future.* New York: Oxford University Press, 2006.

References

Graber, L. *Wilderness as Sacred Space*. Monograph Series, No. 8. Washington, DC: American Society of Geographers, 1976.

Greeley, Andrew. "Religion and attitudes toward the environment." *Journal for the Scientific Study of Religion* 32, no. 1 (1993): 19–28.

Hall, Adrienne. *A Journey North*. Boston: Appalachian Mountain Club Books, 2000.

Harbison, Peter. *Pilgrimage in Ireland: The Monuments and the People*. Syracuse, NY: Syracuse University Press, 1991.

Hargrove, Eugene. *Foundations of Environmental Ethics*. Albany: State University of New York Press, 1992.

Harpur, James. *Sacred Tracks: 2000 Years of Christian Pilgrimage*. Cambridge, MA: Harvard University Press, 2002.

Hawks, S. "Spiritual health: definition and theory." *Wellness Perspectives* 10, no. 1 (1994): 3–13.

Heelas, Paul, and Linda Woodhead. *The Spiritual Revolution: Why Religion is Giving Way to Spirituality*. Oxford: Blackwell Publishing, 2005.

Heffernan, Kevin "Marely." *Blaze: A Dog's Appalachian Trail Adventure*. Victoria, BC: Trafford Publications, 2007.

Heintzman, Paul. "A conceptual model of leisure and spiritual well-being." *Journal of Park and Recreation Administration* 20, no. 4 (2002): 147–69.

———. *Leisure and Spiritual Well-Being: A Social Scientific Exploration*. Ph.D. diss. University of Waterloo, 1999.

Heintzman, Paul, and Roger C. Mannell. "Spiritual functions of leisure and spiritual well-being: Coping with time pressure." *Leisure Sciences* 25 (2003): 207–30.

Hendee, John C., and Chad P. Dawson. *Wilderness Management: Stewardship and Protection Resources and Values*. 3rd ed. Golden, CO: Fulcrum Press, 2002.

Hopper, Sarah. *To Be a Pilgrim: The Medieval Pilgrimage Experience*. Phoenix Mill, UK: Sutton Publishing, 2002.

Howe, Nicholas. *Not Without Peril: 150 Years of Misadventure on the Presidential Range of New Hampshire*. Boston: Appalachian Mountain Club Books, 2000.

Howell, Harold, and Amy Adams. *Encountering God on the Appalachian Trail*. Colorado Springs, CO: Peak Press, 2003.

Hughes, M. E. Postcard. *We're Off to See the Wilderness, The Wonderful Wilderness of Awes*. Bloomington, IN: Xlibris Corporation, 2005.

Huntsinger, Lynn, and Maria Fernandez-Gimenez. "Spiritual pilgrims at Mount Shasta, California." *Geographical Review* 90, no. 4 (2000): 536–58.

Hutter, Denise Marie. "Weaving the Fabric of Culture: The Emergence of Personal and Collective Wisdom in Young Adults Participating in a Wilderness Rite of Passage." Ph.D. diss. Institute of Transpersonal Psychology, Palo Alto, CA, 1999.

References

Irvine, Hunter. *One Pair of Boots: A Journey from Georgia to Maine on the Appalachian Trail.* Lake City, CO: Golden Stone Press, 1996.

Irwin, Bill and David McCasland. *Blind Courage.* Waco, TX: WRS Publishing, 1996.

Jackson, Bernard. *Places of Pilgrimage.* London: Geoffrey Chapman, 1989.

Jenkins, Willis. *Ecologies of Grace: Environmental Ethics and Christian Theology.* New York: Oxford University Press, 2008.

Johnson, Russell, and Kerry Moran. *Tibet's Sacred Mountain: The Extraordinary Pilgrimage to Mount Kailas.* Rochester, VT: Park Street Press, 1989.

Kanagy, Conrad L., and Hart M. Nelson. "Religion and environmental concern: Challenging the dominant assumptions." *Review of Religious Research* 37, no. 1 (1995): 33–45.

Keane, Marc C. *Japanese Garden Design.* Rutland, VT: Charles E. Tuttle, 1996.

Kearns, Laurel, and Catherine Keller, eds. *Ecospirit: Religions and Philosophies for the Earth.* New York: Fordham University Press, 2007.

Korngold, Jamie. *God in the Wilderness: Rediscovering the Spirituality of the Great Outdoors with the Adventure Rabbi.* New York: Doubleday, 2007.

Korrick, Susan A., Lucas M. Neas, Douglas W. Dockery, Diane R. Gold, George A. Allen, L. Bruce Hill, Kenneth D. Kimball, Bernard A. Rosner, and Frank E. Speizer. "Effects of ozone and other pollutants on the pulmonary functions of adult hikers." *Environmental Health Perspectives* 106, no. 2 (1998): 93–99.

Kyle, Gerald, Alan Graefe, Robert Manning, and James Bacon. "An examination of the relationship between leisure activity involvement and place attachment among hikers along the Appalachian Trail." *Journal of Leisure Research* 35, no. 3 (2003): 249–73.

———. "Predictors of behavioral loyalty among hikers along the Appalachian Trail." *Leisure Sciences* 26 (2004): 98–118.

Lane, Belden. *The Solace of Fierce Landscapes: Exploring Desert and Mountain Spirituality.* New York: Oxford University Press, 1998.

Lionberger, John. *Renewal in the Wilderness: A Spiritual Guide to Connecting with God in the Natural World.* Woodstock, VT: Skylight Press, 2007.

Longnecker, Justin G., Joseph A. McKinney, and Carlos W. Moore. "Religious intensity, Evangelical Christianity, and business ethics: An empirical study." *Journal of Business Ethics* 55 (2004): 373–86.

Maas, Leslie. *In Beauty May She Walk: Hiking the Appalachian Trail at 60.* Jacksonville, FL: Rock Spring Press, 2005.

Maas, Leslie, ed. *Appalachian Trail Thru-Hiker's Companion.* Harpers Ferry, WV: Appalachian Trail Conference, 2008.

McGrath, Robert L. *Gods in Granite: The Art of the White Mountains of New Hampshire.* Syracuse, NY: Syracuse University Press, 2001.

References

McKinney, Donald. *Walking the Mist: Celtic Spirituality for the 21st Century.* London: Hodder and Stoughton, 2004.

MacKaye, Benton. "An Appalachian Trail: A project in regional planning." *Journal of the American Institute of Architects,* 9 (October 1921): 325–30.

MacLaine, Shirley. *The Camino: A Journey of the Spirit.* New York: Simon and Schuster, 2001.

Manning, Robert, James Bacon, Alan Graefe, Gerard Kyle, Robert Lee, and Robert Burns. "'I never hike alone': Security on the Appalachian Trail." *Park and Recreation* (July 2001): 50–56.

Maroni, Bill. *When Straight Jacket met Golden Sun: A Journey on the Appalachian Trail.* Bloomington, IN: Xlibris 2003.

Martin, Danie. *Always Another Mountain: A Woman Hiking the Appalachian Trail from Springer to Katahdin.* College Station, TX: Virtual Bookworm, 2005.

Martinez, Teresa, and Steve McMullin. "Factors affecting decisions to volunteer in non-governmental organizations." *Environment & Behavior* 36, no. 1 (2004): 112–26.

Metzger, Bruce, and Roland Murphy. *The New Oxford Annotated Bible.* New York: Oxford University Press, 1994.

Miller, Angela. *The Empire of the Eye: Landscape Representation and American Cultural Politics, 1825–1875.* Ithaca, NY: Cornell University Press, 1993.

Miller, David. *AWOL on the Appalachian Trail.* Livermore, CA: Wingspan Press, 2006.

Mueser, Roland. *Long Distance Hiking: Lessons from the Appalachian Trail.* Camden, ME: Ragged Mountain Press, 1998.

Muir, John. *My First Summer in the Sierra.* Boston: Houghton Mifflin, 1911.

Murray, Michael, and Brian Graham. "Exploring the dialectics of route based tourism: the Camino de Santiago." *Tourism Management* 18, no. 8 (1997): 513–24.

Mursell, Gordon, ed. *Christian Spirituality: Two Thousands Years from East to West.* Minneapolis: Fortress Press, 2001.

Nash, Roderick. *Wilderness and the American Mind.* 4th ed. New Haven, CT: Yale University Press, 2001.

Nash, Steve. *Blue Ridge 2020: An Owner's Manual.* Chapel Hill: University of North Carolina Press, 1999.

Neff, John W. *Katahdin: An Historic Journey.* Boston: Appalachian Mountain Club Books, 2006.

Neilands, Rob. *The Road to Compostela.* Bradford-on-Avon, UK: Dotesis, 1985.

Neville, Gwen K. *Kinship and Pilgrimage: Rituals of Reunion in American Protestant Culture.* New York: Oxford University Press, 1987.

References

Newell, Buddy. *You Won't Get to Maine Unless You Walk in the Rain*. Littleton, NH: Bondcliff Books, 2002.

Newton, Lisa, Catherine Dillingham, and Joanne Choly. *Watershed 4: Ten Cases in Environmental Ethics*. Belmont, CA: Thomas Wadsworth, 2006.

Nolan, Mary Lee, and Sidney Nolan. *Christian Pilgrimage in Modern Western Europe*. Chapel Hill: University of North Carolina Press, 1992.

Novak, Barbara. *Nature and Culture: American Landscape Painting, 1825–1875*. New York: Oxford University Press, 1980.

Oelschalger, Max. *The Idea of Wilderness: From Prehistory to the Age of Ecology*. New Haven, CT: Yale University Press, 1991.

Ogryzlo, Todd. "The Outcomes of a Wilderness Experience: Perception and Trip Intensity of Stress Reduction." Master's thesis, Laurentian University of Sudbury, 1998.

Paper, Jordan. *The Mystic Experience: A Descriptive and Comparative Analysis*. Albany: State University of New York Press, 2004.

Pike, Sarah M. *New Age and Neo-Pagan Religions in America*. New York: Columbia University Press, 2004.

Pinder, Eric. *North to Katahdin*. Minneapolis: Milkweed Editions, 2005.

Platt, Jay. *A Time to Walk: Life Lessons Learned on the Appalachian Trail*. Cartersville, GA: Eagle Eye Publishing, 2000.

Pohl, Sarah, William Borrie, and Michael Patterson. "Women, wilderness and everyday life: A documentation of the connection between wilderness recreation and women's everyday lives." *Journal of Leisure Research* 12, no. 4 (2000): 415–34.

Post, Paul, Jos Pieper and Marinus van Uden. *The Modern Pilgrim: Multidisciplinary Explorations of Christian Pilgrimage*. Lueven, Netherlands: Peeters, 1998.

Price, Joseph L. "Naturalistic recreations." In *Spirituality and the Scared Quest*, edited by Peter van Ness, 414–44. New York: Crossroads Press, 1996.

Ralston, Holmes, III. *Environmental Ethics: Duties to and Values in the Natural World*. Philadelphia: Temple University Press, 2003.

Redick, Kip. "Wilderness as *axis mundi:* Spiritual journeys on the Appalachian Trail." In *Symbolic Landscapes,* edited by Gary Backhuas and John Muungi, 65–90. New York: Springer Verlag, 2009.

Rees, Gwyther, Leslie Francis, and Many Robbins. *Spiritual Health and the Well-Being of Urban Young People*. Bangor, Wales: Commission on Urban Life and Faith, University of Wales, 2005.

Robinson, Martin. "Pilgrimage and Mission." In *Explorations in a Christian Theology of Pilgrimage,* edited by Craig Bartholomew and Fred Hughes, 170–83. Aldershot, UK: Ashgate Publishing, 2004.

References

Ross, Cindy. *A Woman's Journey.* Harpers Ferry, WV: Appalachian Trail Conference, 1990.

Rubin, Robert Alden. *On the Beaten Path: An Appalachian Pilgrimage.* Guilford, CT: Lyons Press, 2001.

Rupp, Joyce. *Walk in a Relaxed Manner: Life Lessons from the Camino.* Mary Knoll, NY: Orbis Books, 2005.

Russell, Keith. "What is wilderness therapy?" *Journal of Experiential Education* 24, no. 2 (2001): 70–79.

Russell, Keith, and Dianne Miller. "Perspectives on the wilderness therapy process and its relation to outcome." *Child and Youth Care Forum* 31, no. 6 (2002): 415–37.

Ryan, David. *Long Distance Hiking on the Appalachian Trail for the Older Adventurer.* Albuquerque: New Mountain Books, 2002.

Ryan, Kelly Gould. *Frederic Edwin Church.* Washington, DC: National Gallery of Art, 1989.

Sanford, A. Whitney. "Pinned on karma rock: Whitewater kayaking as religious experience." *Journal of the American Academy of Religion* 75, no. 4 (2007): 875–95.

Santmire, H. Paul. *The Travail of Nature: The Ambiguous Ecological Promise of Christian Theology.* Philadelphia: Fortress Press, 1985.

Sawatzky, Rick, Pamela Ratner, and Lyren Chiu. "A meta-analysis of the relationship between spirituality and quality of life." *Social Indicators Research* 72 (2005): 153–88.

Schuette, William. *White Blaze Fever: Georgia to Maine on the Appalachian Trail.* College Station, TX: Virtual Bookworm, 2003.

Setzer, Lynn. *A Season on the Appalachian Trail.* Harpers Ferry, WV: Appalachian Trail Conference, 1997.

Shaffer, Earl V. *Walking with Spring.* Harpers Ferry, WV: Appalachian Trail Conference, 1983.

Slack, Nancy, and Allison Bell. *The AMC Field Guide to the New England Alpine Summits.* 2nd ed. Boston: Appalachian Mountain Club Books, 2006.

Slawson, David A. *Secret Teachings in the Art of Japanese Gardens: Design Principles, Aesthetic Values.* Tokyo: Kodansha Int., 1987.

Snyder, Samuel. "New streams of religion: Fly fishing as a lived, religion of nature." *Journal of the American Academy of Religion* 75, no. 4 (2007): 896–922.

Staats, Henk, Birgitta Gatersleben, and Terry Hartig. "Change in mood as a function of environmental design: Arousal and pleasure on a simulated forest hike." *Environmental Psychology* 17 (1998): 283–300.

Stark, Rodney. *What Americans Really Believe.* Waco, TX: Baylor University Press, 2008.

Stoll, Mark. *Protestantism, Capitalism and Nature in America.* Albuquerque: University of New Mexico Press, 1997.

References

Tapon, Francis. *Hike Your Own Hike: 7 Life Lessons from Backpacking Across America.* Burlingame, CA: SonicTrek Press, 2006.

Tate, J. R. "Model T." *Walkin' on the Happy Side of Misery.* Bloomington, IN: Xlibris, 2001.

———. *Walkin' with the Ghost Whisperers.* Bloomington, IN: Xlibris, 2006.

Taylor, Bron. "Earth and nature based spirituality (Part II): From Earth First! and Bioregionalism to Scientific Paganism and the New Age." *Religion* 31 (2001): 225–45.

———. "Focus introduction: Aquatic nature religion." *Journal of the American Academy of Religion* 75, no. 4 (2007): 863–74.

———. "Surfing into spirituality and a new, aquatic nature religion." *Journal of the American Academy of Religion* 75, no. 4 (2007): 923–51.

Taylor-Miller, Cynthia, ed. *Appalachian Trail Thru-Hikers' Companion 2007.* Harpers Ferry, WV: Appalachian Trail Conservancy, 2007.

Taylor-Miller, Cynthia, and Carol Barnes, ed. *Appalachian Trail Thru-Hikers' Companion 2006.* Harpers Ferry, WV: Appalachian Trail Conservancy, 2006.

Thoreau, Henry David. "A week on the Concord and Merrimac Rivers." In Catherine Albanese, *The Spirituality of the American Transcendentalists.* Atlanta: Mercer University Press, 1988, 241–65.

Thoreau, Henry David. *Walden, or Life in the Woods,* edited by Bill McKibben. Boston: Beacon Press, 2004.

Tomlin, Graham. "Protestants and Pilgrimage." In Craig Bartholomew and Fred Hughes, *Explorations in a Christian Theology of Pilgrimage.* Aldershot, UK: Ashgate Publishing, 2004.

Turner, Victor, and Edith Turner. *Image and Pilgrimage in Christian Culture: Anthropological Perspectives.* New York: Columbia University Press, 1978.

Underhill, Evelyn. *Mysticism: A Study in the Nature of Man's Spiritual Consciousness.* New York: Dutton, 1910.

Vale, Thomas. *The American Wilderness: Reflections on Nature Protection in the United States.* Charlottesville: University of Virginia Press, 2005.

Veith, Gene Edward. *Painters of Faith: The Spiritual Landscape in Nineteenth-Century America.* Washington, DC: Regnery Publishing, 2001.

Viles, Brad Wayne. *Dreaming the Appalachian Trail.* Bloomington, IN: Xlibris, 2006.

Waterman, Laura, and Guy Waterman. *Forest and Crag: A History of Hiking, Trail Blazing, and Adventure in the Northeast Mountains.* Boston: Appalachian Mountain Club Books, 2003.

Weidensaul, Scott. *Mountains of the Heart: A Natural History of the Appalachians.* Golden, CO: Fulcrum Publishing, 1994.

References

Weinstein, Netta, Andrew K. Przybylski, and Richard M. Ryan. "Can nature make us more caring? Effects of immersion in nature on intrinsic aspirations and generosity." *Personality and Social Psychology Bulletin* 35 (2009): 1315–29.

Westwood, Jennifer. *On Pilgrimage: Sacred Journeys around the World.* Mahwah, NJ: Hidden Spring of Paulist Press, 2003.

Wilkinson, Loren, ed. *Earthkeeping in the '90s: Stewardship of Creation.* Grand Rapids, MI: William B. Eerdmans, 1991.

Winters, Kelly. *Walking Home: A Woman's Pilgrimage on the Appalachian Trail.* Los Angeles: Alyson Books, 2001.

Wirzba, Norman. *The Paradise of God: Renewing Religion in an Ecological Age.* New York: Oxford University Press, 2003.

Wright, Kevin J. *Catholic Shrines of Western Europe.* Liguori, MO: Liguori Press, 1997.

Zequeira-Russell, D. L. Ben. "Wilderness and Spirituality: Hikers' Experience of God in the Backcountry." Ph.D. diss. Fuller Theological Seminary, 2002.

INDEX